TRUTH, DEDUCTION, AND COMPUTATION

Logic and Semantics for Computer Science

PRINCIPLES OF COMPUTER SCIENCE SERIES

Series Editors
Alfred V. Aho, Bell Telephone Laboratories, Murray Hill, New Jersey
Jeffrey D. Ullman, Stanford University, Stanford, California

Computer Organization
Michael Andrews
Trends in Theoretical Computer Science
Egon Borger, Editor
Truth, Deduction, and Computation: Logic and Semantics for Computer Science
R. E. Davis
The Turing Omnibus
A. K. Dewdney
Formal Languages and Automata Theory
Vladimir Drobot
Advanced C: Food for the Educated Palate
Narain Gehani
C: An Advanced Introduction
Narain Gehani
C: An Advanced Introduction, Ansi C Version
Narain Gehani
C for Personal Computers: IBM PC, AT&T PC 6300, and Compatibles
Narain Gehani
An Introduction to the Theory of Computation
Eitan Gurari
Theory of Relational Databases
David Maier
An Introduction to Solid Modeling
Martti Mantyla
Principles of Computer Design
Leonard R. Marino
UNIX: The Minimal Manual
Jim Moore
A Logical Language for Data and Knowledge Bases
Shamim Naqvi and Shalom Tsur
The Theory of Database Concurrency Control
Christos Papadimitriou
Algorithms for Graphics and Image Processing
Theo Pavlidis
Data Compression: Methods and Theory
James A. Storer
The Elements of Artificial Intelligence
Steven Tanimoto
Computational Aspects of VLSI
Jeffrey D. Ullman
Principles of Database and Knowledge-Base Systems, Volumes I and II
Jeffrey D. Ullman
Algorithmic Studies in Mass Storage Systems
C. K. Wong

OTHER BOOKS OF INTEREST

Jewels of Formal Language Theory
Arto Salomaa
Fuzzy Sets, Natural Language Computations, and Risk Analysis
Kurt J. Schmucker
LISP: An Interactive Approach
Stuart C. Shapiro
Principles of Database Systems, Second Edition
Jeffrey D. Ullman

TRUTH, DEDUCTION, AND COMPUTATION

Logic and Semantics for Computer Science

R. E. DAVIS
Santa Clara University

COMPUTER SCIENCE PRESS

AN IMPRINT OF W. H. FREEMAN AND COMPANY • NEW YORK

Library of Congress Cataloging-in-Publication Data

Davis, Ruth E.
Truth, deduction, and computation: logic and semantics for computer science/R. E. Davis.
p. cm.
Includes index.
ISBN 0-7167-8201-4
1. Programming languages (Electronic computers)—Semantics. 2. Logic, Symbolic and mathematical. 3. Electronic data processing. I. Title.
QA76.7.D386 1989 89-34922
005. 13—dc20 CIP

Printed in the United States of America

Computer Science Press

An imprint of W. H. Freeman and Company
41 Madison Avenue, New York, NY 10010
20 Beaumont Street, Oxford OX1 2NQ, England

1 2 3 4 5 6 7 8 9 0 RRD 8 9

To John, Michael, Kevin, and Peter

CONTENTS

PREFACE

> I always worked with programming languages because it seemed to me that until you could understand those, you really couldn't understand computers. Understanding them doesn't really mean only being able to use them. A lot of people can use them without understanding them.
>
> *Christopher Strachey*

The study of programming languages is central to the study of computer science. When studying a programming language, one must learn both the syntax and the semantics of the language in order to understand it, rather than simply be able to use it. Everyone knows and agrees upon what is meant by the syntax of a language, but what do we mean by "semantics"? What one requires of a description of the semantics of a language is dependent upon one's point of view. A compiler writer is happy with a description of the operational semantics of a language; someone interested in proving properties of a given program might prefer to use the axiomatic semantics of the language. A language designer, being as concerned with *what* can be said as with *how* to say it, may prefer a denotational (mathematical) description. The denotational description is also most useful when attempting to prove the equivalance of different implementations of the same language.

We could argue the advantages and drawbacks of each approach, or we can realize that each has its place and see what we can learn about the relationships between these descriptive devices.

Because a solid foundation in mathematical logic is also critical to the study of computer science, I have combined an introduction to formal logic with the study of three approaches to semantics of languages. In particular, I chose to investigate the concepts of truth (denotational semantics), deduction (axiomatic semantics), and computation (operational semantics) as they apply to mathematical logic and computer science formalisms (i.e., languages) and to observe how the relationships among these ideas vary as the expressive power of the formalism increases.

The investigation of each formalism begins with a description of the syntax of the language. This is simply a description of the symbols allowed and the rules by which the symbols may be combined to form legal sentences of the language.

Truth is an intuitive notion. Since the symbols of a formalism (language) have no intrinsic meaning, we speak of truth in an interpretation of a formalism. An interpretation gives meaning to the symbols and sentences of a language by mapping them onto objects in the domain of interpretation. For example, the French map the sequence of symbols "pomme" onto the object we call "apple."

Deduction involves the formal manipulation of symbols according to prescribed rules. A deductive system, or formal theory, specifies the rules by which derivations can be made. These derivations are strictly syntactic, so they have no intrinsic meaning. In particular, *proof* is a syntactic notion; its relationship with *truth* depends upon the formal theory being investigated.

Computation is also syntactic in nature and closely related to deduction. Computation suggests an algorithm; we are interested not only in *what* the legal moves are, but in *how* we might execute them. Thus a computational scheme must provide some information to control the use of the rules for rewriting symbols.

(Note: We are concerned with deterministic computation only. Thus we always know what to do next. Nondeterministic computation is closer yet to deduction—a set of possible next moves is determined, but the choice of one move to make is not. Nondeterministic computation is discussed in Section 3.4.2 on logic programming.)

We will investigate four languages (formalisms): Propositional Logic, Predicate Calculus, Elementary Number Theory, and Lambda Calculus. In each case, the syntax of the language is described first; then we examine separately the truth, deduction, and computation aspects of the language; and finally, discover the relationships among these concepts.

In Propositional Logic we will find that truth, deduction, and computation are equivalent and that our computation scheme provides a decision procedure for provability in the theory. The model theory of Propositional Logic is explicated by means of truth tables, and a minimal (in number of axioms) formal theory is presented. For computation, the process of complementary literal elimination (CLE), or ground resolution, which provides a decision procedure for the theory, is described. An alternative computation scheme is offered that is simply a method of generating a truth table for a given formula, establishing its truth, and therefore (by completeness) its provability.

For Predicate Calculus our computation scheme is expanded to general resolution. An alternative computation scheme for a subset of Predicate Calculus known as Horn clauses is also discussed. This is the basis for many logic programming systems, such as Prolog and its descendants. Again, we can show the equivalence of our notions of truth, deduction, and computation. However, we cannot decide whether or not our computation will yield any results. *If* a sentence is provable, then computation will terminate successfully, and *if* computation terminates successfully, then the sentence is provable. We cannot, however, put any bound on our computation; we have no way of knowing whether or not the program will terminate.

In Elementary Number Theory we look more closely at what we mean by an algorithm (effectively computable function) and prove that the formal system is undecidable. We also establish the undecidability of Predicate Calculus (which we had left hanging after showing that the procedure we had described did not provide a decision procedure). We sketch Gödel's incompleteness results, exhibiting a sentence that is true under the standard interpretation but not provable.

Thus in moving from Propositional Logic through Predicate Calculus to Elementary Number Theory, we begin with decidability and completeness, first lose decidability, and finally also lose completeness.

When studying the λ-calculus we run into a few surprises. Intuitively, we expect to be able to equate termination of computation with the ability to find a *normal form.* This idea of computation takes the reduction rules (inference rules) of the formal system and uses them as computational rules. A normal form is reached when no more reductions are possible. This might lead us to believe that terms without normal forms should be different (semantically distinguishable) from those with normal forms. However, this turns out not to be the case.

This unexpected fact caused C. Wadsworth to look more closely at the idea of computation. A more adequate analysis of computation involves the concept of a generalized normal form (head normal form), which gives much more satisfying results with respect to the models.

We exhibit several examples of terms that are equal in the models but cannot be proved so in the formalism; thus, the λ-calculus is also incomplete. However, if we restrict our attention to terms with normal forms, we can establish the equivalence of truth, deduction, and computation. We also show that if we allow approximate normal forms, we get completeness in the limit. That is, every term is the limit of its approximate normal forms, so we can compute the approximate normal forms of a term to get a closer and closer approximation of the term itself.

The formalisms presented are arranged in the order of their expressive power. Anything that can be expressed in one formalism can be expressed in the one following it. This is one reason that once we lost decidability and completeness because of statements formalizable within the system, they were gone forever.

Acknowledgments

First and foremost I must acknowledge John R. Allen, who pointed me toward this subject in the first place, insisting that it was prerequisite material for anyone who wanted to pursue study in computer science. I owe an obvious debt to all my sources, but most notably:

Elliott Mendelson, for the formal theories of $\mathcal{L}$, $\mathcal{PC}$, and $\mathcal{ENT}$; and Christopher Wadsworth, for his work on the lambda calculus.

I am also indebted to over six hundred graduate students who suffered through various versions of this text over the past several years. Many provided comments and occasionally some constructive criticism. Donna Potter did an excellent job of providing detailed criticism on an early draft.

I am grateful to Barbara Friedman of Computer Science Press for her helpfulness and understanding when medical complications interfered with the timely completion of the manuscript; and I am most grateful to Fred Schlichting for keeping complications from turning to tragedy.

I also wish to thank John R. Allen, and Michael, Kevin, and Peter Davis-Allen for putting up with each other and with my absence in the early hours of the morning for so very, very long.

CHAPTER 1

PRELIMINARY DEFINITIONS

We define here some of the terminology that is used in each of the following chapters. One of the most important distinctions we must make is between the notions of *truth* and *proof*. Most people are familiar with an informal style of proof, which is best characterized as *a convincing argument*. The point of the proof is to convince someone that a statement is true. (Some people are more easily convinced than others.) However, we shall be concerned with a different, more formal type of proof. Rather than concern ourselves with what can be shown to be true, we simply wish to investigate what follows from what. The definition of "follows from", as well as what we have to begin with, changes from one theory to the next.

A formal theory can be intuitively understood as defining a game — providing us with a language and rules by which it can be manipulated. Something is provable if it is derivable within the rules of the game; changing games changes what is provable. There is no intrinsic relationship between truth and proof — the first is semantic, the second syntactic.

Before we define what is meant by a deductive system, or formal theory, we need to know what it means for a set to be countable.

Definition: A set is ***denumerable*** if it can be put into a one-to-one correspondence with the positive integers — in other words, if there is a way to list (or enumerate) the elements such that each element will eventually be listed, but the entire set can never be completely listed (there are always more elements). A set is ***countable*** if it is either finite or denumerable. ■

Definition: A ***formal theory*** $\mathcal{T}$ consists of the following:

1. A countable set of symbols. (A finite sequence of symbols of $\mathcal{T}$ is called an ***expression*** of $\mathcal{T}$.)

2. A subset of the expressions, called the ***well-formed formulas*** (abbreviated ***wffs***) of $\mathcal{T}$. The wffs are the legal sentences of the theory.

3. A subset of the wffs called the ***axioms*** of $\mathcal{T}$.

4. A finite set of relations $R_1, \ldots, R_n$ on wffs, called ***rules of inference***. For each R_i there is a unique positive integer j such that for every j wffs and each wff A one can effectively decide whether the given j wffs are in the relation R_i to A; if so, A is called a ***direct consequence*** of the given wffs by virtue of R_i. For example, the rule ***modus ponens*** is a relation on three wffs, A, $A \rightarrow B$, and B, by which B is a direct consequence of A and $A \rightarrow B$. ■

The set of axioms of a theory is often infinite. It can usually be specified by providing a finite set of axiom schemata.

Definition: A ***schema*** is a statement form; it provides a template showing the form of a wff while leaving some pieces unspecified. We indicate these unspecified pieces using metavariables. (The prefix *meta-* indicates that we are not referring to variables that may be symbols *in* the theory; we are talking *about* the theory. Metavariables stand for wffs in the theory). In the modus ponens example above, A and B are metavariables. Metavariables are distinguished from symbols of the theory by font. ■

DEFINITION: An ***instance*** of a statement form or schema is a wff obtained from the statement form by substitution. In particular, we can substitute wffs for all metavariables (statement letters in the statement form), all occurrences of the same metavariable being replaced by the same wff. ■

For example, Theory $\mathcal{X}$[1]:

1. The symbols are: A, B, C, ¬ , →,), and (. The symbols ¬ and → can be read "not" and "implies", respectively.

2. A, B, and C are wffs, and if P and Q are any wffs, then $(\neg P)$ and $(P \rightarrow Q)$ are also wffs.

3. The axioms are:

$$(\neg(P{\rightarrow}P))$$
$$(\neg(P{\rightarrow}(Q{\rightarrow}P)))$$

4. There is one rule of inference:

$$Q \text{ is a direct consequence of } (\neg(Q{\rightarrow}P))$$

Theory $\mathcal{X}$ has an infinite number of wffs and an infinite number of axioms. Metavariables P and Q were used to describe both of these sets. Some wffs of $\mathcal{X}$ are:

A

B

C

(¬A)

(B→(¬A))

(¬(B→(¬A)))

[1]Remember that a formal theory is just a game. Do not expect that it must reflect reality, or that something must be true simply because it is provable.

Some of the axioms of $\mathcal{X}$ are:

$$(\neg(\mathsf{B}\rightarrow\mathsf{B}))$$

$$(\neg(\mathsf{A}\rightarrow(\mathsf{B}\rightarrow\mathsf{A})))$$

$$(\neg((\neg\mathsf{A})\rightarrow(\neg\mathsf{A})))$$

$$(\neg((\mathsf{B}\rightarrow(\neg\mathsf{A}))\rightarrow((\neg\mathsf{C})\rightarrow(\mathsf{B}\rightarrow(\neg\mathsf{A})))))$$

Each of the axioms above is constructed by using the templates provided by the axiom schemata. P and Q in the schemata are consistently replaced by wffs.

DEFINITION: Let $\underline{S}$ be a set of wffs, and let P be a wff in the formal theory $\mathcal{T}$. We say that P is ***deducible from $\underline{S}$ in $\mathcal{T}$*** (denoted $\underline{S} \vdash_{\mathcal{T}} P$) if there exists a finite sequence of wffs $P_1, \ldots, P_n$ such that $P_n = P$ and for $1 \leq i \leq n$, P_i is either an axiom, a formula in $\underline{S}$ (called a hypothesis), or a direct consequence of previous P_i's by virtue of one of the rules of inference. ■

DEFINITION: The sequence of P_i's is called a ***derivation*** of P from $\underline{S}$, or a ***proof*** of P from $\underline{S}$. ■

DEFINITION: If P is deducible from the empty set, we write $\vdash_{\mathcal{T}} P$, and say that P is a ***theorem*** or P is ***provable*** in $\mathcal{T}$.[2] ■

When we say that P is deducible from the empty set, it sounds as if we can deduce it from nothing. However, checking the definition of *deducible from*, we see that we always have the set of axioms of the theory as an implicit set of assumptions.

For example, consider the following proof of A in Theory $\mathcal{X}$:

1.	$(\neg(\mathsf{A}\rightarrow\mathsf{A}))$	by the first axiom
2.	A	by 1 and the rule of inference

The following properties of deducibility are consequences of the definition of *deducible from*:

Let $\underline{S1}$ and $\underline{S2}$ be sets of wffs, and A a wff, then

[2] We will not continue to use the subscript $\mathcal{T}$ on the symbol $\vdash_{\mathcal{T}}$; the theory we mean should be clear from context.

1. If $\underline{S1}$ is a subset of $\underline{S2}$ and $\underline{S1} \vdash A$, then $\underline{S2} \vdash A$. (That is, we can always add extra hypotheses, simply ignoring them in the derivation.) This property is sometimes called *monotonicity.*[3]

2. $\underline{S1} \vdash A$ if and only if there is a finite subset $\underline{S2}$ of $\underline{S1}$ such that $\underline{S2} \vdash A$. (That is, since a derivation must be finite, it must require only a finite number of hypotheses.) This property is sometimes called *compactness.*

3. If $\underline{S2} \vdash A$, and for each wff B in $\underline{S2}$, $\underline{S1} \vdash B$, then $\underline{S1} \vdash A$. (If every wff in $\underline{S2}$ can be derived from the set of wffs $\underline{S1}$, then anything that can be derived from $\underline{S2}$ can also be derived from $\underline{S1}$.)

Note that a proof is a sequence of wffs with certain restrictions, and that it is a proof of the *last* statement in the sequence. Therefore, if we consider only the first n elements of the sequence, you have a proof of the nth statement.

We will investigate the relationships among truth, deduction, and computation in each of the languages that we study. When we speak about a theory, we are interested in various metatheoretic properties. (Again, *meta-* indicates that we are speaking *about* the theory rather than *in* the theory — wffs being the sentences of the language in the theory.)

DEFINITION: An ***interpretation*** supplies a meaning for each of the symbols of a formal theory such that any wff can be understood as a statement that is either true or false in the interpretation. ■

The above is only an intuitive definition of interpretation. We will be more precise about what is required to specify an interpretation when we discuss specific languages.

---

[3]All the theories we study in this book are *monotonic.* There is a wealth of research on non-monotonic logics. In such systems it is possible that the addition of new information (axioms) can invalidate proofs that were possible prior to the addition. Such logics are very useful in modelling common sense reasoning, in which, for example, we modify conclusions derived from general rules by learning the exceptions. However interesting, these logics are outside the scope of this text. We refer the interested reader to [1], particularly to [11,27].

DEFINITION: An interpretation is a ***model*** for a set of wffs $\underline{S}$ if every wff in $\underline{S}$ is true in the interpretation. We say that an interpretation provides a model for a formal theory $\mathcal{T}$ if it provides a model for the set of theorems of $\mathcal{T}$. ■

Completeness is a metatheoretic concept used to relate truth and provability in a formal theory; *soundness* is the complementary property.

DEFINITION: A theory is ***complete*** if every sentence that is true in all interpretations is provable in the theory. ■

DEFINITION: A theory is ***sound*** if every provable sentence is true in all interpretations. ■

Our example theory $\mathcal{X}$ is complete. It is possible to prove every sentence that is true in all interpretations. In fact, it is possible to prove *every* sentence in theory $\mathcal{X}$. We gave a sample proof of the wff consisting of the single proposition letter A. Since the axioms and the rule of inference are schemata we could use the form of that proof, instantiated with different specific wffs to prove any wff. For example, we will prove $(A \rightarrow A)$.

1. $(\neg((A \rightarrow A) \rightarrow (A \rightarrow A)))$ by the first axiom
2. $(A \rightarrow A)$ by 1 and the rule of inference

But theory $\mathcal{X}$ is not sound. If a wff A is true in all interpretations, then certainly its negation, $\neg A$, must be false. However, both of these sentences are provable in $\mathcal{X}$. Thus, something that is not true in all interpretations is provable; therefore, $\mathcal{X}$ is unsound.

A theory in which we can prove false results is not of much use, so we will insist that every theory we use be sound. It is easy to legislate, but we cannot ignore enforcement; although it is obvious that we want our theories to be sound, it is not always so obvious how we can *prove* that they are sound. Soundness must be demonstrated, not simply assumed.

If a theory is both sound and complete, we will say truth and deduction are equivalent and write "truth $\Leftrightarrow$ deduction." We will also be concerned with the relationships between truth and computation, and between deduction and computation. So, for each theory we discuss, we will define precisely what we mean by computation.

DEFINITION: A computation method is ***complete*** if for every sentence S the algorithm will terminate on input S in a finite amount of time, indicating whether or not S is true in all interpretations. ■

Besides general completeness, we can speak of completeness with respect to a particular class of interpretations, narrowing the focus of our discussion from *truth in all interpretations* to *truth in some chosen interpretations.* This idea surfaces in Elementary Number Theory ($\mathcal{ENT}$), where we show that the theory is incomplete with respect to the standard model (Intuitive Number Theory or $\mathcal{INT}$), and is useful in the study of programming formalisms.

Two other metatheoretic concepts of interest are the decidability and consistency of a theory.

DEFINITION: A *formal theory* is ***decidable*** if there exists an effective procedure that will determine, for any sentence of the theory, whether or not that sentence is provable in the theory. ■

We will occasionally wish to speak of the decidability of a property in a more general sense.

DEFINITION: Any *property* is said to be ***decidable*** if there exists an effective procedure (i.e., terminating algorithm) that will determine whether or not the property holds. ■

This definition is purposefully vague definition since we may wish to apply it to properties of symbols (is x a symbol of $\mathcal{T}$?), strings of symbols (is x a wff?), sets of wffs (is P deducible from set x?), sequences of wffs (is x a proof?), and so on.

DEFINITION: A theory is ***consistent*** if it contains no wff such that both the wff and its negation are provable. ■

An inconsistent theory is usually not very useful, altough there are exceptions, particularly in the field of artificial intelligence; hence, all the theories we study in detail will be consistent. However, it is important to realize that not all theories are consistent; consistency must be demonstrated, particularly when dealing with programming languages.

We defined above what is meant by a decidable theory — that there exists an effective procedure capable of determining whether or not any given well-formed formula is a theorem. So if, within a given theory, we can find some rule by which we can always tell whether a given wff is provable or not, our theory is decidable. The example theory $\mathcal{X}$ is decidable. In fact, the decision procedure is very simple: given any wff, terminate immediately with the answer "Yes, it is provable."

We also know that $\mathcal{X}$ is inconsistent. We proved $(\mathsf{A} \rightarrow \mathsf{A})$ as an example above. We know that $(\neg(\mathsf{A} \rightarrow \mathsf{A}))$ is also provable, as is any axiom. Thus we have exhibited a wff such that both it and its negation are provable, implying that the theory is not consistent. (Aside: Look again at the definitions of "sound" and "consistent." The terms are closely related, but not the same. For example, one might be able to conceive of a theory in which one could prove only false statements. Such a theory would be consistent but not sound.)

Wffs are strictly syntactic objects; they have meaning only when an interpretation is given for the symbols. However, our definition of consistency has assumed something about the meaning of $\neg$. We have said that it means negation. We shall fix the meaning of some of our symbols — for example, the logical connectives $\neg$ and $\rightarrow$ with which we build complicated wffs from the atomic wffs. The meaning assigned to these symbols will be defined precisely in Section 2.2.

The meaning attached to wffs of a theory is determined by the meaning of the connectives, together with an interpretation. To supply an interpretation for our theory $\mathcal{X}$, we must specify the domain of interpretation, and a relation over that domain for each of the symbols A, B, and C. For example:

domain = integers
A means "2 is an even number"
B means "3 is an even number"
C means "21 is divisible by 7"

Under this interpretation, the wff $(\mathsf{A} \rightarrow (\mathsf{B} \rightarrow (\neg\mathsf{C})))$ means: If 2 is an even number, then (3 is an even number implies that it is not the case that 21 is divisible by 7).

Well, no one said that every interpretation has to make sense. However, interpretations are our means of connecting the purely syntactic world of formal theories with the world of semantics.

Exercises 1.0

1. Review the definitions of sound, complete, consistent, and decidable. Is it conceivable that a theory might be:

   a. sound, but not complete?

   b. sound, but not consistent?

   c. consistent, but not sound?

   d. complete, but not decidable?

   e. consistent and complete, but not sound?

   Give a rationale or an example or both justifying each answer.

CHAPTER 2

PROPOSITIONAL LOGIC

2.1 The Language

The first two requirements for a description of a formal theory are precisely what we need to describe the syntax of the language. Thus, we describe the language of Propositional Logic by giving the symbols of the language and the rules for generating well-formed formulas of the language.

1. A countable set of symbols:

   a. Proposition (or predicate) letters: A, B, C, ..., Z and the same letters subscripted by positive integers: A_1, B_1, ..., Z_1; A_2, B_2, ..., Z_2; A_3, ...

   b. Logical connectives: $\rightarrow$ and $\neg$.

   c. Two auxiliary symbols:) and (.

2. The class of well-formed formulas consists of:

   a. Atomic formulas — that is, the proposition letters A, B, ...

   b. Compound Formulas — if P and Q are wffs, then $(\neg P)$ and $(P\rightarrow Q)$ are also wffs. (For ease in reading, we can anticipate the interpretation of $\neg$ as negation and $\rightarrow$ as implication, thus $\neg P$ may be read as "not P" and $P \rightarrow Q$ as "if P then Q" or "P implies Q.")

DEFINITION: If P is a wff in which no proposition letters other than those in the set $\{\mathsf{A}_1, \ldots, \mathsf{A}_n\}$ occur, then P is said to be a *formula in the proposition letters* $\mathsf{A}_1, \ldots, \mathsf{A}_n$. ■

For example, each of the following is a formula in the proposition letters A, B, C, D:

$$((\mathsf{A} \rightarrow (\neg \mathsf{C})) \rightarrow (\mathsf{D} \rightarrow \mathsf{B}))$$

$$(\neg(\mathsf{A} \rightarrow (\mathsf{B} \rightarrow (\mathsf{C} \rightarrow \mathsf{D}))))$$

$$(((\neg \mathsf{A}) \rightarrow \mathsf{B}) \rightarrow (\mathsf{C} \rightarrow \mathsf{D}))$$

$$(\mathsf{D} \rightarrow \mathsf{D})$$

We use the symbols A, B, C, ..., Z, subscripted as needed, for metavariables — that is, they stand for arbitrary wffs as opposed to the individual proposition letters. We rarely need to be concerned with specific proposition letters of the language. Most results are stated using metavariables and therefore apply to any wff in which the metavariables have been consistently replaced.

We introduce three more propositional connectives as abbreviations:

$$\begin{array}{lll} (A \wedge B) & \text{for} & (\neg(A \rightarrow (\neg B))) \\ (A \vee B) & \text{for} & ((\neg A) \rightarrow B) \\ (A \equiv B) & \text{for} & ((A \rightarrow B) \wedge (B \rightarrow A)) \end{array}$$

Any formula can be seen as a logical function; the proposition letters appearing in the formula are the arguments, and the value of the function for a given set of arguments is either true or false. Any formula written using any of the five connectives can be reexpressed as a formula using only the connectives $\neg$ and $\rightarrow$.

DEFINITION: $\underline{S}$ is a ***sufficient set of connectives*** if any logical function can be expressed in terms of connectives in the set $\underline{S}$. ■

The set $\{\neg, \rightarrow\}$ is a sufficient set of connectives. Sometimes it is more convenient to use one set of connectives than another. It makes no difference, formally, as long as the set of connectives chosen is sufficient to express all formulas. When we consider computation we will use a different set of sufficient connectives than the one we chose for our formal system of Propositional Logic.

DEFINITION: The ***scope*** of a connective is the wff or wffs to which the connective applies. ■

To make complicated expressions easier to read, we will adopt some conventions for elimination of parentheses. First, we will omit the outer pair of parentheses; thus, $(A \rightarrow B)$ may be written as $A \rightarrow B$, and $(\neg A)$ as $\neg A$.

Second, when a form contains only one binary connective, parentheses are omitted by association to the left. Thus,

$$A \rightarrow B \rightarrow A \rightarrow C \quad \text{stands for} \quad (((A \rightarrow B) \rightarrow A) \rightarrow C)$$

Last, the connectives are ordered from greatest to least scope, or lowest to highest precedence as follows: $\equiv$, $\rightarrow$, $\vee$, $\wedge$, $\neg$. Parentheses are eliminated according to the rule that $\equiv$ has the greatest scope and $\neg$ has the least, or, if you prefer to think in terms of precedence, $\neg$ has the highest precedence and $\equiv$ has the least. That is, $\neg$ applies to the smallest wff following it, then $\wedge$ connects the smallest wffs surrounding it, then $\vee$, $\rightarrow$, and finally $\equiv$.

For example, $\neg A \vee B \equiv A \rightarrow B \vee \neg C \wedge A$ stands for the fully parenthesized formula $(((\neg A) \vee B) \equiv (A \rightarrow (B \vee ((\neg C) \wedge A))))$. Omitting the unnecessary parentheses in the wffs given above,

((A→(¬C))→(D→B))	becomes	A→¬C→(D→B)
(¬(A→(B→(C→D))))	becomes	¬(A→(B→(C→D)))
(((¬A)→B)→(C→D))	becomes	¬A→B→(C→D)
(D→D)	becomes	D→D

Exercises 2.1

1. Remove all redundant pairs of parentheses (i.e., those that are not needed due to the conventions described above) from each of the following wffs:

   a. $(((A \wedge (\neg(B \rightarrow C))) \vee (A \wedge (B \rightarrow (\neg A)))) \rightarrow (C \wedge (\neg B)))$

   b. $(((B \rightarrow (C \rightarrow A)) \rightarrow B) \rightarrow (C \rightarrow A))$

2. Fully parenthesize each of the following wffs according to the conventions described above.

   a. $A \wedge \neg B \rightarrow C \vee A \wedge B \rightarrow \neg A \rightarrow C \wedge \neg B$

   b. $B \rightarrow C \rightarrow A \rightarrow B \rightarrow C \rightarrow A$

2.2 Truth

For Propositional Logic, an interpretation consists of an assignment of a truth value (**t** or **f**, for "true" and "false", respectively) to each proposition letter. The interpretation of a wff is determined by the truth values of the proposition letters in the formula. By giving truth tables to define the meaning of the connectives, we can describe how the truth value of a wff is built from the truth values of its component wffs. In constructing a truth table we exhibit all possible interpretations of a wff. Each line of the truth table assigns a unique combination of truth values to the proposition letters of the wff, thus determining an interpretation; we consider all possible interpretations by listing all possible assignments. In the following truth tables we use metavariables to emphasize that the definitions apply to arbitrarily complex wffs.

DEFINITION: The logical connective "not," written $\neg$, represents negation; $\neg A$ is true iff A is false, as shown by the following truth table:

A	$\neg A$
t	**f**
f	**t**

■

DEFINITION: $\rightarrow$ is a conditional; $A \rightarrow B$ is read "A implies B" or "if A then B". A is the ***antecedent*** (or ***hypothesis***) of the implication, B is the ***consequent*** (or ***conclusion***). The meaning of $A \rightarrow B$ is given by the following truth table:

A	B	$A \rightarrow B$
t	**t**	**t**
t	**f**	**f**
f	**t**	**t**
f	**f**	**t**

■

In informal usage, "if A then B" implies some sort of causal relationship. However, the (perhaps surprising) truth table entries of lines 3 and 4 can be explained by considering the following:

$$A \wedge B \rightarrow B \qquad \text{(If } A \text{ and } B\text{, then } B\text{)}$$

Certainly this implication should be true in all situations; *if* we know two things, then we must certainly know the second of them.

f $\rightarrow$ **t** is **t**: Suppose that A is false and B is true. Then the conjunction $A \wedge B$ is false, and the conclusion B is true.

f $\rightarrow$ **f** is **t**: If B is false, we have that false implies false is true.

Intuitively, we simply do not want to consider cases in which the hypothesis of an implication is false as counterexamples to the truth of the implication. We define the implication to be true unless we can show it to be false by exhibiting a case in which the hypothesis is satisfied but the conclusion does not follow.

If we know the meaning of the proposition letters, we can always determine the meaning of a complicated wff by repeated use of the truth tables given above. Note that an interpretation is free to change only the meaning of individual proposition letters. The meaning of the connectives is fixed by the truth tables just given.

The truth tables for the connectives $\wedge$, $\vee$, and $\equiv$ can be determined by considering the formulas they are abbreviations of. Given separately, they are:

A	B	$A \vee B$
t	**t**	**t**
t	**f**	**t**
f	**t**	**t**
f	**f**	**f**

A	B	$A \wedge B$
t	**t**	**t**
t	**f**	**f**
f	**t**	**f**
f	**f**	**f**

A	B	$A \equiv B$
t	**t**	**t**
t	**f**	**f**
f	**t**	**f**
f	**f**	**t**

Remember, each row of a truth table corresponds to one possible interpretation. If a wff P is made up of the proposition letters $\mathsf{P}_1, \ldots,$ P_n and propositional connectives, there are 2^n possible interpretations assigning truth values to the proposition letters.

The propositional connectives are *logical functions* in that they take truth-valued arguments and define a truth-valued result. The connectives defined above are unary ($\neg$), or binary ($\wedge$, $\vee$, $\rightarrow$, $\equiv$), but we can easily define a function of any number of arguments by supplying a truth table that specifies the value of the function for all possible values of its arguments, as we used truth tables to define the connectives $\neg$, $\rightarrow$, $\vee$, $\wedge$, and $\equiv$. If a function takes n arguments, then to define the values of the function under all possible combinations of values of its arguments will require a truth table with 2^n lines.

We can demonstrate that $\{\neg, \wedge, \vee\}$ is a sufficient set of connectives by showing that any logical function $f(x_1, \ldots, x_n)$ can be expressed in terms of $\neg$, $\wedge$, and $\vee$.

THEOREM 2.2.1 $\{\neg, \wedge, \vee\}$ is a sufficient set of connectives.

Proof: Consider an arbitrary logical function $f(x_1, \ldots, x_n)$ of n arguments. We represent each argument by a proposition letter P_i and construct a truth table exhibiting the value of the function under all possible combinations of values of the arguments. (If there are n proposition letters, then there are 2^n lines in the truth table.)

For each line of the truth table that contains the value **t** as value of the function, construct the conjunction

$$\mathsf{P}'_1 \wedge \mathsf{P}'_2 \wedge \cdots \wedge \mathsf{P}'_\mathsf{n}$$

where

$\mathsf{P}'_\mathsf{i} = \mathsf{P}_\mathsf{i}$ if P_i is **t** in that row
$\mathsf{P}'_\mathsf{i} = \neg\mathsf{P}_\mathsf{i}$ if P_i is **f** in that row

The disjunction ($\vee$) of all these conjunctions is an expression representing the given function in terms of connectives from $\{\neg, \wedge, \vee\}$. ■

For example, $A \vee \neg C \equiv B$ has the following truth table:

A	B	C	$\neg C$	$(A \vee \neg C)$	$(A \vee \neg C \equiv B)$
t	**t**	**t**	**f**	**t**	**t**
t	**t**	**f**	**t**	**t**	**t**
t	**f**	**t**	**f**	**t**	**f**
t	**f**	**f**	**t**	**t**	**f**
f	**t**	**t**	**f**	**f**	**f**
f	**t**	**f**	**t**	**t**	**t**
f	**f**	**t**	**f**	**f**	**t**
f	**f**	**f**	**t**	**t**	**f**

Reading across each line with a **t** in the last column, it is easy to see that $A \vee \neg C \equiv B$ is equivalent to

$$(A \wedge B \wedge C) \vee (A \wedge B \wedge \neg C) \vee (\neg A \wedge B \wedge \neg C) \vee (\neg A \wedge \neg B \wedge C)$$

DEFINITION: The ***principal connective*** of a wff is the one that is applied last in constructing the wff (i.e., the one that has the greatest scope). ■

Truth tables can be abbreviated by writing the wff once, listing the possible assignments of truth values under each proposition letter, and then, step by step, entering the truth values of each component sentence under the principal connective of that component.

Thus, we have the alternative form shown below for the truth table above (we have numbered the columns to indicate the order in which they are filled in).

$(A$	$\vee$	$(\neg$	$C))$	$\equiv$	B
t	**t**	**f**	**t**	**t**	**t**
t	**t**	**t**	**f**	**t**	**t**
t	**t**	**f**	**t**	**f**	**f**
t	**t**	**t**	**f**	**f**	**f**
f	**f**	**f**	**t**	**f**	**t**
f	**t**	**t**	**f**	**t**	**t**
f	**f**	**f**	**t**	**t**	**f**
f	**t**	**t**	**f**	**f**	**f**
1	3	2	1	4	1

DEFINITION: A wff that is always true, no matter what the truth values of its statement letters (proposition letters) may be, is called a ***tautology***. Such a statement P is said to be ***logically valid*** or ***true in all interpretations***, is denoted $\models P$, and is read "P is logically valid." ■

DEFINITION: A wff is ***satisfiable*** if it is true in some interpretation (i.e., there exists an assignment of truth values to the proposition letters that makes the wff true). ■

If P is true in all models, then $\neg P$ is false in all models; that is, there does not exist an interpretation in which $\neg P$ is true.

DEFINITION: P is ***unsatisfiable*** if $\neg P$ is logically valid. An unsatisfiable wff is also called a ***contradiction***. ■

The validity of any statement P is decidable. $\models P$ if and only if the column under P in its truth table (or under its main connective in the abbreviated form) contains only **t**'s — that is, P is true for every possible interpretation (assignment of truth values to its proposition letters).

LEMMA 2.2.2 $(P \wedge (P \rightarrow Q)) \rightarrow Q$ is a tautology.

Proof:

P	Q	$P \rightarrow Q$	$P \wedge (P \rightarrow Q)$	$(P \wedge (P \rightarrow Q)) \rightarrow Q$
t	**t**	**t**	**t**	**t**
t	**f**	**f**	**f**	**t**
f	**t**	**t**	**f**	**t**
f	**f**	**t**	**f**	**t**

■

Exercises 2.2

1. Demonstrate, via the truth table, that the wff

$$((A \rightarrow (B \rightarrow C)) \rightarrow ((A \rightarrow B) \rightarrow (A \rightarrow C)))$$

is a tautology.

2. Determine whether each of the following wffs is unsatisfiable, a tautology, both, or neither.

   a. $(\neg A \rightarrow B) \rightarrow (\neg B \rightarrow A)$
   b. $(A \rightarrow B) \rightarrow (B \rightarrow A)$
   c. $\neg(A \rightarrow (B \rightarrow A))$
   d. $\neg(A \rightarrow B) \rightarrow A$
   e. $\neg(A \rightarrow B) \rightarrow \neg(B \rightarrow A)$

3. Show that $\vee$, and $\wedge$ are commutative and associative.

   a. commutativity:
   $A \vee B \equiv B \vee A$
   $A \wedge B \equiv B \wedge A$

   b. associativity:
   $A \vee (B \vee C) \equiv (A \vee B) \vee C$
   $A \wedge (B \wedge C) \equiv (A \wedge B) \wedge C$

4. Is $\rightarrow$ associative?

5. Show that $\{\neg, \wedge\}$ is a sufficient set of connectives.

6. A NAND B, written $A \mid B$, is defined to be $\neg(A \wedge B)$. Show that {NAND} is a sufficient set of connectives.

7. A NOR B, written $A \uparrow B$, is defined to be $\neg(A \vee B)$. Is {NOR} a sufficient set of connectives?

2.3 Deduction

The first two requirements for a formal theory — the set of symbols and the class of well-formed formulas we presented in Section 2.1 — describe the syntax of the language. It remains to describe the axioms and rules of inference of our formal theory for Propositional Logic (which we shall call $\mathcal{L}$).

There are many ways of axiomatizing Propositional Logic. The following set of axioms is a minimal one. If A, B, and C are any wffs of $\mathcal{L}$, then the following are axioms of $\mathcal{L}$.

Axioms:

L1 $(A \rightarrow (B \rightarrow A))$

L2 $((A \rightarrow (B \rightarrow C)) \rightarrow ((A \rightarrow B) \rightarrow (A \rightarrow C)))$

L3 $(((\neg B) \rightarrow (\neg A)) \rightarrow (((\neg B) \rightarrow A) \rightarrow B))$

Rule of inference: There is only one rule of inference in $\mathcal{L}$. It is ***modus ponens*** (MP): B is a direct consequence of A and $A \rightarrow B$, written

$$A,\ A \rightarrow B \vdash B$$

In other words, assuming A and $A \rightarrow B$, we can derive B. We shall abbreviate modus ponens by the initials MP.

The axioms are presented as schemata expressed in metavariables over $\mathcal{L}$. They actually describe an infinite number of axioms. Any instance of one of these statement forms is an axiom.

DEFINITION: An ***instance*** of a statement form is obtained by replacing each metavariable with a wff consistently throughout the statement form (that is, each occurrence of the same metavariable must be replaced by the same wff). ■

For example,

$$((C \rightarrow D) \rightarrow (\neg A \rightarrow (C \rightarrow D)))$$

is an instance of axiom **L1**, with $(C \rightarrow D)$ for A, and $\neg A$ for B.

We have chosen to define our theory using only the connectives $\neg$ and $\rightarrow$. We have also chosen to use a minimal set of axioms; none of the three can be proven from the other two, and together they are sufficient to prove any true statement of Propositional Logic (i.e., $\mathcal{L}$ is *complete*, as we shall see in Section 2.5). Providing many more axioms, even though they might be redundant, would make it easier to prove theorems, so what is the benefit of using a minimal set? Although it may be more difficult to prove theorems *in* the theory, a minimal axiom set makes it easier to prove theorems *about* the theory (metatheorems).

For example, suppose we wish to prove something about all theorems of a theory (such as the fact that they are all tautologies). Every theorem must be derivable from the axioms and rules of inference. Thus, the smaller the set of axioms and rules of inference the fewer the cases we must consider.

Clearly, from the definition of proof given in Section 1, we have the following lemma.

Lemma 2.3.1 $\vdash A$, for any axiom A.

We must be careful to distinguish two uses of the word *proof*. A proof *in* the theory, as defined previously, is a sequence of wffs of the theory such that the last is the statement we wish to prove and each preceding wff in the sequence is an axiom or follows by a rule of inference from two previous members of the sequence. As is the case with the axioms, we can represent an infinite number of actual theorems and proofs by using metavariables to establish a proof schema. Any instance of a theorem schema is a theorem of the theory, just as any instance of an axiom schema is an axiom.

We also give proofs of statements *about* the theory. Lemma 2.3.1 is such a statement, as are the Deduction Theorem (Theorem 2.3.3) and the completeness theorems. These proofs are constructed by the usual mathematical methods and are written in English supplemented by mathematical symbols and symbols from the theory we are discussing. These are actually metatheorems, that is, theorems *about* the theory rather than *in* the theory. However, we will refer only to theorems, lemmas, etc., without continuing the distinction by using the terms metatheorems, metalemmas, and so on. (Note: Each theorem *in* a theory must be a well-formed formula of the theory.)

We shall prove the following lemma *in* the theory $\mathcal{L}$. That is, we will construct a sequence of wffs in $\mathcal{L}$ such that the last element of the sequence is the statement we wish to prove, and every other wff in the sequence is an (instance of an) axiom or follows from previous members of the sequence by MP.

Lemma 2.3.2 $A \rightarrow A$

Proof:

1. $(A \rightarrow ((A \rightarrow A) \rightarrow A)) \rightarrow ((A \rightarrow (A \rightarrow A)) \rightarrow (A \rightarrow A))$
   an instance of axiom schema **L2**, with A for A, $(A \rightarrow A)$ for B, and A for C

2. $A \rightarrow ((A \rightarrow A) \rightarrow A)$ axiom schema **L1**with A for A, $(A \rightarrow A)$ for B

3. $(A \to (A \to A)) \to (A \to A)$ — by MP on 1 and 2

4. $A \to (A \to A)$ — axiom schema **L1**, A for A, A for B

5. $A \to A$ — by MP on 3 and 4

■

We can extend our idea of proof in two ways. First, we allow abbreviations of proofs; that is, we can use any previously proved theorem in our sequence of statements as an abbreviation for its own proof. Another helpful extension is the common mathematical practice of proving a statement B on the assumption of some other statement A, and then concluding that we have A implies B. In Propositional Logic this procedure is justified by the Deduction Theorem.

THEOREM 2.3.3 (Deduction Theorem for $\mathcal{L}$) If $\underline{S}$ is a set of wffs, and A and B are wffs, and $\underline{S}, A \vdash B$, then $\underline{S} \vdash A \to B$. In particular (when $\underline{S}$ is empty), if $A \vdash B$, then $\vdash A \to B$. (If you can derive B given the assumption A, then, with no assumptions, you can derive that A implies B.)

Proof: Let $B_1, \ldots, B_n$ be a derivation of B from $\underline{S}$, A; then $B_n = B$. We shall use induction on i to show that if it is the case that $\underline{S}$, $A \vdash B_i$, then $\underline{S} \vdash A \to B_i$, for every i, $1 \leq i \leq n$.

Basis case: $i = 1$. B_1 must be either an axiom or a hypothesis.

1. If B_1 is an axiom:

   $\vdash B_1$ — Lemma 2.3.1

   $\vdash B_1 \to (A \to B_1)$ — **L1**

   $\vdash A \to B_1$ — MP on the previous two steps

   $\underline{S} \vdash A \to B_1$ — property 1 of deducibility (Section 1)

2. If B_1 is an assumption:

   a. If $B_1 \in \underline{S}$:

   $\underline{S} \vdash B_1$ — def. of "deducible from" (Section 1)

   $\underline{S} \vdash B_1 \to (A \to B_1)$ — **L1**

   $\underline{S} \vdash A \to B_1$ — MP on the previous two steps

b. If B_1 is A:

$\vdash A \to B_1$ Lemma 2.3.2

$\underline{S} \vdash A \to B_1$ property 1 of deducibility

Induction step. Assume the theorem is true for $i < k$, then (by the definition of proof)

1. B_k is an axiom, or

2. B_k is an assumption

   a. $B_k \in \underline{S}$, or

   b. B_k is A, or

3. B_k follows by MP from B_i and B_j, where $i,j < k$, and B_j is $B_i \to B_k$.

The first two cases are treated exactly as in the basis case above. We now consider the third case.

$\underline{S} \vdash A \to (B_i \to B_k)$ inductive hypothesis

$\underline{S} \vdash A \to B_i$ inductive hypothesis

$\vdash (A \to (B_i \to B_k)) \to ((A \to B_i) \to (A \to B_k))$ **L2**

$\underline{S} \vdash ((A \to B_i) \to (A \to B_k))$ MP

$\underline{S} \vdash A \to B_k$ MP

The theorem follows as the special case where $i = n$. ∎

Now that we have the Deduction Theorem, the proof of Lemma 2.3.2 is simplified to the point of being trivial. We used Lemma 2.3.2 in proving the Deduction Theorem, but we could have simply used the proof (without the Deduction Theorem) given earlier to derive what we needed without ever making reference to Lemma 2.3.2. Thus the following proof, although quite trivial, is not circular.

LEMMA 2.3.2 $A \to A$

Proof:

1. $A \vdash A$ — definition of "deducible from "
2. $\vdash A \to A$ — Deduction Theorem

■

The following lemma gives us a transitivity rule for implication.

LEMMA 2.3.4 $A \to B,\ B \to C \vdash A \to C$

Proof:

1. $A \to B$ — hypothesis
2. $B \to C$ — hypothesis
3. A — hypothesis
4. B — MP 1,3
5. C — MP 2,4

   Thus $A \to B,\ B \to C, A \vdash C$, so,

6. $A \to B,\ B \to C \vdash A \to C$ — Deduction Theorem, 3, 5

■

Lemma 2.3.5 states one direction of the equivalence of an implication with its contrapositive.[1]

LEMMA 2.3.5 $(\neg B \to \neg A) \to (A \to B)$

Proof:

1. $\neg B \to \neg A$ — hypothesis
2. $(\neg B \to \neg A) \to ((\neg B \to A) \to B)$ — **L3**
3. $A \to (\neg B \to A)$ — **L1**
4. $(\neg B \to A) \to B$ — MP 1,2

[1] The contrapositive of an implication $(A \to B)$ is $(\neg B \to \neg A)$.

5. $A \to B$ 3 and 4, Lemma 2.3.4 Thus $\neg B \to \neg A \vdash A \to B$, and,
6. $(\neg B \to \neg A) \to (A \to B)$ Deduction Theorem, 1, 5

■

Exercises 2.3

Prove each of the following theorems of $\mathcal{L}$:

1. $\neg\neg A \to A$
2. $A,\ B \vdash \neg(A \to \neg B)$ (i.e., $A,\ B \vdash A \wedge B$)
3. $A \equiv \neg\neg A$ (i.e., $(A \to \neg\neg A) \wedge (\neg\neg A \to A)$)
   (First prove $A \to \neg\neg A$, then use this result together with 1 and 2.)
4. $(A \to B) \to (\neg B \to \neg A)$
5. $\neg(A \to \neg B) \vdash B$ (i.e., $A \wedge B \vdash B$)
6. If $A,\ B \vdash C$ then $\neg(A \to \neg B) \vdash C$ (i.e., $A \wedge B \vdash C$)
7. $A \vdash \neg\neg(A \to \neg B) \to \neg B$ (i.e., $A \vdash \neg(A \wedge B) \to \neg B$)
8. If $\vdash P \to A$ and $\vdash P \to B$, then $\vdash P \to \neg(A \to \neg B)$
   (i.e., $\vdash P \to (A \wedge B)$)
9. $\neg A \to (A \to B)$

2.4 Computation

Now that we have developed the ideas of truth and deducibility (provability), we need to know how we can compute in Propositional Logic. Then we can discuss the relationships among these ideas.

Computation for Propositional Logic will be based on *Complementary Literal Elimination* (CLE), also called *ground resolution.* In order to develop this idea we introduce two new symbols, τ and $\Box$ ($\Box$ may be read "box," or "the empty clause"). These symbols are intended to represent statements that are always true and always false, respectively. In order to relate our language of computation with that of truth and deduction, we can consider the symbols $\mathcal{T}$ and $\Box$ as abbreviations for $\mathsf{A} \vee \neg\mathsf{A}$ and $\neg\mathsf{A} \wedge \mathsf{A}$, respectively. (It is convenient to assume that our wffs are expressed using only the connectives $\vee$, $\wedge$, and $\neg$. Clearly this is possible since we have already shown (page 16) that $\{\neg, \wedge, \vee\}$ is a sufficient set of connectives.)

DEFINITION: A wff P is in ***conjunctive normal form***, abbreviated ***cnf***, if *all* of the following are satisfied:

1. No subformula Q of P whose principal connective is $\neg$ contains another occurrence of $\neg$, or an occurrence of $\vee$, $\wedge$, $\mathcal{T}$, or $\Box$. For example, the following are *not* in conjunctive normal form: $\neg(\neg Q)$, $\neg(P \vee Q)$, $\neg(P \wedge Q)$, $\neg(\mathcal{T})$, and $\neg(\Box)$.

2. No subformula of P whose principal connective is $\vee$ contains $\wedge$, $\mathcal{T}$, or $\Box$. That is, no $\wedge$, $\mathcal{T}$, or $\Box$ occurs within the scope of any $\vee$. (The scope of a connective is the wff(s) to which it applies.)

3. Neither $\mathcal{T}$ nor $\Box$ occurs within the scope of any $\wedge$. ■

For example, the following well-formed formula is in conjunctive normal form:

$$(\mathsf{A} \vee \neg\mathsf{B} \vee \neg\mathsf{A}) \wedge (\neg\mathsf{C} \vee \neg\mathsf{B}) \wedge (\mathsf{C} \vee \neg\mathsf{A} \vee \mathsf{C} \vee \mathsf{B})$$

DEFINITION: P is in ***reduced conjunctive normal form*** if, in addition to satisfying the three conditions above,

4. No proposition letter appears more than once within the scope of any $\vee$. ■

The reduced conjunctive normal form of the example given above is:

$$(\mathsf{C} \vee \neg\mathsf{B}) \wedge (\mathsf{C} \vee \neg\mathsf{A} \vee \mathsf{B})$$

Every wff P can be reduced to an equivalent formula P' such that P' is in reduced conjunctive normal form.

1. By repeated application of the following reduction rules we get a formula satisfying criterion 1 of the definition of reduced conjunctive normal form.

a. $\neg\neg Q$ reduces to Q

b. $\neg(Q_1 \vee Q_2)$ reduces to $\neg Q_1 \wedge \neg Q_2$

c. $\neg(Q_1 \wedge Q_2)$ reduces to $\neg Q_1 \vee \neg Q_2$

d. $\neg\tau$ reduces to $\Box$

e. $\neg\Box$ reduces to τ

2. The following rules eliminate occurrences of $\wedge, \tau$, or $\Box$ within the scope of any $\vee$.

a. $Q_1 \vee (Q_2 \wedge Q_3)$ reduces to $(Q_1 \vee Q_2) \wedge (Q_1 \vee Q_3)$

b. $\vee$ and $\wedge$ are commutative operations

c. $Q \vee \tau$ reduces to τ

d. $Q \vee \Box$ reduces to Q

3. We ensure no occurrences of τ or $\Box$ within the scope of any $\wedge$ by:

a. $Q \wedge \tau$ reduces to Q

b. $Q \wedge \Box$ reduces to $\Box$

4. To put our formula in reduced conjunctive form we eliminate repetitions of the same proposition letter within the scope of any $\vee$ as follows: Assume P is in conjunctive normal form. Let Q be a subformula of P of the form $P_1 \vee P_2$. By condition 2 of conjunctive normal form we know P_1 and P_2 are built up by $\vee$'s from P_i's and $\neg P_i$'s, where each P_i is a proposition letter. Since $\vee$ is both commutative and associative, we can rearrange the P_i's and $\neg P_i$'s so that if Q contains two occurrences of some P_k we can assume Q contains a subformula of one of the forms:

a. $P_k \vee P_k$, which reduces to P_k

b. $\neg P_k \vee P_k$, which reduces[2] to τ

c. $\neg P_k \vee \neg P_k$, which reduces to $\neg P_k$

For example, we can use the reductions above to transform the wff

$$\neg((A\rightarrow(B\rightarrow C))\rightarrow((A\rightarrow B)\rightarrow(A\rightarrow C)))$$

[2]Note that the introduction of τ may require that we again make use of the elimination rules 2c and 3a above.

to its reduced conjunctive normal form. First we eliminate the implications.

$$\neg(\neg(A\rightarrow(B\rightarrow C)) \vee ((A\rightarrow B)\rightarrow(A\rightarrow C)))$$
$$\neg(\neg(\neg A \vee (B\rightarrow C)) \vee (\neg(A\rightarrow B) \vee (A\rightarrow C)))$$
$$\neg(\neg(\neg A \vee (\neg B \vee C)) \vee (\neg(\neg A \vee B) \vee (\neg A \vee C)))$$

Then we move the negations inside the parentheses.

$$\neg\neg(\neg A \vee (\neg B \vee C)) \wedge \neg(\neg(\neg A \vee B) \vee (\neg A \vee C))$$

Last, we eliminate double negations and superfluous parentheses.

$$(\neg A \vee \neg B \vee C) \wedge (\neg\neg(\neg A \vee B) \wedge \neg(\neg A \vee C))$$
$$(\neg A \vee \neg B \vee C) \wedge ((\neg A \vee B) \wedge \neg\neg A \wedge \neg C)$$
$$(\neg A \vee \neg B \vee C) \wedge (\neg A \vee B) \wedge A \wedge \neg C$$

To describe the process of CLE on formulas in reduced conjunctive form, we need to define a few more terms. The following style of syntax specification is called a *context-free grammar.* Each line represents a rule for transforming a nonterminal symbol into a string of symbols. A terminal symbol is placed inside quotation marks; the symbol ::= is to be read "is a"; the symbol | is to be read "or" (representing alternative reduction rules on the same line); and juxtaposition of x and y indicates that x is followed by y. Thus the first clause below can be read "a plus-or-minus literal is a plus-literal or a minus-literal."

±literal ::= +literal | −literal
+literal ::= proposition_letter
−literal ::= "¬" proposition_letter
ground_clause ::= "□" | ±literal
  | ±literal "∨" ground_clause
ground_sentence ::= ground_clause
  | ground_clause "∧" ground_sentence

The empty clause is □. A wff in reduced conjunctive normal form is a ground sentence. The adjective "ground" refers to the fact that the clause or sentence it precedes contains no variables. Since there are no variables in Propositional Logic, all clauses and sentences are ground.

The distinction will become more important in the next chapter. We abbreviate "ground" by gr.

Sometimes it is convenient in the following to think of a gr sentence as a set of gr clauses, and a gr clause as a set of literals. This will cause no confusion since we know that a gr sentence is always a conjunction ($\wedge$) of its elements (gr clauses), and a gr clause is a disjunction ($\vee$) of its elements ($\pm$literals). In the following definitions we use the form of a context-free grammar, but indicate some alternatives using set notation rather than the strictly syntactic juxtaposition of symbols ($\cup$ indicates set union).

gr_clause ::= "$\Box$" | $\pm$literal
 | $\pm$literal $\cup$ gr_clause
gr_sentence ::= gr_clause
 | gr_clause $\cup$ gr_sentence

Now we are prepared to define complementary literal elimination (CLE) on formulas in reduced conjunctive normal form.

DEFINITION: P_k and $\neg P_k$ (where P_k is a proposition letter) are ***complementary literals***. ∎

DEFINITION: If A and B are gr clauses, and $P_k \in A$ and $\neg P_k \in B$, then the ***ground resolvent*** of A and B with respect to P_k and $\neg P_k$ is:[3]

$$(A - \{P_k\}) \cup (B - \{\neg P_k\})$$ ∎

That is, the resolvent clause is the union of the two original clauses, with the exception that the complementary literals have been eliminated. Since we consider $\Box$ to be the empty clause, the ground resolvent of P_k and $\neg P_k$ is $\Box$.

Ground resolution, or CLE, is a more general application of MP, which states that from A and $A \rightarrow B$, we can deduce B. This could also be written: From A and $(\neg A \vee B)$ (which are in reduced conjunctive

---

[3] $A - B$ indicates the set difference of A and B. It consists of those elements of A that are not in B.

normal form) we can deduce B. Eliminating A and $\neg A$ results in the gr resolvent B. Pictorially,

$$A \qquad\qquad \neg A \vee B$$

$$B$$

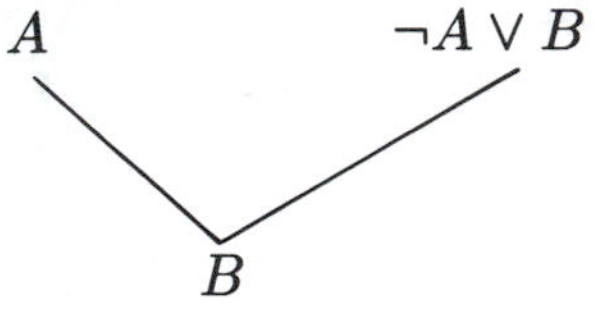

We exhibit several examples:

(a) $(P \vee Q)$ $\wedge$ $(R \vee \neg P)$

$$Q \vee R$$

(b) $(\neg P \vee Q \vee \neg R)$ $\wedge$ R $\wedge$ $\neg Q$

$$\neg P \vee Q$$

$$\neg P$$

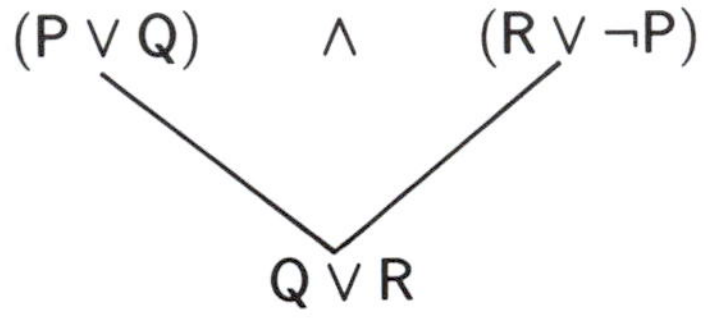

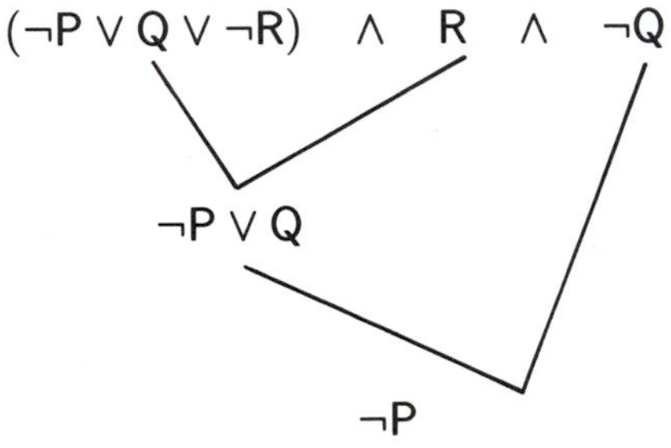

Note that in the second example, the same result could have been obtained by resolving first the Q's and then the R's. Having selected the clauses we wish to resolve on, we also have a choice of literals to eliminate. It is important to remember that although the choice will not matter, only one pair of complementary literals can be eliminated in the resolvent.

(c) $(P \vee Q)$ $\wedge$ $(\neg P \vee \neg Q)$

$$Q \vee \neg Q$$

(d) $(P \vee Q)$ $\wedge$ $(\neg P \vee \neg Q)$

$$P \vee \neg P$$

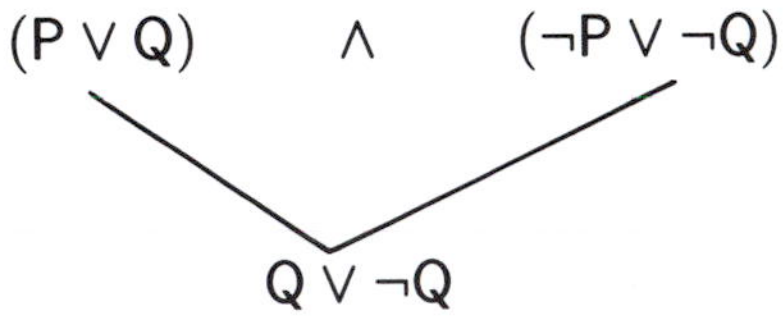

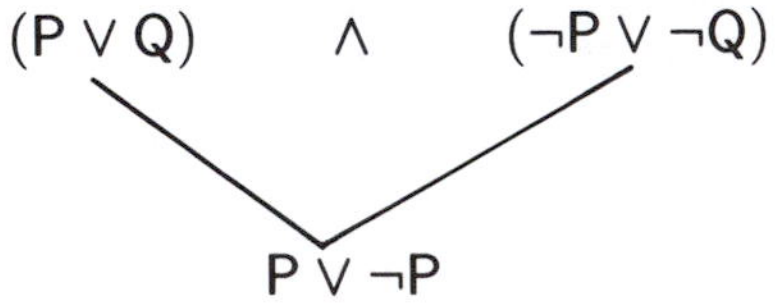

These examples are both legal resolutions. However, it would *not* be possible to eliminate both pairs of complementary literals at once in order to derive □.

DEFINITION: A ***resolution deduction*** of a clause A from a set of clauses $\underline{S}$ is a finite sequence of clauses $B_1, \ldots, B_n$ such that

1. B_n is A
2. For every i, $1 \leq i \leq n$, B_i is either
   a. an element of $\underline{S}$, or
   b. a ground resolvent of B_j and B_k, where $j, k < i$ ■

If C is a ground resolvent of a pair of clauses in $\underline{S}$, we sometimes write: $\underline{S} \longrightarrow C$. We write $\underline{S} \stackrel{*}{\longrightarrow} A$ if a resolution deduction of A from $\underline{S}$ exists.

DEFINITION: A resolution deduction of □ from $\underline{S}$ is called a ***resolution refutation***, or simply a ***refutation***, of $\underline{S}$. ■

For example:

$$\underline{S} = \{(\mathsf{P} \lor \mathsf{Q}),\ (\neg\mathsf{Q} \lor \mathsf{R}),\ (\neg\mathsf{P} \lor \mathsf{R}),\ \neg\mathsf{R}\}$$

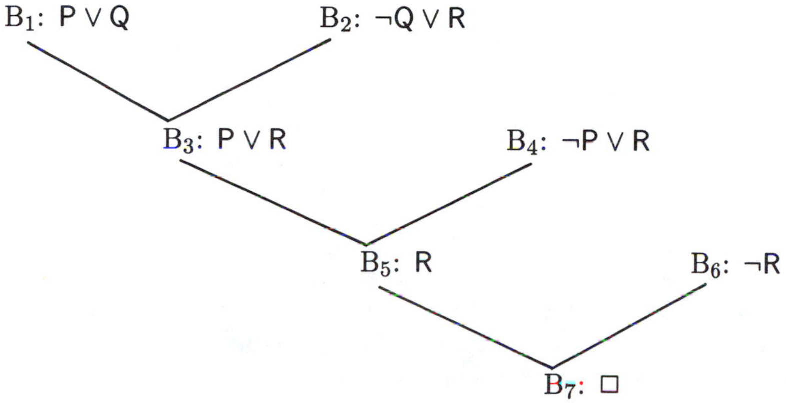

Note that in B_5 there is only one occurrence of R in the resolvent, although there was an occurrence of R in each of the clauses being resolved upon. Note also that you do not *use up* clauses in the process of resolution; the same clause may be used several times. Each time a resolvent is generated, the set of clauses available for use is increased. Another possible refutation of the set of clauses $\underline{S}$ above is:

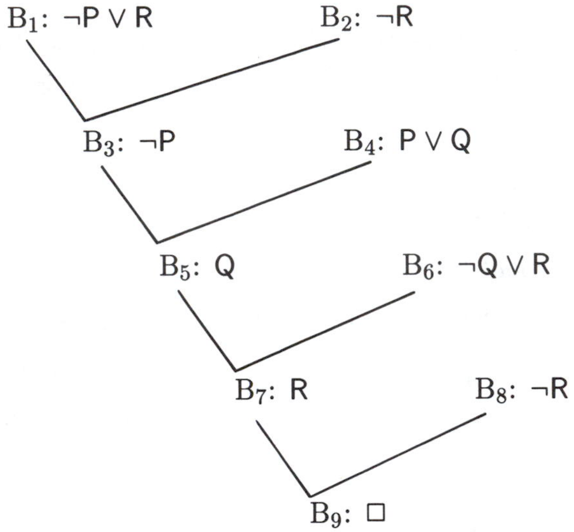

Our computation method, CLE or ground resolution, has been described as a means of producing *refutations* of sets of clauses. The terminology stems from the fact that by refuting a conjunction of clauses we hope to show that the conjunction is contradictory, or impossible to satisfy. Thus, when we relate this computation method with our understanding of truth and proof, we will attempt to refute the *negation* of what we know to be true and/or provable. If a wff is always true, then its negation is always false and we hope to exhibit its refutation. Likewise, if we can refute the negation of a wff A, then we hope to be able to prove the un-negated A in our formal theory.

Clearly, a resolution may take many possible paths. One way to mechanize the process is to take all possible paths — that is, at each step generate all possible resolvents from the current set of clauses.

DEFINITION: Given an initial set of clauses $\underline{S}$, we define $\Re(\underline{S})$ to be the union of $\underline{S}$ with the set of all possible ground resolvents of clauses in $\underline{S}$. We define $\Re^n$ as follows:

$$\begin{aligned} \Re^0(\underline{S}) &= \underline{S} \\ \Re^{n+1}(\underline{S}) &= \Re(\Re^n(\underline{S})) \end{aligned}$$

■

By definition, $\underline{S} \subset \Re(\underline{S}) \subset \Re^2(\underline{S}) \subset \cdots$ ($\subset$ denotes "is a subset of"). Also, each $\Re^n(\underline{S}) \subset \underline{S}^*$, the set of all possible clauses using literals contained in $\underline{S}$, since no new literals are generated by ground resolution. $\underline{S}^*$ is finite; therefore, for some integer m, which depends upon $\underline{S}$, we have $\Re^m(\underline{S}) = \Re^k(\underline{S})$ for all $k > m$. Thus the operation of taking resolvents *closes out* (we get no new resolvent clauses) after a finite number of steps. If $\Box \in \Re^m(\underline{S})$, then a refutation of $\underline{S}$ exists. If $\Box \notin \Re^m(\underline{S})$, then there is no refutation of $\underline{S}$. Thus, given any set $\underline{S}$ of clauses, whether or not $\underline{S} \xrightarrow{*} \Box$ is decidable. Since we are only interested in whether or not $\underline{S} \xrightarrow{*} \Box$, as soon as $\Box$ appears we need not continue computing $\Re^m(\underline{S})$.

Exercise 2.4

1. Exhibit a refutation of the *negation* of each of the following wffs. (Note: This requires that each wff be negated and then converted to reduced conjunctive normal form before resolution begins.)

   a. $(((\mathsf{A}\rightarrow\mathsf{B})\rightarrow\mathsf{C})\rightarrow((\mathsf{A}\rightarrow\mathsf{B})\rightarrow(\mathsf{A}\rightarrow\mathsf{C})))$

   b. $((\neg\mathsf{A}\rightarrow\mathsf{B})\rightarrow(\neg\mathsf{B}\rightarrow\mathsf{A}))$

   c. $((\neg\mathsf{B}\rightarrow\neg\mathsf{A})\rightarrow((\neg\mathsf{B}\rightarrow\mathsf{A})\rightarrow\mathsf{B}))$

2.5 Completeness Results

Now we investigate the relationships among logical validity, provability, and refutability by CLE. First we will show that every theorem of $\mathcal{L}$ is logically valid — i.e., a tautology.

Lemma 2.5.1 If P is an axiom, then P is a tautology.

Proof: (of **L1** and **L3**, **L2** is left to the reader)

A	B	$B\rightarrow A$	$A\rightarrow(B\rightarrow A)$
t	t	t	t
t	f	t	t
f	t	f	t
f	f	t	t

A	B	$\neg B$	$\neg A$	$\neg B \rightarrow A$	$(\neg B \rightarrow \neg A) \rightarrow ((\neg B \rightarrow A) \rightarrow B)$		
t	t	f	f	t	t	t	t
t	f	t	f	t	f	t	f
f	t	f	t	t	t	t	t
f	f	t	t	f	t	t	t

■

THEOREM 2.5.2 ($\mathcal{L}$ is sound) If $\vdash P$ then $\models P$ (if P is provable, then P is a tautology).

Proof: $\vdash P$ implies that there is a derivation of P — say, $P_1, \ldots, P_n$, where $P_n = P$ — such that for all i, $1 \leq i \leq n$, P_i is an axiom or P_i follows by MP from P_j and P_k (where $P_k = P_j \rightarrow P_i$ and $j, k < i$). We shall prove by induction on i that each P_i in the derivation is a tautology:

Basis case: $i = 1$. By the definition of proof, P_1 must be an axiom, and by Lemma 2.5.1 it is a tautology.

Induction step. Assume that P_i is a tautology for all i, $1 \leq i < k$; we must show that P_k is a tautology.

1. If P_k is an axiom then by Lemma 2.5.1 it is a tautology.
2. If P_k follows by MP from P_i and P_j where $i, j < k$ then, since P_i and P_j are tautologies by the inductive assumption, P_k is a tautology by the definition of $\rightarrow$. (In the truth table given in Section 2.2, we see that B is true whenever A and $A \rightarrow B$ are true.)

Therefore, P_i is a tautology for all i, $1 \leq i \leq n$. Since $P = P_n$, it follows that P is a tautology. ■

Thus deducibility implies truth, meaning that our theory $\mathcal{L}$ is sound. Now we look at truth and computation. We want to show that if P is a tautology, then we can find a refutation of $\neg P$, the negation of P. By definition, if P is a tautology, then $\neg P$ is unsatisfiable. So, we wish to show that if $\neg P$ is unsatisfiable, then $\neg P \xrightarrow{*} \Box$.

We will assume that our wff $\neg P$ has been put into reduced conjunctive normal form. Thus $\neg P$ is a set of clauses, which we understand to be the conjunction of those clauses.

DEFINITION: If $\underline{S}$ is a set of clauses, the phrase "$\underline{S}$ with A replaced by B" denotes the set

$$(\underline{S} - \{A\}) \cup \{B\}$$

That is, the clause A is removed from the set of clauses $\underline{S}$ and then the clause B is added to the result. ■

LEMMA 2.5.3 If $\underline{S}$ is an unsatisfiable set of gr clauses with $A \in \underline{S}$, and $B \subset A$, then $\underline{S}$ with A replaced by B is an unsatisfiable set.

Proof: By the definition of clause, A is a disjunction of literals; $B \subset A$, so B is also a disjunction of literals. If $\underline{S}$ with A replaced by B is satisfiable, then there exists an interpretation under which $\underline{S}$ with A replaced by B is true. Since $\underline{S}$ is a conjunction of clauses, we know that B must be true under this interpretation.

B is a disjunction of literals; it is true only if one of its literals is true. Since $B \subset A$, the same interpretation renders A true and therefore $\underline{S}$ is satisfiable, which contradicts our initial assumption.

Thus $\underline{S}$ with A replaced by B is unsatisfiable. ■

Lemma 2.5.3 assures us that an unsatisfiable set of clauses cannot be made satisfiable by eliminating literals in its clauses. Contrast this with the idea of eliminating an entire clause. Since a clause is a disjunction, eliminating elements (literals) makes it more difficult to satisfy. However, since a wff is a conjunction, eliminating elements (clauses) makes it easier to satisfy.

DEFINITION: A set $\underline{S}$ of clauses is a ***minimal unsatisfiable set*** if $\underline{S}$ is unsatisfiable but no proper subset of $\underline{S}$ is unsatisfiable. A minimal unsatisfiable set is finite by the compactness theorem for satisfiability (see [17]). ■

Every unsatisfiable set contains a minimal unsatisfiable subset, but such a subset is not necessarily unique. For example, {A, B, ¬A, ¬B} has two minimally unsatisfiable subsets.

We introduce the notions of unit, multiunit, and nonunit clauses, and excess literals, in order to simplify the proof of Lemma 2.5.4.

DEFINITION: A clause that contains exactly one literal is a ***unit clause***. A ***multiunit*** clause is a clause with two or more literals. A ***nonunit*** clause is either the empty clause or a multiunit clause. ■

DEFINITION: Let $\#\underline{S}$ denote the number of clauses in the finite set $\underline{S}$, and $\#\#\underline{S}$ the number of literal occurrences in $\underline{S}$. The number of ***excess literals*** in $\underline{S}$ is $\#\#\underline{S} - \#\underline{S}$, which is nonnegative if $\Box \notin \underline{S}$. ■

For example:

$$\begin{aligned} \underline{S} &= \{\mathsf{P} \lor \mathsf{Q},\ \neg\mathsf{Q} \lor \mathsf{R},\ \neg\mathsf{P} \lor \mathsf{R},\ \neg\mathsf{R}\} \\ \#\underline{S} &= 4 \text{ (the number of clauses in } \underline{S}) \\ \#\#\underline{S} &= 7 \text{ (the number of literal occurrences in } \underline{S}) \\ \#\#\underline{S} - \#\underline{S} &= 3 \text{ (the number of excess literals in } \underline{S}) \end{aligned}$$

The only clause with no literals is $\Box$, so if $\Box \notin \underline{S}$, then $\underline{S}$ must have at least one literal occurrence in each clause, making $\#\#\underline{S} \geq \#\underline{S}$ and the number of excess literals nonnegative.

LEMMA 2.5.4 If $\underline{S}$ is a minimal unsatisfiable set of ground clauses then $\underline{S} \xrightarrow{*} \Box$.

Proof: If $\Box \in \underline{S}$, then $\underline{S} = \{\}$ since $\underline{S}$ is minimal, and $\{\} \xrightarrow{*} \Box$. Now assume $\Box \notin \underline{S}$ and let n be the number of excess literals in $\underline{S}$. We will prove that $\underline{S} \xrightarrow{*} \Box$ by induction on n.

Basis case: $n = 0$. If the number of excess literals n is 0, there are no nonunit clauses in $\underline{S}$. Thus $\underline{S}$ is of the form $\{P, \neg P\}$ for some literal P. In this case, ground resolution on these two unit clauses yields $\Box$.

Induction step: Assume that $\underline{S} \xrightarrow{*} \Box$ for all minimal unsatisfiable sets of ground clauses $\underline{S}$ with k excess literals, for all $0 \leq k < n$. We must show that $\underline{S} \xrightarrow{*} \Box$ where $\underline{S}$ is a minimal unsatisfiable set of ground clauses with n excess literals.

Since $n > 0$, a multiunit clause A exists in $\underline{S}$. Let $P \in A$ and let $\underline{S}_1$ be $\underline{S}$ with A replaced by $A - \{P\}$. By Lemma 2.5.3, $\underline{S}_1$ is unsatisfiable. Let $\underline{S}'$ be a minimal unsatisfiable subset of $\underline{S}_1$. Now, $\underline{S}_1$ (and thus $\underline{S}'$) has less than n excess literals. Therefore, by the induction hypothesis, $\underline{S'} \xrightarrow{*} \Box$ by some resolution refutation $B_1, \ldots, B_{(k-1)}, B_k = \Box$.

Some B_i is $A - \{P\}$, otherwise $\underline{S}$ would not have been minimal. We make $B_1, \ldots, B_k$ into a deduction from $\underline{S}$ by replacing P in $A - \{P\}$, to yield A, and adjusting subsequent resolvents to include P if necessary. Let $B'_1, \ldots, B'_k$ denote the deduction from $\underline{S}$ so obtained. If $B'_k = \Box$ we are done. If not, then $B'_k = \{P\}$, and we must obtain a refutation of $\underline{T} \cup \{P\}$ for some subset $\underline{T}$ of $\underline{S}$, and append it to $B'_1, \ldots, B'_k$ to get a refutation of $\underline{S}$.

Let $\underline{S}_2$ be $\underline{S}$ with A replaced by $\{P\}$. $\underline{S}_2$ is unsatifiable, again by Lemma 2.5.3. Let $\underline{S}'_2$ be a minimal unsatisfiable subset of $\underline{S}_2$. Now, $\underline{S}'_2$ is $T \cup \{P\}$ for some $T \subset S$ as $\{P\}$ must be in $\underline{S}'_2$. (Otherwise $\underline{S}'_2$ would be a proper subset of $\underline{S}$, which contradicts the hypothesis that $\underline{S}$ was a minimal unsatisfiable set.) $T \cup \{P\}$ has fewer than n excess literals, so by the induction hypothesis a refutation $C_1, \ldots, C_r$ of $T \cup \{P\}$ exists. Then $B'_1, \ldots, B'_k, C_1, \ldots, C_r$ is the desired refutation of $\underline{S}$. ∎

Now that the hard work has been done we can prove Theorem 2.5.5.

Theorem 2.5.5 $\models P$ implies $\neg P \xrightarrow{*} \Box$.
(If P is logically valid, then there exists a refutation of $\neg P$.)

Proof: $\models P$ if and only if $\neg P$ is unsatisfiable, and $\neg P$ is unsatisfiable implies that there exists a minimal unsatisfiable subset $\underline{S}$ of $\neg P$. By Lemma 2.5.4, $\underline{S} \xrightarrow{*} \Box$; thus by the same refutation $\neg P \xrightarrow{*} \Box$. ∎

Thus, if a wff P is valid we can compute a refutation of $\neg P$. This means that our computation scheme is complete. So far, we know that deducibility implies truth, and truth implies computation; now we compare computation with deduction.

We begin by establishing that if Q is a ground resolvent of clauses in a set of clauses P, we can prove that $P \rightarrow Q$. We then generalize this to consider the case in which there exists a resolution deduction of Q from P (perhaps involving several steps of CLE).

Lemma 2.5.6 If Q is a ground resolvent of clauses in P, then $\vdash P \rightarrow Q$. (i.e., if $P \longrightarrow Q$ then $\vdash P \rightarrow Q$)

Proof: $P \longrightarrow Q$ implies that P is of the form $(P_1 \vee R) \wedge (\neg R \vee P_2) \wedge P_3$ where R is a proposition letter, P_1 and P_2 are clauses, P_3 is a conjunction of clauses, and $Q = (P_1 \vee P_2)$; then we wish to show

$$((P_1 \vee R) \wedge (\neg R \vee P_2) \wedge P_3) \vdash Q$$

which, by the definition of $\vee$ as an abbreviation (see page 12), can also be written

$$(\neg P_1 \rightarrow R) \wedge (\neg\neg R \rightarrow P_2) \wedge P_3 \vdash (\neg P_1 \rightarrow P_2)$$

1. $\neg P_1 \rightarrow R$ hypothesis
2. $R \rightarrow \neg\neg R$ Exercise 3 page 25
3. $\neg P_1 \rightarrow \neg\neg R$ 1, 2, Lemma 2.3.4
4. $\neg\neg R \rightarrow P_2$ hypothesis
5. $\neg P_1 \rightarrow P_2$ 3, 4, Lemma 2.3.4
6. $(\neg P_1 \rightarrow R) \wedge (\neg\neg R \rightarrow P_2) \vdash (\neg P_1 \rightarrow P_2)$ 1, 4, 5 Exercise 6 page 25
7. $(\neg P_1 \rightarrow R) \wedge (\neg\neg R \rightarrow P_2),\ P_3 \vdash (\neg P_1 \rightarrow P_2)$
   property 1 of deducibility (Section 1)
8. $(\neg P_1 \rightarrow R) \wedge (\neg\neg R \rightarrow P_2) \wedge P_3 \vdash (\neg P_1 \rightarrow P_2)$ Exercise 6 page 25
   or, $(P_1 \vee R) \wedge (\neg R \vee P_2) \wedge P_3 \vdash (P_1 \vee P_2)$

that is, $P \vdash Q$, and by the Deduction Theorem for $\mathcal{L}$ we have $\vdash P \rightarrow Q$. ■

Lemma 2.5.7 $\neg P \xrightarrow{*} Q$ implies $\vdash \neg P \rightarrow Q$

Proof: $\neg P \xrightarrow{*} Q$ implies that a resolution deduction of Q from $\neg P$ exists (i.e., there exists a sequence, $P_1, \ldots, P_n = Q$ such that for all i, $1 \leq i \leq n$, P_i is either a clause of $\neg P$ or a ground resolvent of two previous P_i's in the sequence).

We show by induction on i that for all i, $\vdash \neg P \rightarrow P_i$.

Basis case: $i = 1$.

P_1 is a clause of $\neg P$ (i.e., $\neg P = P_1 \wedge Q_1$)

$P_1 \vdash P_1$	definition of proof
$P_1,\ Q_1 \vdash P_1$	property 1 of deducibility (Sec 1)
$P_1 \wedge Q_1 \vdash P_1$	Exercise 6 page 25
$\vdash (P_1 \wedge Q_1) \rightarrow P_1$	Deduction Theorem for $\mathcal{L}$

that is, $\vdash \neg P \rightarrow P_1$

Induction step. Assume $\vdash \neg P \rightarrow P_i$ for all $i < k$. We must show $\vdash \neg P \rightarrow P_k$.

1. If P_k is a clause of $\neg P$, then, as in the case for $i = 1$, we have $\vdash \neg P \rightarrow P_k$.

2. If P_k is a ground resolvent of two previous P_i's (that is, P_k is a ground resolvent of P_i and P_j, $i, j < k$, then

$\vdash \neg P \rightarrow P_i$	induction hypothesis
$\vdash \neg P \rightarrow P_j$	induction hypothesis
$\vdash \neg P \rightarrow (P_i \wedge P_j)$	Exercise 8 page 25
$\vdash (P_i \wedge P_j) \rightarrow P_k$	Lemma 2.5.6
$\vdash \neg P \rightarrow P_k$	Lemma 2.3.4

for $i = n$, we have $\vdash \neg P \rightarrow P_n$ and $P_n = Q$; therefore, $\neg P \xrightarrow{*} Q$ implies $\vdash \neg P \rightarrow Q$. ∎

Finally, Theorem 2.5.8 provides the statement we really want: If there exists a refutation of $\neg P$ (by CLE) then we can prove P in $\mathcal{L}$.

THEOREM 2.5.8 $\neg P \xrightarrow{*} \Box$ implies $\vdash P$

Proof: $\neg P \xrightarrow{*} \Box$ implies that there exists a resolution deduction $P_1, \ldots, P_n = \Box$ from $\neg P$.

1. If $\Box \in \neg P$ then $\neg P = \{\Box\}$, since $\neg P$ is in reduced conjunctive form. But then $P = \neg(\neg P) = \neg\Box = \tau$. (Recall that τ is an abbreviation for $\mathsf{A} \vee \neg\mathsf{A}$, which, by definition, is equivalent to: $\neg\mathsf{A} \rightarrow \neg\mathsf{A}$, thus P is simply $\neg\mathsf{A} \rightarrow \neg\mathsf{A}$, which is provable by Lemma 2.3.2.)

2. $\Box$ must be a ground resolvent of P_i and P_j, $i, j < n$. Recall that $\Box$ is an abbreviation for $\neg A \wedge A$; thus, by the proof of Lemma 2.5.7, we have $\vdash \neg P \rightarrow (A \wedge \neg A)$.

a.	$\vdash \neg P \rightarrow \neg(A \rightarrow \neg\neg A)$	definition of $\wedge$
b.	$\vdash A \rightarrow \neg\neg A$	Exercise 3, page 25
c.	$\vdash (\neg P \rightarrow \neg(A \rightarrow \neg\neg A)) \rightarrow ((A \rightarrow \neg\neg A) \rightarrow P)$	Lemma 2.3.5
d.	$\vdash (A \rightarrow \neg\neg A) \rightarrow P$	MP a,c
e.	$\vdash P$	MP b,d

■

THEOREM 2.5.9 In Propositional Logic:

$$\vdash P \Leftrightarrow \models P \Leftrightarrow \neg P \xrightarrow{*} \Box$$

Proof:

$\vdash P$ implies $\models P$	Theorem 2.5.2
$\models P$ implies $\neg P \xrightarrow{*} \Box$	Theorem 2.5.5
$\neg P \xrightarrow{*} \Box$ implies $\vdash P$	Theorem 2.5.8

■

Thus, for Propositional Logic we have shown that a statement is provable if and only if it is logically valid if and only if its negation reduces to the empty clause by ground resolution (Complementary Literal Elimination).

Exercises 2.5

1. In each of the following cases, determine, if possible, whether the theory described is sound, consistent, complete, and/or decidable. If the information given is insufficient to determine any of these, state why. (Assume that all axioms and rules are given as schemata, standing for many axioms or rules as instances.)

   a. The language and axioms of $\mathcal{L}$,
   with one rule of inference: $A \vdash A \vee B$

b. The language of $\mathcal{L}$, with one axiom: $A \to \neg B$
and one rule of inference: $A \to B,\ B \to C \vdash B$

c. A theory in which some tautology is not provable

d. The language of $\mathcal{L}$, with one axiom: $A \to B$
and one rule of inference: Modus Ponens

e. A theory in which some nontautological wff is provable

f. The language of $\mathcal{L}$ with one axiom schema and no rules of inference

2. What relationships, if any, exist among the metatheoretic notions of completeness, soundness, consistency, and decidability? (Are they totally independent, or does knowing one property imply that another must hold?)

3. For each of the following, invent a formal theory that satisfies the given conditions.

   a. sound, not complete, consistent

   b. not sound, complete, not consistent

   c. not sound, not complete, consistent

CHAPTER 3

PREDICATE CALCULUS

Propositional Logic is comfortable because we can easily define theories for it that are sound and complete, as well as describe algorithms for determining the truth and provability (equivalent, in an appropriately defined theory) of propositional statements. However, Propositional Logic is too restrictive as a language to enable us to describe the kinds of problems we need to deal with in a realistic computational world.

Our language gets more complicated because we wish to express more complicated ideas. We want to be able to consider the truth or falsity of compound statements made up of atomic statements that (unlike proposition letters) may be sometimes true and sometimes false under a single interpretation. For example the statement "if x is even then $x+1$ is odd," is an implication between the two atomic statements "x is even" and "$x+1$ is odd." It is easy to convince oneself that in the world of integers the implication is true. However, we cannot say that "x is even" is true, or that it is false; that depends on the value of x. So we add to our language the ability to make parametric statements. These statements are atomic, but rather than being simply true or false (as with proposition letters), they state that some relationship holds among their arguments. These relationships are expressed with *predicates* applied to arguments.

These concerns lead us to consider *first-order theories*. First-order theories are distinguished from higher-order theories in that what may appear as arguments to predicates are restricted to terms constructed from constants, variables, and function applications. We also allow quantification only over variables. In higher-order theories, functions and predicates may take functions and predicates as arguments and we can make statements about all functions and predicates by quantifying over function and predicate symbols. These concepts will be precisely defined in the next section.

3.1 The Language

We will describe here the class of *first-order languages*. The language of Predicate Calculus is an element (in fact, the largest element) of this class. Recall that a set is denumerable if it can be put into one-to-one correspondence with the set of positive integers, and it is countable if it is finite or denumerable.

DEFINITION: The countable set of symbols of a ***first-order language*** is defined as follows:

logical connectives: $\neg$, $\rightarrow$, and $\forall$
auxiliary symbols:), (, and ,
a denumerable number of variables:

$$\mathsf{x}, \mathsf{x}_1, \mathsf{x}_2, \mathsf{x}_3, \ldots$$

a countable, possibly empty, set of constant symbols:

$$\mathsf{a}, \mathsf{a}_1, \mathsf{a}_2, \mathsf{a}_3, \ldots$$

a countable, possibly empty, set of function letters:

$\mathsf{f}^{\mathsf{n}}_{\mathsf{k}}$ for all positive integers **n** and **k**

a countable, nonempty set of predicate letters:

$\mathsf{A}^{\mathsf{n}}_{\mathsf{k}}$ for all positive integers **n** and **k** ■

The subscript on variables, constants, function letters, and predicate letters is just an indexing number to distinguish different symbols. There may be function and predicate letters that take n arguments for any value of n. This is indicated by superscripts giving the arity (number of arguments) of each function and predicate symbol. As this notation is very cumbersome, we will not give the superscripts. The arity of a function or predicate letter will be obvious from context. We also eliminate the need for subscripts by using different letters for different symbols. We follow convention in using lowercase letters from the beginning of the alphabet to represent constants, lowercase letters from the end of the alphabet to symbolize variables, and f, g, and h to represent function letters. Predicate letters are uppercase.

Now we need to describe the well-formed formulas of a first-order language. They are built up from atomic formulas, which are predicate letters applied to terms. Terms are variables, constants, and function letters applied to terms.

DEFINITION: ***The well-formed formulas*** of a first-order language are defined as follows:

term ::= variable | constant | function_letter "(" termlist ")"
termlist ::= term | term "," termlist
atomic_formula ::= predicate_letter "(" termlist ")"
wff ::= atomic_formula | "(¬" wff ")" | "(" wff "→" wff ")"
| "((∀" variable ")" wff ")"

■

DEFINITION: ∀ is the ***universal quantifier***, and may be read "for all." ∃ is the ***existential quantifier***, read "there exists." It was unnecessary to define ∃ as a primitive symbol, since we can define it as an abbreviation as follows:

$$((\exists x)A) \text{ stands for } \neg((\forall x)\neg A)$$ ■

DEFINITION: The ***scope*** of a quantifier is the wff to which it applies — for example, in $((\forall y)\neg A \vee B)$, $\neg A \vee B$ is the scope of the quantifier $(\forall y)$. ■

The symbols ∨, ∧, and ≡ are defined as for $\mathcal{L}$. We use the same conventions as before for eliminating parentheses, with the additional rule that the quantifiers $(\forall y)$ and $(\exists y)$ rank between →and ∨. We also omit parentheses around quantified formulas when they are preceded by other quantifiers.

For example,

$$\forall x)\mathsf{A}(\mathsf{x}) \vee \mathsf{B}(\mathsf{y},\mathsf{f}(\mathsf{x}))\rightarrow\mathsf{C}(\mathsf{x},\mathsf{y},\mathsf{f}(\mathsf{y},\mathsf{x}))$$

stands for

$$(((\forall \mathsf{x})\mathsf{A}(\mathsf{x}) \vee \mathsf{B}(\mathsf{y},\mathsf{f}(\mathsf{x})))\rightarrow\mathsf{C}(\mathsf{x},\mathsf{y},\mathsf{f}(\mathsf{y},\mathsf{x})))$$

and

$$(\forall x)(\exists z)A(h(a,x,a),y,z)$$

stands for

$$((\forall x)((\exists z)A(h(a,x,a),y,z)))$$

DEFINITION: An ***occurrence*** of a variable x is ***bound*** in a wff if and only if it is either the variable of a quantifier, $(\forall x)$ or $(\exists x)$, in the wff, or it is the same variable that is quantified and is within the scope of the quantifier. Otherwise the ***occurrence*** is said to be ***free*** in the wff. ■

DEFINITION: A ***variable*** is said to be ***free*** (*bound*) in a wff if and only if it has a free (bound) occurrence in the wff. ■

A variable may have both bound and free occurrences in a given wff. Thus, a variable may be both bound and free in the same wff.

For example:

$$A(x,y) \rightarrow (\forall x)B(x) \tag{3.1}$$

The first occurrence of x is free, the second and third are bound.

$$(\forall x)P(f(x),y,z) \rightarrow \neg P(z,x,f(y)) \tag{3.2}$$

The first and second occurrences of x are bound, the third occurrence of x is free; y and z are free throughout the entire formula.

$$(\forall x)(P(f(x),y,z) \rightarrow \neg P(z,x,f(y))) \tag{3.3}$$

x is bound throughout (notice the parentheses), and y and z are free throughout the entire formula.

$$(\forall z)P(x,y,z) \wedge (\forall y)S(f(x),z,y) \wedge R(z) \tag{3.4}$$

x is free throughout, z is bound throughout, and y is free in its first occurrence and bound in its second and third occurrences.

We shall often indicate that a wff A has some of the free variables $x_1, \ldots, x_k$ by writing it as $A(x_1, \ldots, x_k)$. This does not mean that A contains precisely these variables as free variables. It is simply a convenient notation, as we then agree to write $A(t_1, \ldots, t_k)$ as the result of substituting in A the terms $t_1, \ldots, t_k$ for all free occurrences (if any) of $x_1, \ldots, x_k$, respectively.

A is used here as a metavariable standing for an arbitrarily complex wff. Make note of the difference between $A(x_1, \ldots, x_k)$ just defined, and $\mathsf{A}(\mathsf{x}_1, \ldots, \mathsf{x}_k)$, which is an atomic formula consisting of the predicate letter A applied to precisely the k arguments: $\mathsf{x}_1, \ldots, \mathsf{x}_k$.

DEFINITION: If A is a wff and t is a term, then t is said to be ***free for*** x_i ***in*** A if and only if no free occurrences of x_i in A lie within the scope of any quantifier $(\forall x_j)$ where x_j is a variable in t. ■

Although the definition of "free for" is quite complicated, several special cases are easily checked. We will look at some examples of these and then give an algorithm for checking whether an arbitrary variable is free for a term in a given wff.

- y is free for x in $\mathsf{A}(\mathsf{x})$, but is not free for x in $(\forall \mathsf{y})\mathsf{A}(\mathsf{x})$.

- $\mathsf{f}(\mathsf{g}(\mathsf{a}, \mathsf{y}))$ is free for x, y, and z in 3.2, and it is free for y and z but not for x in 3.4.

- Any term t containing no variables is free for any variable in any wff (e.g., $\mathsf{g}(\mathsf{f}(\mathsf{a}), \mathsf{c})$ is free for any term in any wff).

- A term t is free for any variable in A if none of the variables of t is bound in A (e.g., $\mathsf{h}(\mathsf{a}, \mathsf{f}(\mathsf{g}(\mathsf{y}, \mathsf{z})))$ is free for any variable in 3.1–3.3).

- Any variable is always free for itself in any wff.

The definition of "free for" is a little difficult to grasp on first sight. The idea is that a term t *is* free for a variable x *unless* there is a problem. A problem is defined as capture of a variable in the term t by a quantifier in the wff. This can only happen if there is a free occurrence of x within the scope of a quantifier binding a variable in t.

To determine whether a given term t is free for a given variable x in a wff A:

1. Find all free occurrences of x. You can ignore bound occurrences; they never cause a problem. If there are no free occurrences of x — there can be no problem — t is free for x.

2. For each free occurrence of x ask: Is the occurrence of x within the scope of a quantifier binding a variable that appears in t? If the answer is "Yes," there is a problem and t is not free for x. If the answer is "No," then check the next occurrence of x. When all occurrences of x have been checked, and have yielded no problems, then t is free for x.

Exercises 3.1

1. Determine whether each of the variables x, y, and z is *free*, *bound*, or *both* in each of the wffs a–d.

   a. $(\forall x)P(f(x), y, z) \rightarrow \neg P(z, x, y)$
   b. $(\forall z)P(g(z), a, y) \wedge (\forall y)\neg Q(x, y)$
   c. $(\forall x)(P(x, y, z) \wedge (\forall y)S(f(x), z, y) \vee R(z))$
   d. $(\forall y)P(y, a, z) \rightarrow (\forall z)(Q(x, z) \wedge P(x, a, z))$

2. Determine whether or not each of the terms:

$$h(x, y) \text{ and } g(a, f(y, z))$$

   is free for each of the variables x, y, and z in each of the following wffs (that is 18 questions):

   a. $(\forall z)(P(z, y, a) \wedge (\forall x)Q(g(z)))$
   b. $(\forall x)P(f(x), y) \rightarrow \neg P(f(x), z)$
   c. $P(f(x), x) \rightarrow (\forall z)\neg P(f(y), z)$

3.2 Truth

Wffs of Propositional Logic were made up of statement letters and logical connectives. To supply an interpretation, all we needed to know was whether the individual statement letters were true or false. We could list all possible interpretations using a truth table. Now the situation is more complex. We can express relationships that are true of some objects and not of others, instead of only simple statements that must be true or false. In order to determine the truth or falsity of a wff in an interpretation we need to know what values the variables can take on, as well as the values of the constants and what functions and relationships are to be represented by the function and predicate symbols.

DEFINITION: An ***interpretation*** of a wff, or set of wffs of a first-order language, consists of:

1. A nonempty set $\mathcal{D}$, called the *domain*
2. An assignment to each n-ary predicate letter A_j^n of an n-place relation in $\mathcal{D}$
3. An assignment to each n-ary function letter f_j^n of an n-place operation closed over $\mathcal{D}$, (that is, a function: $\mathcal{D}^n \rightarrow \mathcal{D}$)
4. An assignment to each individual constant a_i of some fixed element of $\mathcal{D}$ ■

Variables range over $\mathcal{D}$ and the logical connectives $\neg$ and $\rightarrow$, and thus $\wedge$, $\vee$, and $\equiv$ are given their usual meaning. $((\forall \mathsf{y})A)$ means that for all values of y, taken from the domain, property A holds. If A does not contain the variable y, $((\forall \mathsf{y})A)$ means the same as A. $((\exists \mathsf{y})A)$ means that there exists some value for y, taken from the domain, such that A holds.

DEFINITION: A ***closed*** wff is a wff containing no free variables. ■

For a given interpretation, a closed wff represents a statement that is true or false. A wff with free variables represents a relation on the domain that may be true for some values of the free variables and false for others.

For example consider the wffs:

1. $\mathsf{P(x,y)} \rightarrow \mathsf{Q(x)}$
2. $(\forall \mathsf{x})(\mathsf{Q(x)} \rightarrow \mathsf{Q(f(x))})$
3. $(\forall \mathsf{x})(\exists \mathsf{y})\mathsf{P(x,y)} \rightarrow (\exists \mathsf{y})(\forall \mathsf{x})\mathsf{P(x,y)}$

Two possible interpretations are:

A	B
Domain = Integers	Domain = Integers
P(x, y) means $x = y$	P(x, y) means $x * y = 0$
Q(x) means $x > 1$	Q(x) means $x = 0$
f(x) means $x + 1$	f(x) means $x * x$

Under interpretation A, the formulas read:

1. If $x = y$ then $x > 1$.

   This cannot be said to be either true or false, since the relation it describes will hold for some values in the domain and not for others.

2. For all integers x, if $x > 1$ then $x + 1 > 1$.

   This is a true statement.

3. If for each integer x there exists an integer y such that $x = y$, then there exists an integer y such that for each integer x, $x = y$.

   This statement is false.

Under interpretation B, the formulas read:

1. If $x * y = 0$, then $x = 0$.

   Again, this is neither true nor false, since the relation it describes will hold for some values in the domain and not for others.

2. For all integers x, if $x = 0$ then $x * x = 0$.

   This is a true statement.

3. If for each integer x there exists an integer y such that $x * y = 0$, then there is an integer y such that for each integer x, $x * y = 0$.

   This is also a true statement.

We define precisely what we mean by satisfiability and truth in an interpretation as follows: Given an interpretation with domain $\mathcal{D}$, let Σ be the set of denumerable sequences of elements of $\mathcal{D}$. We will define what it means for a sequence $\mathbf{s} = (\mathbf{b_1}, \mathbf{b_2}, \ldots)$ in Σ to satisfy a wff A under the given interpretation. First we define a function $\mathbf{s}^*$ of one argument, with terms as arguments and values in $\mathcal{D}$.

DEFINITION: $\mathbf{s}^*(t)$ is defined by cases. A term can be: (1) a variable; (2) a constant; or (3) a function symbol applied to terms.

1. If t is $\mathsf{x_i}$, then $\mathbf{s}^*(t) = \mathbf{b_i}$.[1] Thus, we can consider a sequence $\mathbf{s}$ to be a symbol table, and $\mathbf{s}^*$ applied to a variable simply retrieves the value assigned to that variable in the table.

2. If t is an individual constant, then $\mathbf{s}^*(t)$ is the fixed element of $\mathcal{D}$ assigned to that constant by the interpretation.

3. If $\mathsf{f_j}$ is a function letter, g is the corresponding operation in $\mathcal{D}$ (assigned by the interpretation), and $t_1, \ldots, t_n$ are terms, then $\mathbf{s}^*(f_j(t_1, \ldots, t_n) = g(\mathbf{s}^*(t_1), \ \ldots, \ \mathbf{s}^*(t_n))$ ■

Thus $\mathbf{s}^*$ is a function, determined by the sequence $\mathbf{s}$, from the set of terms into $\mathcal{D}$. Intuitively, $\mathbf{s}^*$ maps a syntactic expression onto its intended value. For a sequence $\mathbf{s} = (\mathbf{b_1}, \mathbf{b_2}, \ldots)$ and a term t, $\mathbf{s}^*(t)$ is the element of $\mathcal{D}$ obtained by substituting, for each i, $\mathbf{b_i}$ for all occurrences of x_i in t, and then performing the operations of the interpretation corresponding to the function letters of t. Another way of looking at it is to consider a sequence $\mathbf{s}$ as a symbol table containing values for all the variables of the language; $\mathbf{s}^*$ is then an interpreter that evaluates a term t in the context of the symbol table $\mathbf{s}$.

> For example, if t is $\mathsf{f_2(x_3, f_1(x_1, a_1))}$ and the interpretation is such that $\mathcal{D}$ = set of integers; $\mathsf{f_2}$ and $\mathsf{f_1}$ are assigned to ordinary multiplication and addition, respectively; and $\mathsf{a_1}$ is the constant $\mathbf{2}$; then for any sequence of integers $\mathbf{s} = (\mathbf{b_1}, \mathbf{b_2}, \mathbf{b_3}, \ldots)$, $\mathbf{s}^*(t)$ is the integer $\mathbf{b_3}(\mathbf{b_1} + \mathbf{2})$.

---

[1]Since we have a countable number of variable symbols it would suffice to use only the letter x subscripted by natural numbers to represent all the variable symbols. For ease in describing the mapping $\mathbf{s}^*$, we assume this is the case. For ease in reading formulas we will make use of other letters, such as w, y, and z.

DEFINITION: We define what it means for a sequence **s** to ***satisfy*** a wff, A, in a given interpretation by cases. A wff can be: (1) atomic, (2) a negated wff, (3) an implication, or (4) a quantified wff.

1. If A is an atomic wff $\mathsf{A_j}(t_1, \ldots, t_n)$ and $\mathbf{A_j}$ is the corresponding relation of the interpretation, then the sequence **s** ***satisfies*** A if and only if $\mathbf{A_j}(\mathbf{s}^*(t_1), \ldots, \mathbf{s}^*(t_n))$ — that is, if the n-tuple $(\mathbf{s}^*(t_1), \ldots, \mathbf{s}^*(t_n))$ is in the relation $\mathbf{A_j}$.[2]

2. **s** ***satisfies*** $\neg A$ if and only if **s** does not satisfy A.

3. **s** ***satisfies*** $A \rightarrow B$ if and only if either **s** does not satisfy A, or **s** satisfies B.

4. **s** ***satisfies*** $(\forall x_i)A$ iff every sequence of Σ that differs from **s** in at most the ith component satisfies A. ■

Intuitively, a sequence $\mathbf{s} = (\mathbf{b_1}, \mathbf{b_2}, \ldots)$ satisfies a wff A if and only if, when we substitute $\mathbf{b_i}$ for all free occurrences of $\mathsf{x_i}$ in A, for every i, the resulting proposition is true under the given interpretation. For example, again we make use of interpretations A and B given on page 50, and consider the formula $\mathsf{P}(\mathsf{x_1}, \mathsf{x_2}) \rightarrow \mathsf{Q}(\mathsf{x_1})$.

Under interpretation A, the sequence **(2, 3, ...)** satisfies the formula (as would any sequence whose first two elements are not equal, or whose first element is greater than **1**) and the sequence **(1, 1, ...)** does not.

Under interpretation B, the sequence **(0, 4, ...)** satisfies the formula (as would any sequence in which the first element is **0** or both the first two elements are nonzero) and the sequence **(4, 0, ...)** does not.

DEFINITION: A wff A is ***true*** (for a given interpretation) iff every sequence in Σ satisfies A. A is ***false*** iff no sequence in Σ satisfies A. ■

Note that we are now talking about true and false at a higher level. A wff is true for a given interpretation only if it is true for all possible assignments of values for its free variables. It is false in a given interpretation only if it is false for *all* possible assignments of values to its

[2]Note the difference between A (a metavariable), $\mathsf{A_j}$ (a specific predicate letter), and $\mathbf{A_j}$ (a relation on the domain).

free variables. Thus it is possible for a wff to be neither true nor false for a given interpretation.

The following Remarks are consequences of the above definitions. (These consequences are "obvious," but it may require some effort to determine that they are obvious.)

3.2.1 Remarks

1. A is false for a given interpretation iff $\neg A$ is true for that interpretation; and A is true iff $\neg A$ is false.

2. If A and $A \rightarrow B$ are true for a given interpretation, so is B.

3. For a given interpretation $A \rightarrow B$ is false iff A is true and B is false.

4. **s** satisfies $A \wedge B$ iff **s** satisfies A and **s** satisfies B; **s** satisfies $A \vee B$ iff **s** satisfies A or **s** satisfies B; **s** satisfies $A \equiv B$ iff **s** satisfies both A and B, or neither A nor B; **s** satisfies $(\exists x)A$ iff there exists a sequence **s**$'$, differing from **s** in at most the ith place, such that **s**$'$ satisfies A.

5. $A(x)$ is true iff its closure $(\forall x)A(x)$ is true. By the *closure* of A we mean the closed wff obtained from A by prefixing A with universal quantifiers of those variables that appear free in A.

6. Every instance of a tautology is true for any interpretation. (All instances of the axioms **L1**– **L3** are true. By 2 above, if A and $A \rightarrow B$ are true then so is B; thus, every theorem of Propositional Logic is true. Since $\mathcal{L}$ is complete, we know that every tautology is a theorem of $\mathcal{L}$, and it follows that every instance of a tautology is true.)

7. If the free variables (if any) of a wff A occur in the list $\mathsf{x}_1, \ldots, \mathsf{x}_k$ and if the sequences **s** and **s**$'$ have the same components in the 1st, ..., kth places, then **s** satisfies A iff **s**$'$ satisfies A.

8. If A does not contain x_i free, then $(\forall x_i)(A \rightarrow B) \rightarrow (A \rightarrow (\forall x_i)B)$ is true for all interpretations. (For proof see [27].)

Lemma 3.2.1 If t and u are terms, and **s** is a sequence in Σ, and t' results from t by substitution of u for all occurrences of x_i in t, and **s**$'$

results from $\mathbf{s}$ by substituting $\mathbf{s}^*(u)$ for the ith component of $\mathbf{s}$, then $\mathbf{s}^*(t') = (\mathbf{s}')^*(t)$. (For sketch of proof, see [27].)

Intuitively, this lemma states that the symbol table can be used to simulate substitution correctly. For example, it makes no difference to the value of the result if

1. We substitute x_2 for x_1 in the expression $\mathsf{x}_1 + \mathsf{x}_2$, getting $\mathsf{x}_2 + \mathsf{x}_2$, and then evaluate the result using the sequence $\mathbf{s} = \mathbf{(5,\ 3,\ \ldots)}$.

   or

2. We substitute the value of x_2 in $\mathbf{s}$ for the value of x_1 in $\mathbf{s}$, getting a new sequence $\mathbf{s}' = (\mathbf{3},\ \mathbf{3},\ \ldots)$, and then evaluate the original expression $\mathsf{x}_1 + \mathsf{x}_2$ in $\mathbf{s}'$.

Corollary 3.2.1.1 If $(\forall x_i)A(x_i)$ is satisfied by $\mathbf{s}$, so is $A(t)$. Hence $(\forall xi)A(x_i) \rightarrow A(t)$ is true for all interpretations.

Definition: A wff A is said to be ***logically valid*** iff A is true for every interpretation. ■

Now we've jumped to another level. A wff A is logically valid only if it is true in *every* interpretation. It is true in an interpretation only if it is satisfied by *every* sequence.

Definition: A wff A is said to be ***satisfiable*** iff there is an interpretation for which A is satisfied by at least one sequence in Σ. ■

Note the two levels of existence requirements: (1) An interpretation exists in which (2) a sequence exists that satisfies A. Thus it is possible that a formula may be satisfiable but not true for any interpretation.

A is logically valid iff $\neg A$ is unsatisfiable; and A is satisfiable iff $\neg A$ is not logically valid. If A is a closed wff, then A is either true or false for any given interpretation (i.e., A is satisfied by all sequences or by none). Thus, if A is closed, then A is satisfiable iff A is true for some interpretation.

Definition: A is ***contradictory*** (*unsatisfiable*) iff $\neg A$ is logically valid (i.e., iff A is false for every interpretation). ■

DEFINITION: A is said to ***logically imply*** B iff, in every interpretation, any sequence satisfying A also satisfies B. B is a ***logical consequence*** of a set $\underline{S}$ of wffs if and only if, in every interpretation, every sequence that satisfies every wff in $\underline{S}$ also satisfies B. ■

DEFINITION: A and B are ***logically equivalent*** iff they logically imply each other. ■

DEFINITION: Any sentence of a formal language that is an instance of a logically valid wff is called ***logically true***, and an instance of a contradictory wff is said to be ***logically false***. ■

Immediate consequences of the above definitions include:

1. A logically implies B iff $A \rightarrow B$ is logically valid.

2. A and B are logically equivalent iff $A \equiv B$ is logically valid.

3. If A logically implies B, and A is true in a given interpretation, then so is B.

4. If B is a logical consequence of a set $\underline{S}$ of wffs, and all wffs in $\underline{S}$ are true in a given interpretation, so is B.

5. Every instance of a tautology is logically valid. (By definition, and 6 of Remarks 3.2.1 on page 53.)

6. If A does not contain x free, then $(\forall x)(A \rightarrow B) \rightarrow (A \rightarrow (\forall x)B)$ is logically valid. (By 8 of Remarks 3.2.1, page 53.)

7. If t is free for x in A, then $(\forall x)A(x) \rightarrow A(t)$ is logically valid. (By Corollary 3.2.1.1.)

8. The wff $(\forall \mathsf{x}_2)(\exists \mathsf{x}_1)\mathsf{A}_1(\mathsf{x}_1,\mathsf{x}_2) \rightarrow (\exists \mathsf{x}_1)(\forall \mathsf{x}_2)\mathsf{A}_1(\mathsf{x}_1,\mathsf{x}_2)$ is not logically valid. As a counterexample, consider the following:

   $\mathcal{D}$ is the set of integers; $\mathsf{A}_1(\mathsf{x}_1,\mathsf{x}_2)$ is $\mathbf{x_1} < \mathbf{x_2}$. Then $(\forall \mathsf{x}_2)(\exists \mathsf{x}_1)\mathsf{A}_1(\mathsf{x}_1,\mathsf{x}_2)$ is true, (i.e., for every integer $\mathbf{x_2}$, there exists an integer $\mathbf{x_1}$, such that $\mathbf{x_1} < \mathbf{x_2}$). However, $(\exists \mathsf{x}_1)(\forall \mathsf{x}_2)\mathsf{A}_1(\mathsf{x}_1,\mathsf{x}_2)$ is false, (i.e., there is no least integer).

Exercises 3.2

1. Determine whether each of the following wffs is true, false, or neither in the interpretation:

$$\text{Domain} = \text{Integers}$$
$$P(x, y) \text{ means } x \leq y$$

   a. $(\forall x)(\exists y)P(x,y) \rightarrow (\exists y)(\forall x)P(x,y)$
   b. $(\forall x)(\forall y)P(x,y) \rightarrow (\forall y)(\forall x)P(x,y)$
   c. $(\exists x)(\forall y)P(x,y)$
   d. $(\forall y)(\exists x)P(x,y)$

2. Indicate *as many* of the following as apply to each of the wffs listed below:

   a. logically valid
   b. true in an interpretation, but not logically valid
   c. satisfiable but not true, in some interpretation
   d. false in an interpretation
   e. unsatisfiable

      i. $\forall x A(z,x) \vee B(x,y) \rightarrow (\forall x A(z,x) \vee \forall x B(x,y))$
      ii. $\forall x \forall y P(x,y) \rightarrow \forall x \forall y P(y,x)$
      iii. $P(x,y) \rightarrow P(y,x)$
      iv. $P(f(x)) \rightarrow P(x)$
      v. $\forall x P(x) \rightarrow P(f(x))$

3. Make up a wff of $\mathcal{PC}$ for each set of conditions given below. Justify your answer (providing interpretations wherever appropriate).

   a. true in a given interpretation, but not logically valid
   b. neither true nor false for a given interpretation
   c. satisfiable and not logically valid
   d. true in some interpretation and false in some interpretation
   e. false, but not contradictory
   f. logically valid
   g. contradictory (unsatisfiable)

3.3 Deduction

In Section 3.1 we described the symbols and wffs of a first-order theory. To complete the definition we need to specify the axioms and rules of inference. In doing so, we define first-order theories in general, as well as the specific first-order theory of Predicate Calculus, which we shall call $\mathcal{PC}$.

DEFINITION: The symbols and wffs of a ***first-order theory*** are those of a first-order language (see Definition page 44). The ***axioms*** of a first-order theory are split into classes: ***logical axioms*** and ***proper*** (or ***nonlogical***). The logical axioms of any first-order theory are those given below for $\mathcal{PC}$. The proper axioms vary from one first-order theory to another. A first-order theory that contains no proper axioms is called a ***first-order predicate calculus***.

The rules of inference of a first-order theory are Modus Ponens (defined in Section 2.3) and Generalization (defined below). ■

Axioms:

If A, B, and C are wffs, then the following are axioms of $\mathcal{PC}$:

PC1: $A \rightarrow (B \rightarrow A)$

PC2: $(A \rightarrow (B \rightarrow C)) \rightarrow ((A \rightarrow B) \rightarrow (A \rightarrow C))$

PC3: $(\neg B \rightarrow \neg A) \rightarrow ((\neg B \rightarrow A) \rightarrow B)$

PC4: $(\forall x)A(x) \rightarrow A(t)$, if $A(x)$ is a wff and t is a term free for x in $A(x)$. Note that if t is x, we have the axioms $(\forall x)A(x) \rightarrow A(x)$.

PC5: $(\forall x)(A \rightarrow B) \rightarrow (A \rightarrow (\forall x)B)$ if A is a wff containing no free occurrences of x.

Note that the first three axioms are just those used for $\mathcal{L}$ in Section 2.3. We have added two new axioms that deal with variables and quantifiers. We have two rules of inference for Predicate Calculus ($\mathcal{PC}$).

Rules of Inference:

Modus Ponens (MP): $A,\ A \rightarrow B \vdash B$
(B follows from A and $A \rightarrow B$)

Generalization (Gen): $A \vdash (\forall x)A$
($(\forall x)A$ follows from A)

As one might expect, adding two new axioms and one rule of inference does not diminish the number of theorems we had in $\mathcal{L}$.

Lemma 3.3.1 Every wff A that is an instance of a tautology is a theorem of $\mathcal{PC}$ and may be proved using only axioms **PC1**– **PC3** and MP.

Proof: A arises from a tautology P by substitution. By completeness for $\mathcal{L}$, P has a proof in $\mathcal{L}$. In such a proof, make the same substitutions of wffs of $\mathcal{PC}$ for the proposition letters as were used in obtaining A from P, and for all proposition letters in the proof that do not occur in P, substitute an arbitrary wff of $\mathcal{PC}$. The resulting sequence of wffs is a proof of A, and this proof uses only **PC1**– **PC3** and MP. ■

So, we can prove all that we could prove in $\mathcal{L}$, and more. Now, we wish to establish that the theory $\mathcal{PC}$ is consistent (i.e., that we have not added so much that we could prove some wff and its negation). In order to do so we introduce a function that maps formulas of Predicate Calculus back into formulas of Propositional Calculus.

Definition: For each wff A, let $\mathbf{h}(A)$ be the expression obtained by deleting all quantifiers and terms in A. ■

For example,

$$\mathbf{h}(\neg(\forall x)\mathsf{A}(x, y) \rightarrow \mathsf{B}(z)) = (\neg\mathsf{A} \rightarrow \mathsf{B})$$

Then $\mathbf{h}(A)$ is a wff of $\mathcal{L}$ with the predicate symbols of A as proposition letters.

Lemma 3.3.2 $\mathbf{h}(A)$ is a tautology whenever A is a theorem of $\mathcal{PC}$.

Proof: To show that $\mathbf{h}(A)$ is a tautology whenever A is a theorem, we must show that $\mathbf{h}(A)$ is a tautology for each axiom A, and that the rules of inference lead from wffs whose images under $\mathbf{h}$ are tautologies to wffs whose images under $\mathbf{h}$ are also tautologies.

By definition, $\mathbf{h}(\neg A) = \neg(\mathbf{h}(A))$ and $\mathbf{h}(A \to B) = \mathbf{h}(A) \to \mathbf{h}(B)$. For every axiom A given by **PC1–PC5**, $\mathbf{h}(A)$ is a tautology. For **PC1–PC3**, this is immediate, since they are already free of quantifiers and terms.

PC4: An instance of $(\forall x)A(x) \to A(t)$ under $\mathbf{h}$ is transformed into a tautology of the form $A \to A$.

PC5: An instance of the axiom $(\forall x)(A \to B) \to (A \to (\forall x)B)$ becomes $(A \to B) \to (A \to B)$.

Now we check the rules of inference. If $\mathbf{h}(A)$ and $\mathbf{h}(A \to B)$ are tautologies, then by the definition of $\to$, so is $\mathbf{h}(B)$; and if $\mathbf{h}(A)$ is a tautology so is $\mathbf{h}((\forall x)A)$, which is just $\mathbf{h}(A)$.

Hence $\mathbf{h}(A)$ is a tautology whenever A is a theorem of $\mathcal{PC}$. ■

Now we can prove the consistency result we wanted.

Theorem 3.3.3 Predicate Calculus is consistent.

Proof: If there were a wff B such that $\vdash B$ and $\vdash \neg B$ then, by Lemma 3.3.2, both $\mathbf{h}(B)$ and $\mathbf{h}(\neg B)$ (or $\neg\mathbf{h}(B)$), would be tautologies, which is impossible. Therefore $\mathcal{PC}$ is consistent. ■

We found the Deduction Theorem for $\mathcal{L}$, page 22, to be a very powerful tool in proving theorems. The Deduction Theorem for $\mathcal{PC}$ is also useful, but must be stated carefully to avoid problems like the following:

> For any wff A, $A \vdash (\forall x)A$, the Deduction Theorem for $\mathcal{L}$ would then allow us to conclude that $\vdash A \to (\forall x)A$, but this is certainly not the case, as the following (interpreted) example shows.
>
> Let A be $\mathbf{x} \neq \mathbf{0}$; by applying Gen we get $\mathbf{x} \neq \mathbf{0} \vdash (\forall \mathbf{x})\mathbf{x} \neq \mathbf{0}$. However, we would not want to conclude that we can prove $\mathbf{x} \neq \mathbf{0} \to (\forall \mathbf{x})\mathbf{x} \neq \mathbf{0}$, which could lead us to such results as $\vdash \mathbf{x} \neq \mathbf{0} \to \mathbf{0} \neq \mathbf{0}$.

The problem lies in using the Deduction Theorem to discard a hypothesis by making it the antecedent of an implication when we could not have derived the consequent without first using Gen on the hypothesis. To state the conditions precisely, we first need to define "depends upon."

DEFINITION: Let A be a wff in a set $\underline{S}$ of wffs; assume we are given a deduction $B_1, \ldots, B_n$ from $\underline{S}$, together with justification for each step of the deduction. We say that B_i ***depends upon*** A in this proof iff:

1. B_i is A and the justification for B_i is that it belongs to $\underline{S}$

   or

2. B_i is justified as a direct consequence by MP or Gen of some preceding wffs of the sequence, where at least one of those wffs depends upon A. ■

For example,

$$A,\ (\forall x)A \rightarrow C \vdash (\forall x)C$$

B_1 :	A	hypothesis
B_2 :	$(\forall x)A$	Gen, B_1
B_3 :	$(\forall x)A \rightarrow C$	hypothesis
B_4 :	C	MP B_2, B_3
B_5 :	$(\forall x)C$	Gen B_4

B_1 depends upon A
B_2 depends upon A
B_3 depends upon $(\forall x)A \rightarrow C$
B_4 depends upon A and $(\forall x)A \rightarrow C$
B_5 depends upon A and $(\forall x)A \rightarrow C$

LEMMA 3.3.4 If B does not depend upon A in a deduction $\underline{S}, A \vdash B$, then $\underline{S} \vdash B$. (If the conclusion does not depend upon an assumption, then you could have proven it without the assumption.)

Proof: Let $B_1, \ldots, B_n = B$ be a deduction of B from $\underline{S}$ and A, in which B does not depend upon A. We will prove by induction on n, the number of steps in the proof, that $\underline{S} \vdash B_n$.

Basis Case: $n = 1$.
$B_1 = B$, which does not depend upon A, therefore $B \in \underline{S}$, or B is an axiom, thus $\underline{S} \vdash B$.

Induction Step: Assume $\underline{S} \vdash B_i$, for $i < n$; show $\underline{S} \vdash B$.

If B belongs to $\underline{S}$ or is an axiom, then $\underline{S} \vdash B$. If B is a direct consequence of one or two preceding wffs, then, since B does not depend upon A, neither do these preceding wffs. By the inductive hypothesis, these preceding wffs are deducible from $\underline{S}$ alone; therefore, so is B. ■

THEOREM 3.3.5 (Deduction Theorem for PC) Assume there is a proof $\underline{S}, A \vdash B$, where in the deduction, no application of Gen to a wff that depends upon A has as its quantified variable a free variable of A. Then $\underline{S} \vdash A \to B$.

Proof: Let $B_1, \ldots, B_n = B$ be a deduction of B from $\underline{S}, A$ that satisfies the assumption of the theorem. We shall show by induction on i that $\underline{S} \vdash A \to B_i$ for each $i \leq n$.

Basis Case: $i = 1$.

1. B_i is an axiom or belongs to $\underline{S}$.

$\underline{S} \vdash B_i$	def. of "deducible from" (page 4)
$B_i \to (A \to B_i)$	**PC1**
$\underline{S} \vdash A \to B_i$	MP

2. B_i is A.

$\vdash A \to A$	Lemma 2.3.2
$\underline{S} \vdash A \to B_i$	property 1, def. of "deducible from," page 4

Induction Step: Assume $\underline{S} \vdash A \to B_i$ for $i < k$; show $\underline{S} \vdash A \to B_k$.

1. If B_k is an axiom or an element of $\underline{S}$, the result follows as in case 1 above.
2. If B_k is A, the result follows as in case 2 above.
3. If B_k follows by MP from B_i and $B_j = B_i \to B_k$, $i, j < k$, then

$\underline{S} \vdash A \to B_i$	induction hypothesis
$\underline{S} \vdash A \to (B_i \to B_k)$	induction hypothesis
$\vdash (A \to (B_i \to B_k)) \to ((A \to B_i) \to (A \to B_k))$	**PC2**
$\underline{S} \vdash ((A \to B_i) \to (A \to B_k))$	MP
$\underline{S} \vdash A \to B_k$	MP

4. If B_k follows by Gen from B_j, $j < k$, (i.e., $B_k = (\forall x)B_j$), then

$\underline{S} \vdash A \rightarrow B_j$ induction hypothesis

a. If B_j does not depend upon A in the deduction of B from $\underline{S}$ and A, then

$\underline{S} \vdash B_j$		Lemma 3.3.4
$\underline{S} \vdash (\forall x)B_j$	(i.e., $\underline{S} \vdash B_k$)	Gen
$\vdash B_k \rightarrow (A \rightarrow B_k)$		**PC1**
$\underline{S} \vdash A \rightarrow B_k$		MP

b. If x is not a free variable of A, then

$\vdash (\forall x)(A \rightarrow B_j) \rightarrow (A \rightarrow (\forall x)B_j)$	**PC5**
$\underline{S} \vdash A \rightarrow B_j$	induction hypothesis
$\underline{S} \vdash (\forall x)(A \rightarrow B_j)$	Gen
$\underline{S} \vdash A \rightarrow (\forall x)B_j$	MP
(i.e., $\underline{S} \vdash A \rightarrow B_k$)	

The theorem follows as the case where $i = n$. ■

The hypothesis of the Deduction Theorem for $\mathcal{PC}$ is cumbersome; the following corollaries are more transparent and often more useful.

Corollary 3.3.5.1 If a deduction $\underline{S}$, $A \vdash B$ involves no application of Gen in which the quantified variable is free in A, then $\underline{S} \vdash A \rightarrow B$.

Corollary 3.3.5.2 If A is closed (contains no free variables) and $\underline{S}$, $A \vdash B$, then $\underline{S} \vdash A \rightarrow B$.

Note that in the proof of the Deduction Theorem for $\mathcal{PC}$, B_j depends upon a premise C of $\underline{S}$ in the original proof iff $A \rightarrow B_j$ depends upon C in the new proof. This conclusion is useful when we wish to apply the Deduction Theorem several times in a row to a given derivation, (e.g., to obtain $\underline{S} \vdash D \rightarrow (A \rightarrow B)$ from $\underline{S}$, D, $A \vdash B$).

The following sequence of questions may be asked when checking to see whether or not the Deduction Theorem for $\mathcal{PC}$ can be applied to a derivation $\underline{S}$, $A \vdash B$ to get $\underline{S} \vdash A \rightarrow B$. The questions must be answered in the order in which they are given — in particular, question 4 assumes that all of questions 1–3 have been answered affirmatively.

1. Does A have any free variables? If not, the Deduction Theorem can be used.

2. Was Gen used in the proof? If not, the Deduction Theorem can be used.

3. Do any of the Gen'd variables appear free in A? If not, the Deduction Theorem can be used.

4. Did any of the wffs that were Gen'd depend upon A? If not, the Deduction Theorem can be used, otherwise the deduction theorem cannot be used.

THEOREM 3.3.6 $\forall x(A \rightarrow B) \rightarrow (\forall x A \rightarrow \forall x B)$

Proof:

1.	$\forall x(A \rightarrow B)$	hypothesis
2.	$\forall x(A \rightarrow B) \rightarrow (A \rightarrow B)$	**PC4**
3.	$A \rightarrow B$	MP 1,2
4.	$\forall x A$	hypothesis
5.	$\forall x A \rightarrow A$	**PC4**
6.	A	MP 4,5
7.	B	MP 3,6
8.	$\forall x B$	Gen 7
9.	$\forall x A \rightarrow \forall x B$	Theorem 3.3.5 4,8
10.	$\forall x(A \rightarrow B) \rightarrow (\forall x A \rightarrow \forall x B)$	Theorem 3.3.5 1,9

■

Exercise 3.3

1. Prove each of the following in the formal theory $\mathcal{PC}$:

   a. $\forall x \forall y(P(x,y) \rightarrow Q(x)) \rightarrow \forall y \forall x(P(x,y) \rightarrow Q(x))$
   b. $\neg \forall x \neg \forall y A \rightarrow \forall y \neg \forall x \neg A$
   c. $\forall x \forall y P(x,y) \rightarrow \forall x \forall y P(y,x)$
   d. $\forall x_1 \ldots \forall x_n(P \wedge Q) \rightarrow (\forall x_1 \ldots \forall x_n P) \wedge ((\forall x_1 \ldots \forall x_n Q)$
   e. $\forall x_1 \ldots \forall x_n P \rightarrow \forall x_n \forall x_1 \ldots \forall x_{n-1} P$

3.4 Computation

The computation scheme we use for Predicate Calculus, called *general resolution*, is described in this section. Later (Section 3.4.2) we also include a description of logic programming to show how the resolution principle is applied in the evaluation mechanism of an actual programming language (Prolog).

3.4.1 Resolution

In describing the process of computation for the propositional case we discussed *ground* resolution. We can now define what is meant by the adjective "ground."

DEFINITION: A ***ground*** expression, term, or clause is one that contains no variables. ■

In Propositional Logic we dealt only with ground clauses, since the language contained no variables. Ground resolution alone is not sufficient to handle the more expressive language of Predicate Calculus. For $\mathcal{PC}$ we use a more general form of resolution that consists of unification together with complementary literal elimination. Again, we shall use refutation procedures — establishing a theorem by showing its negation is contradictory.

Since we have introduced some new symbols in $\mathcal{PC}$, we redefine some old notions and add some new ones as follows:

term ::= constant | variable | function_letter "(" termlist ")"

termlist ::= term | term "," termlist

atomic_formula ::= predicate_letter "(" termlist ")"

±literal ::= atomic_formula | "¬" atomic_formula

clause ::= "□" | {±literal} | {±literal} ∪ clause

sentence ::= {clause} | {clause} ∪ sentence

DEFINITION: A wff of $\mathcal{PC}$ is in ***clausal form*** if it is a sentence as described by the grammar above. ■

Again, we understand a clause to be a disjunction ("or") of its elements (literals), and a sentence to be a conjunction ("and") of its elements (clauses). As always, $\cup$ indicates set union.

One might notice the absence of quantifiers. We know that a wff of $\mathcal{PC}$ is provable if and only if its closure is provable (by **PC4** and Gen). We have also seen that a wff is logically valid if and only if its closure is logically valid. Every wff in clausal form is implicitly closed. We consider each variable to be universally quantified over the clause in which it appears. We will see shortly (pages 67–71) how an arbitrary wff of $\mathcal{PC}$ can be transformed into an equivalent wff in clausal form.

Resolution depends on the basic operation of substituting terms for variables in wffs. A substitution provides an assignment of terms to variables. Each such assignment is indicated by an ordered pair (term, variable).

DEFINITION: A ***substitution*** σ is a set of independent substitution components:

$$\sigma = [(t_1, v_1), \ \ldots, \ (t_n, v_n]$$

The first element of each component is a term and the second element is a variable, such that

1. $v_i \neq v_j$ if $i \neq j$

2. v_i does not occur in t_j for any i and j.

(We use [and] instead of { and } to indicate the set of substitution components.) ■

DEFINITION: If a variable v is replaced at each of its occurrences in the wff C by the term t, the resulting wff is called a ***substitution instance*** of C, and is denoted $C[(t, v)]$, read "C with t for v." Similarly, the result of *simultaneously* replacing all occurrences of different variables $v_1, \ldots, v_n$ in C by terms $t_1, \ldots, t_n$ respectively, is denoted by $C[(t_1, v_1), \ \ldots, \ (t_n, v_n)]$. ■

The independence of the components of a substitution, which is ensured by the two conditions given above, guarantees that two substitutions will be set-theoretically equal if and only if they have the same effect on all expressions. Thus, in applying a substitution to an expression, the ordering of the components in the substitution makes no difference to the result. $C\sigma$, the result of applying σ to C, is the substitution instance

$$C[(t_1, v_1),\ \ldots,\ (t_n, v_n]$$

For example, let

$$\begin{aligned} C &= \mathsf{P(x, z, y) \vee P(e, f(u, y), f(a, b))} \\ \sigma &= \mathsf{[(e, x), (f(u, v), z), (f(a, b), y)]} \\ \tau &= \mathsf{[(f(a, b), v)]} \end{aligned}$$

then

$$\begin{aligned} C\sigma &= \mathsf{P(e, f(u, v), f(a, b)) \vee P(e, f(u, f(a, b)), f(a, b))} \\ (C\sigma)\tau &= \mathsf{P(e, f(u, f(a, b)), f(a, b)) \vee P(e, f(u, f(a, b)), f(a, b))} \end{aligned}$$

Again, because of the condition that v_i does not occur in t_j, we know that no new occurrences of any variables affected by the substitution can be introduced through any of the substitution components.

In order to describe an algorithm for computation we need to impose an ordering on the expressions of $\mathcal{PC}$. Wffs and sequences of wffs can be lexically ordered as follows:

1. The primitive symbols are ordered according to type (variables, constants, function letters, predicate letters, then connectives); then, within each type, according to the number of arguments (i.e., superscripts, for function and predicate letters), then subscripts (we assume that symbols without subscripts come before those that are subscripted), and finally, alphabetically. The connectives are ordered according to their scope, as described earlier, with the least in scope coming first (i.e., $\neg$, $\wedge$, $\vee$, $\rightarrow$, and $\equiv$).

2. Wffs and terms are first ordered by length; then, two wffs of equal length are placed in the order of the symbols in the position at which they first differ. Similarly, sequences of wffs are ordered by length and then by the order of the first members at which they differ.

Graphically, the symbols are ordered as follows:

variables
    subscripts
        alphabetically
constants
function letters
    number of arguments
        subscripts
            alphabetically
predicate letters
    number of arguments
        subscripts
            alphabetically
$\neg$, $\wedge$, $\vee$, $\rightarrow$, $\equiv$

For example, x_1 comes before y_1 comes before x_3; $\mathsf{f(f(x))}$ before $\mathsf{f(f(y))}$; $\mathsf{f(y)}$ before $\mathsf{g(x)}$; $\mathsf{f(g_1(y))}$ before $\mathsf{f(f_2(x))}$, etc.

We will require that the wffs we operate on be in Skolem free variable form, defined as follows.

DEFINITION: A wff is in ***prenex form*** if every variable is quantified, and all quantifiers (the ***prefix*** of the wff) precede a quantifier-free sentence (the ***matrix*** of the wff). ■

Every wff of Predicate Calculus is equivalent to some wff in prenex form. To put a wff in prenex form, we first eliminate any occurrences of the connectives $\equiv$ and $\rightarrow$by applying the following rewrite rules:

$$\begin{array}{lcc} A \equiv B & \text{becomes} & (A \rightarrow B) \wedge (B \rightarrow A) \\ A \rightarrow B & \text{becomes} & \neg A \vee B \end{array}$$

We then move all quantifiers to the left of all logical connectives. At this point we know that the wff can contain only the connectives $\neg$, $\wedge$, and $\vee$. Thus we show how to move each quantifier across each type of connective.

$$\begin{array}{lcl} \neg \exists x A & \text{becomes} & \forall x \neg A \\ \neg \forall x A & \text{becomes} & \exists x \neg A \end{array}$$

We rename all bound variables so all distinct variables have distinct names; then

$$
\begin{array}{lll}
(\wedge \ldots \forall x A \ldots) & \text{becomes} & \forall x(\wedge \ldots A \ldots) \\
(\wedge \ldots \exists x A \ldots) & \text{becomes} & \exists x(\wedge \ldots A \ldots) \\
(\vee \ldots \forall x A \ldots) & \text{becomes} & \forall x(\vee \ldots A \ldots) \\
(\vee \ldots \exists x A \ldots) & \text{becomes} & \exists x(\vee \ldots A \ldots)
\end{array}
$$

The following special cases can be used to simplify the prefix:

$$
\begin{array}{lll}
(\wedge \forall x_1 A_1(x_1) \ldots \forall x_n A_n(x_n)) & \text{becomes} & (\wedge \forall x A_1(x) \ldots \forall x A_n(x)) \\
 & \text{becomes} & \forall x(\wedge A_1(x) \ldots A_n(x)) \\
(\vee \exists x_1 A_1(x_1) \ldots \exists x_n A_n(x_n)) & \text{becomes} & (\vee \exists x A_1(x) \ldots \exists x A_n(x)) \\
 & \text{becomes} & \exists x(\vee A_1(x) \ldots A_n(x))
\end{array}
$$

We then form the *closure* of the wff by universally quantifying all free variables (by 5 of Remarks, page 53, we know that a wff is true iff its closure is true).

For example,

$$\forall x(A(z,x) \vee B(x,y)) \rightarrow (\exists x A(z,x) \vee \forall x B(x,y))$$

Eliminating $\rightarrow$ gives

$$\neg \forall x(A(z,x) \vee B(x,y)) \vee (\exists x A(z,x) \vee \forall x B(x,y))$$

Moving $\forall$ across $\neg$ and renaming variables where necessary gives

$$\exists x \neg(A(z,x) \vee B(x,y)) \vee \exists x A(z,x) \vee \forall x_2 B(x_2,y)$$

Pulling the quantifiers out front, we have

$$\exists x \forall x_2 \neg(A(z,x) \vee B(x,y)) \vee A(z,x) \vee B(x_2,y)$$

and forming the closure of the formula yields

$$\forall z \forall y \exists x \forall x_2 \neg(A(z,x) \vee B(x,y)) \vee A(z,x) \vee B(x_2,y)$$

The prenex form thus obtained is not necessarily unique, but it is guaranteed to be equivalent to the original formula. It is sometimes easier to visualize this process when done graphically.

We can represent a wff by a tree whose leaves are atomic formula(s) and whose nonleaf nodes contain connectives ($\neg$, $\wedge$, $\vee$) or quantifiers ($\forall$, $\exists$), and have descendants representing the wff(s) to which the connective or quantifier in the node applies. Taking the same example used above, after having eliminated any occurrences of $\rightarrow$ and $\equiv$ in the wff, we have

$$\neg\forall x(A(z,x) \vee B(x,y)) \vee (\exists x A(z,x) \vee \forall x B(x,y))$$

or, graphically,

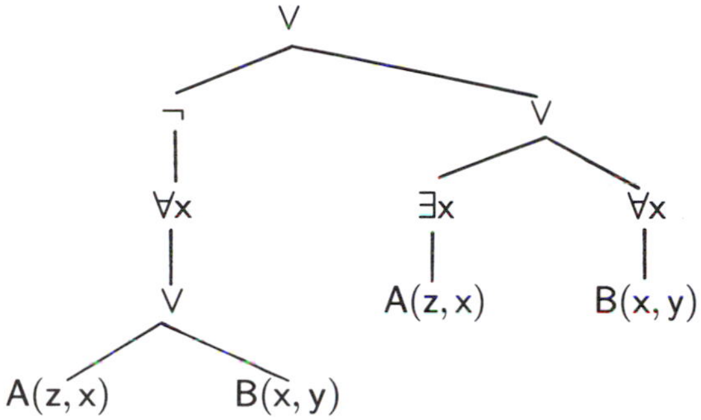

Moving quantifiers to the front of the wff is accomplished by moving them toward the root of the tree representing the wff. Any quantifier that is *uppermost* in the tree (has no quantifiers on a path from it to the prefix of the wff at the root) may be moved up the tree to (the bottom of) the prefix. If there are an even number of ¬'s on the path to the prefix, the quantifier is unchanged; if there are an odd number of ¬'s on the path to the prefix, then ∀ is transformed to ∃, and vice versa. The original position of the quantifier in the tree is taken by its descendant node.

Of course we cannot ignore the unwanted capture of free variables. If a quantifier is moved to a position governing a previously free occurrence of the variable it is binding, then we must change the name of the bound variable (in all its occurrences).

Continuing with the example above:

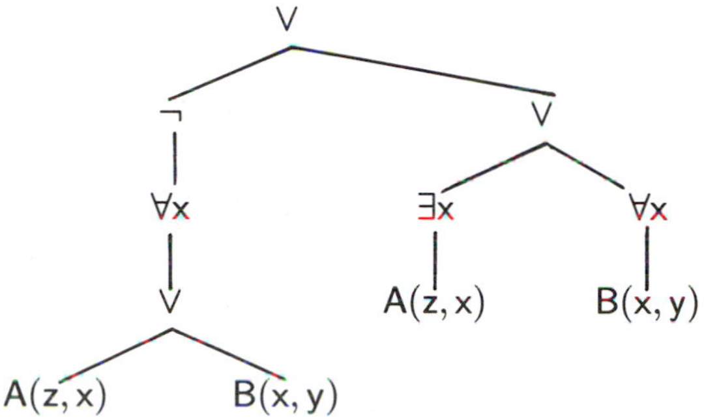

$\Longrightarrow$

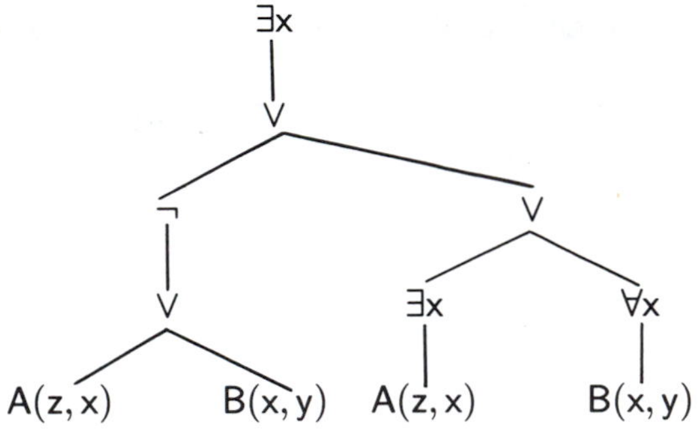

$\Longrightarrow$

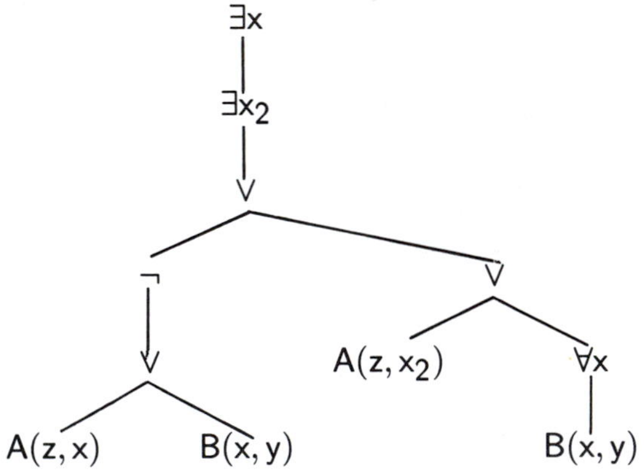

$\Longrightarrow$

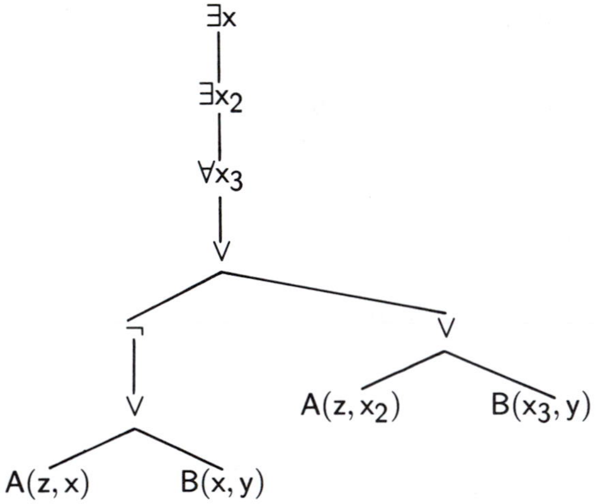

Finally, forming the closure of the wff, we get:

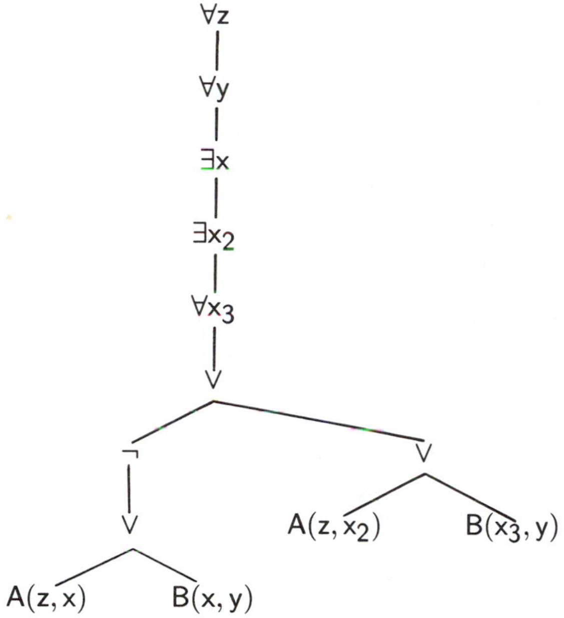

We can now put the matrix of the wff (the quantifier-free part) into reduced conjunctive normal form, using the same rules we had for rewriting formulas of Propositional Calculus.

Suppose sentence A is a proposed theorem of $\mathcal{PC}$. We consider $\neg A$ and assume it is in prenex form, and that the quantifier-free sentence is in reduced conjunctive normal form. For example, consider:

$$\neg A = (\exists x_1)(\forall x_2)(\exists x_3)(\forall x_4)R(x_1, x_2, x_3, x_4)$$

Each existentially quantified variable is replaced by a Skolem function[3] of the universally quantified variables governing it (a 0-ary function being a constant), and the universal quantifiers are dropped, yielding:

$$A' = R(a, x_2, f(x_2), x_4)$$

[3]Skolem functions are named after the logician T. Skolem. If we assert that for every x there exists a y such that some property holds, we are claiming that we can find such a y, though its choice may depend upon the value of x — that is, the choice of y can be seen as a function of x. A Skolem function simply assigns an arbitrary function symbol to represent this choice function.

This is called *Skolem free variable form.* Clearly, $\neg A$ is satisfiable iff A' is satisfiable, since A' logically implies $\neg A$, and if $\neg A$ is true in some interpretation with domain **D**, then there are functions over **D** satisfying A'.

Note that, in general, A' is a finite conjunction of clauses, each of which is a disjunction of literals (possibly negated atomic formulas). We assume that all the variables of A' are universally quantified, since it is in Skolem free variable form. Moreover, since

$$\forall x(A_1(x) \wedge \ldots \wedge A_n(x)) \equiv (\forall x A_1(x)) \wedge \ldots (\forall x A_n(x))$$

we consider each variable of A' to be universally quantified over the clause in which it appears.

DEFINITION: The ***Herbrand domain*** of A' is the set of terms $\mathcal{H}$ obtained from A' using the following rules:

1. If a is a constant (or 0-ary function symbol) in A' then $a \in \mathcal{H}$. If A' has no constants an arbitrary constant symbol a is included in $\mathcal{H}$.

2. If $t_1, \ldots, t_n$ are terms in $\mathcal{H}$, and f is an n-ary function symbol in A' then $f(t_1, \ldots, t_n) \in \mathcal{H}$. ■

The notation $P(\!(\underline{S})\!)$ denotes the set of instances obtained by applying to a set $\underline{S}$ of wffs all possible substitutions with terms belonging to a set P of terms.

DEFINITION: The set of all substitution instances of A', obtainable by replacing each variable in A' by a term from $\mathcal{H}$, is called the ***Herbrand expansion*** of A', denoted $\mathcal{H}(\!(A')\!)$. ■

For example:

x_2	x_4	$R(a, x_2, f(x_2), x_4)$
a	a	R(a, a, f(a), a)
a	f(a)	R(a, a, f(a), f(a))
f(a)	a	R(a, f(a), f(f(a)), a)
f(a)	f(a)	R(a, f(a), f(f(a)), f(a))
a	f(f(a))	R(a, a, f(a), f(f(a)))
⋮	⋮	⋮

where x_2 and x_4 are replaced in all possible ways by the terms a, f(a), f(f(a)), f(f(f(a))), ..., in $\mathcal{H}$, each variable being replaced in all of its occurrences by the same term.

At certain intervals we can test the conjunction of the instances so far generated for inconsistency. If this conjunction is consistent, we generate further instances and test the larger conjunction, and continue in this way until an inconsistent set of instances is found. That this will happen precisely in the case that A' is unsatisfiable (and hence, our original A is logically valid) follows from Herbrand's theorem.

Theorem 3.4.1 (Herbrand's theorem) If A is a finite conjunction of clauses, and $\mathcal{H}$ is its Herbrand domain, then A is unsatisfiable iff some finite subset of $\mathcal{H}((A))$ is inconsistent.

For proof see [3].

The problem with this approach to showing that A is unsatisfiable is not the time taken to test a subset of $\mathcal{H}((A))$, but that if $\mathcal{H}((A))$ is generated according to the increasing complexity of the ground terms in the instances, a prohibitively large number of instances may have to be generated before an inconsistent conjunction arises. Often a small inconsistent subconjunction can be found. Therefore, the problem is to avoid generating the consistent instances. One way to do this is to predict which instances of two clauses will contain complementary literals (or, will *clash*) using the information we have at hand about the way in which the terms of the Herbrand domain are constructed. For example, suppose that the clauses of A are:

1. $\mathsf{P}(\mathsf{x}, \mathsf{e}, \mathsf{x})$

2. $\neg\mathsf{P}(\mathsf{y}, \mathsf{z}, \mathsf{v}) \vee \neg\mathsf{P}(\mathsf{y}, \mathsf{v}, \mathsf{w}) \vee \mathsf{P}(\mathsf{e}, \mathsf{z}, \mathsf{w})$

3. $\mathsf{P}(\mathsf{a}, \mathsf{f}(\mathsf{u}, \mathsf{v}), \mathsf{e})$

4. $\neg\mathsf{P}(\mathsf{e}, \mathsf{f}(\mathsf{f}(\mathsf{b}, \mathsf{c}), \mathsf{a}), \mathsf{a})$

Recall our convention that letters from the beginning of the alphabet, in this case, a, b, c, and e, are constant symbols, and letters from the end of the alphabet, u, v, w, x, y, and z, are variables.

Any instance of 1 will clash with any instance of 2 in which v is replaced by e, and y and w are replaced by the term that replaces x in 1; such an instance of 2 will have the form

$$\neg P(x, z, e) \vee \neg P(x, e, x) \vee P(e, z, x)$$

Thus there will be a family of resolvents (defined precisely a little later) of instances of 1 and 2 of the form

5. $\neg P(x, z, e) \vee P(e, z, x)$

Some of these will clash with instances of 3, namely those instances of 5 of the form

$$\neg P(a, f(u, v), e) \vee P(e, f(u, v), a)$$

the resolvents being of the form

6. $P(e, f(u, v), a)$

This family contains the clause

7. $P(e, f(f(b, c), a), a)$

which clearly contradicts 4. Thus a small segment of $\mathcal{H}(\!(A)\!)$ is contradictory; however, if $\mathcal{H}(\!(A)\!)$ is generated by the increasing-complexity-of-terms method, the first contradictory segment would contain between 4^6 and 20^6 clauses!

Such arguments involve applying a succession of substitutions of terms (not necessarily ground terms) for variables, each substitution being chosen so that the result of applying it to two clauses is that some of the literals in the first clause become equal (or collapse) to a literal L and some of the literals in the second clause collapse to $\neg L$. In order to formalize these notions we introduce the concept of a *most general unifier.*

DEFINITION: Let $\underline{L} = \{L_1, \ldots, L_n\}$ be a set of expressions. $\underline{L}$ is ***unified*** by σ if $L_1\sigma = L_2\sigma = \cdots = L_n\sigma$. L_1 is the ***common instance*** of the elements of $\underline{L}$ determined by σ. ■

Thus a unifier is a substitution that makes the expressions it is applied to look alike. It is important to realize that the resulting expressions are the same in appearance, not just in value. Unification is a strictly syntactic process. Thus $\mathsf{x} + 2$ can be unified with $3 + 2$ by binding x to 3, but $\mathsf{x} + 2$ cannot be unified with 5 or with $2 + 3$.

DEFINITION: σ is a ***most general unifying substitution*** (or ***most general unifier***) of the set of expressions $\underline{L}$, if for any other unifier θ there is a substitution λ such that $\underline{L}\theta = \underline{L}\sigma\lambda$. ■

Intuitively, we understand that a most general unifier is one that makes the fewest and most general (in the sense of leaving variables wherever possible) substitutions necessary to unify the given set of expressions. In many cases there will be no most general unifier. However, if a set of literals $\underline{L}$ is unifiable, then there is a most general substitution unifying $\underline{L}$ and, moreover, we can give an algorithm for finding such a substitution. This procedure, due to Robinson, starts with the empty substitution and builds up, step by step, a most general σ_0 that unifies the set $\underline{L}$ of literals. If, at the kth step, the substitution so far obtained is σ_k, and the literals $L_1\sigma_k, \ldots, L_n\sigma_k$ in $\underline{L}\sigma_k$ are not all equal, the procedure changes σ_k on the basis of a disagreement set containing the first well-formed expression in each $L_i\sigma_k$ that needs to be changed.

DEFINITION: Let each $L_i\sigma_k$ be a sequence of symbols. The ***disagreement set*** of $\underline{L}\sigma_k$ is the set of all well-formed subexpressions of the literals in $\underline{L}\sigma_k$ that begin at the first symbol position at which not all the literals have the same symbol. ■

The disagreement set is either $\underline{L}$ itself (in which case $\underline{L}$ is not unifiable) or it contains a term or subterm from each literal in $\underline{L}\sigma_k$. For example, the disagreement set of $\{\mathsf{P}(\mathsf{x}, \mathsf{f}(\mathsf{x}, \mathsf{g}(\mathsf{y})), \mathsf{v}), \mathsf{P}(\mathsf{x}, \mathsf{f}(\mathsf{x}, \mathsf{z}), \mathsf{w})\}$ is $\{\mathsf{z}, \mathsf{g}(\mathsf{y})\}$.

We will construct our unifying substitution component by component. We can combine the substitution component (t, x) with the substitution $\sigma = [(t_1, v_1), \ldots, (t_n, v_n)]$, provided that $x \neq v_i$ and v_i does not occur in t, for all i, $1 \leq i \leq n$, as follows:

$$\sigma[(t, x)] = [(t_1[(t, x)], v_1), \ \ldots, \ (t_n[(t, x)], v_n), (t, x)]$$

Now we are prepared for the algorithm.

Robinson's unification procedure:

1. Set $\sigma_1 = []$ (the empty substitution), set $k = 0$, and go to step 2.

2. Set $k = k + 1$. If the elements of $\underline{L}\sigma_k$ are all equal, set $\sigma_0 = \sigma_k$ and stop; otherwise go to step 3.

3. Let s_k, t_k be the two earliest expressions in the lexical ordering (page 66) of the disagreement set of $\underline{L}\sigma_k$; if s_k is a variable and does not occur in t_k, set $\sigma_{k+1} = \sigma_k[(t_k, s_k)]$ and go to 2; otherwise stop (there is no unifier).

Since $\underline{L}\sigma_{k+1}$ contains one less variable than $\underline{L}\sigma_k$, the procedure must stop in at most m steps, if $\underline{L}$ has m variables. Also, it is clear that if the procedure stops at step 2, σ_0 is uniquely determined and its terms contain only function symbols occurring in $\underline{L}$. It is also true that if $\underline{L}$ is unifiable then σ_0 is defined and is a most general unifying substitution. For a proof of this statement see [24].

Finally, we are in a position to extend the concept of a resolvent of two clauses to the case where the clauses are not necessarily ground clauses.

DEFINITION: A ***resolvent*** of two clauses C_1 and C_2 is a third clause C_3 obtained as follows:

1. If $v_1, \ldots, v_m$ are the variables of C_2 and the highest variable of C_1 in the lexical order is u_k, let $\theta = [(u_{k+1}, v_1), \ldots, (u_{k+m}, v_m)]$. Thus, none of the variables in $C_2\theta$ occurs in C_1. This is called ***standardizing apart*** the clauses C_1 and C_2.

2. If there is a pair of sets of literals $\underline{L}$ and $\underline{M}$, such that $\underline{L} = \{L_1, \ldots, L_k\} \subseteq C_1$ and $\underline{M} = \{M_1, \ldots, M_n\} \subseteq C_2$, and the set $\{L_1, \ldots, L_k, \neg M_1, \ldots, \neg M_n\}$ is unifiable, let σ_0 be the most general unifying substitution (chosen by the procedure above) so that $\underline{L}\sigma_0$ and $\underline{M}\theta\sigma_0$ are complementary literals (actually they are singleton sets whose elements are complementary literals). Then C_3 is the set of literals:

$$(C_1 - \underline{L})\sigma_0 \cup (C_2 - \underline{M})\theta\sigma_0 \qquad \blacksquare$$

Any pair of clauses has at most a finite number of resolvents, because there are only finitely many pairs of sets of literals $\underline{M}$ and $\underline{L}$, and for each pair at most one substitution σ_0. The resolvents of a pair of ground clauses are ground resolvents. A resolution deduction is defined as before, with the more general term "resolvent" replacing "ground resolvent."

DEFINITION: There is a ***refutation*** of a set of clauses $\underline{S}$ (i.e., $\underline{S} \xrightarrow{*} \Box$) if and only if $\Box \in \Re^n(\underline{S})$ for some n, where $\Re^n$ is defined as in Section 2.4, page 32, omitting the adjective "ground." ■

For example, suppose we wish to show that the following set of clauses is unsatisfiable. As in the propositional case, our goal is to show that the clauses are inconsistent by exhibiting a resolution refutation of them. Matters are substantially more complicated now that we must concern ourselves with unification, but the general strategy is the same.

1. $P(x, e, x)$
2. $\neg P(y, z, v) \vee \neg P(y, v, w) \vee P(e, z, w)$
3. $P(a, f(u, v), e)$
4. $\neg P(e, f(f(b, c), a), a)$

An easy way to standardize apart is to subscript all variables in one of the clauses you intend to resolve upon. Increasing the subscript each time a resolution step is taken can also indicate the length of the derivation. In the above set of clauses, we choose to resolve upon 1 and 2. First we write down a new version of clause 1:

$$1'.\ P(x_1, e, x_1)$$

Unifying this literal with the second literal of clause 2, we find the most general unifier $\sigma_1 = [(x_1, y), (e, v), (x_1, w)]$. We apply σ_1 to $1'$ and 2 and derive the resolvent 5:

$1'.\ P(x_1, e, x_1)$ $\qquad$ $2'.\ \neg P(x_1, z, e) \vee \neg P(x_1, e, x_1) \vee P(e, z, x_1)$

$5.\ \neg P(x_1, z, e) \vee P(e, z, x_1)$

We rename the variables in 3, getting

$$3'.\ \mathsf{P(a, f(u_2, v_2), e)}$$

to unify with the first literal in 5, and get $\sigma_2 = [((\mathsf{a}, \mathsf{x_1}), (\mathsf{f(u_2, v_2)}, \mathsf{z})]$. We apply σ_2 to $3'$ and 5 and derive 6:

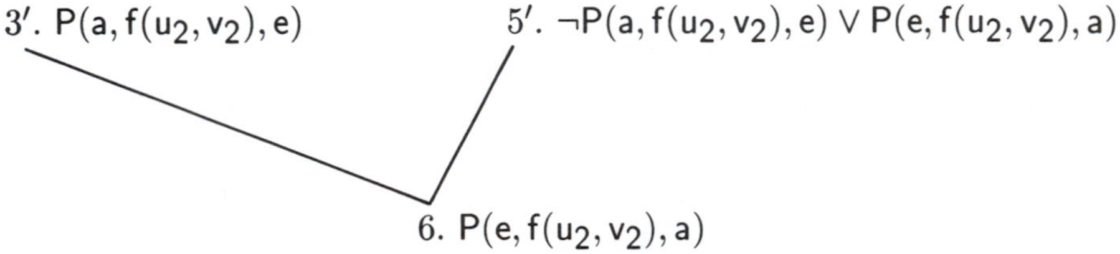

Unifying 6 with the literal in clause 4, (there are no variables in 4 to rename), we get $\sigma_3 = [(\mathsf{f(b, c)}, \mathsf{u_2}), (\mathsf{a}, \mathsf{v_2})]$ and derive $\Box$.

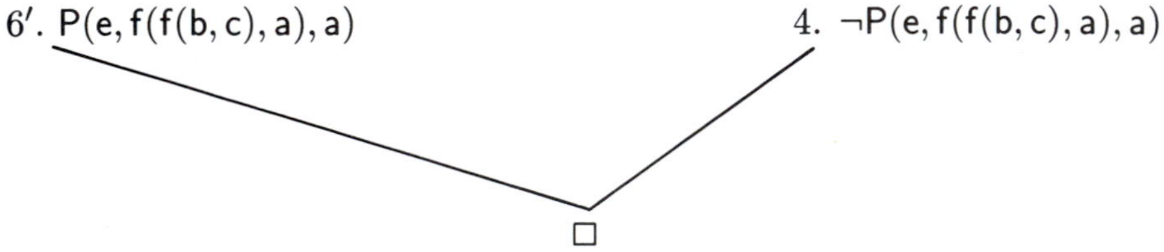

None of the renaming of variables done in the above example was necessary, as there were no clashes of variable names in the clauses being considered. However, it can never hurt to rename variables consistently throughout a clause as done above, and it is a good habit to form as it can prevent errors when derivations get complicated.

As in the previous example, in the following we list the three clauses in the set to be refuted individually, assigning each a number. To ensure that clauses are standardized apart we generate a new instance of a clause, subscripting all the variables. We refer to this new instance with a prime on the number assigned to the original clause. Each step of the resolution deduction of $\Box$ from the clauses 1–3 proceeds as follows: (1) we list the clauses we intend to resolve (standardized apart); (2) we provide a most general unifier of the selected literals of the clauses in (1); (3) we list the clauses again, having applied the unifying substitution to each; and (4) we show the resolvent derived from the clauses.

1. $\mathsf{M(x, h(x, y))}$

2. $\mathsf{M(x, h(y, z)) \lor \neg M(x, z)}$

3. $\mathsf{\neg M(c, h(b, h(a, h(c, d))))}$

$2'$. $\mathsf{M(x_1, h(y_1, z_1)) \lor \neg M(x_1, z_1)}$ 3. $\mathsf{\neg M(c, h(b, h(a, h(c, d))))}$

$$\mathsf{[(c, x_1), (b, y_1), (h(a, h(c, d)), z_1)]}$$

$\mathsf{M(c, h(b, h(a, h(c, d))))) \lor \neg M(c, h(a, h(c, d)))}$

$\mathsf{\neg M(c, h(b, h(a, h(c, d))))}$

$\mathsf{\neg M(c, h(a, h(c, d)))}$ $2''$. $\mathsf{M(x_2, h(y_2, z_2)) \lor \neg M(x_2, z_2)}$

$$\mathsf{[(c, x_2), (a, y_2), (h(c, d), z_2)]}$$

$\mathsf{\neg M(c, h(a, h(c, d)))}$ $\mathsf{M(c, h(a, h(c, d))) \lor \neg M(c, h(c, d))}$

$\mathsf{\neg M(c, h(c, d))}$ $1'$. $\mathsf{M(x_3, h(x_3, y_3))}$

$$\mathsf{[(c, x_3), (d, y_3)]}$$

$\mathsf{\neg M(c, h(c, d))}$ $\mathsf{M(c, h(c, d))}$

$$\Box$$

The above example shows that a clause may be used more than once in a refutation. Each clause, if it contains any variables, actually stands for an infinite number of possible instantiations of itself. As in CLE, we do not eliminate clauses by using them, nor are we required to use all of the clauses we are given.

In each of the examples given above the sets of literals $\underline{L}$ and $\underline{M}$ (from the definition of resolvent) were singletons. Usually we choose clauses to resolve upon and fix our attention on a single literal in each clause. However, we must be careful to treat each clause as a *set* of literals, since several literals may collapse to one literal after unification. Ignoring this fact can cause us to miss a refutation when one does exist. For example, consider the two clauses:

$$C_1 : \mathsf{P(a)} \vee \mathsf{P(x)}$$
$$C_2 : \neg\mathsf{P(a)} \vee \neg\mathsf{P(y)}$$

Looking only at a single literal at a time from each clause, and ignoring the collapse of a set to a singleton after unification, we can generate the following resolvents.

1. Resolving upon the first literal in each clause, we get

$$\mathsf{P(x)} \vee \neg\mathsf{P(y)}$$

2. Resolving upon the first literal of C_1 and the second literal of C_2, using the unifier $[(\mathsf{a}, \mathsf{y})]$, we get

$$\mathsf{P(x)} \vee \neg\mathsf{P(a)}$$

3. Resolving upon the second literal of C_1 and the first literal of C_2, using $[(\mathsf{a}, \mathsf{y})]$, we get

$$\mathsf{P(a)} \vee \neg\mathsf{P(y)}$$

4. Resolving upon the second literal in each clause, using $[(\mathsf{x}, \mathsf{y})]$, we get

$$\mathsf{P(a)} \vee \neg\mathsf{P(a)}$$

Allowing a clause, which is a *set* of literals, to contain two copies of the same literal and eliminating only one when deriving a resolvent, forces us to derive only two element clauses from C_1 and C_2, thus, making it impossible to derive $\Box$. If we look more carefully at the resolutions performed above we find that in the second case we should have gotten just $\mathsf{P(x)}$, which, when used properly with C_2, would allow us to derive $\Box$. In the third example, we should have gotten $\neg\mathsf{P(y)}$, which could be used with C_1 to derive $\Box$.

We might also have chosen to consider the entire clauses C_1 and C_2 as the sets $\underline{L}$ and $\underline{M}$, respectively, of the definition of resolvent (page 76). Then, using the most general unifier $[(\mathsf{a}, \mathsf{x}), (\mathsf{a}, \mathsf{y})]$, we would have derived $\Box$ immediately. Note carefully that this is *not* resolving on two pairs of literals at the same time, which, as discussed on page 31, is not allowed. The reason we seem to eliminate two literals from each clause is that before unification there are two literals in each clause, but after unification there is only one in each, and the result of resolving upon these singletons is $\Box$.

Thus our computation scheme for $\mathcal{PC}$ is very similar to that used in $\mathcal{L}$. However, we can no longer be assured that the process of taking resolvents will ever close out, as we now have an infinite number of possible instances of a literal any time our Herbrand domain contains a single constant and a single function letter. Herbrand's theorem assures us that, given an inconsistent set of clauses $\underline{S}$, some finite subset of $\mathcal{H}(\underline{S})$ is inconsistent — thus $\Box \in \Re^n(\underline{S})$ for some n. But we cannot put a bound on that n; we have no idea how long the program must run to establish the inconsistency of $\underline{S}$ even though we know that given enough time it will in fact do so. The problem arises when $\underline{S}$ is consistent; our process of taking resolvents may close out, or it may keep running. Thus, we have not found a decision procedure for determining whether or not $\Box \in \Re^n(\underline{S})$ for any n, for an arbitrary set of clauses $\underline{S}$. (This is not to say that a general decision procedure does not exist; however, a corollary of a future result, Theorem 4.4.11, concerning the undecidability of elementary number theory will indeed establish this.)

Exercises 3.4.1

1. On page 68, we described the process of transforming an arbitrary wff of $\mathcal{PC}$ into a wff in prenex form graphically, by making transformations on the tree representation of the wff. Provide the tree transformations that would enable one to graphically derive the Skolem free variable form and then the reduced conjunctive normal form of the matrix of the wff.

2. Supply a most general unifier for each of the following pairs of terms. If no unifier exists for a pair, state why not (w, x, y, and z are variables; a, b, c, and d are constant symbols).

a.	h(x, f(a, x))	h(b, y)
b.	h(x, f(g(a, x), z))	h(b, f(g(a, f(w, c)), h(y, x)))
c.	f(a, f(b, f(c, x)))	f(a, y)
d.	h(x, f(g(a, y), z))	h(b, f(g(a, f(w, c)), h(y, x)))
e.	f(x, f(a, f(y, c)))	f(z, f(z, f(f(a, c), w)))

3. Exhibit a resolution refutation of each of the following sets of clauses. (Recall that f, g, and h are function symbols; a, b, c, and d are constant symbols; and w, x, y, and z are variables.) Remember to:

   - Standardize apart a pair of clauses *before* attempting unification.
   - Indicate each unifying substitution *clearly.*
   - Make the unifying substitution throughout *both* clauses.

   Also, remember that there is no limit (upper or lower) to the number of times that you may use a particular clause.

   a. $P(a, x, x)$
   $P(f(x, y), w, f(x, z)) \lor \neg P(y, w, z)$
   $\neg P(f(a, f(b, a)), f(c, a), x)$

   b. $Q(x, a, a)$
   $Q(x, f(x, y), z) \lor \neg Q(x, y, z)$
   $Q(x, f(y, z), f(y, w)) \lor \neg Q(x, z, w)$
   $\neg Q(b, f(b, f(c, f(b, a))), x)$

   c. $L(a, b)$
   $L(f(x, y), g(z)) \lor \neg L(y, z)$
   $\neg L(f(x, f(c, f(d, a))), w)$

4. How do you know that the conditions required in order to combine a substitution component with a substitution are met as needed in Robinson's unification procedure?

3.4.2 Logic Programming[4]

The resolution procedure described above — a breadth-first generation of $\Re^n(\underline{S})$ — provides the basis for execution of logic programs. Although improvements have been made to the algorithm to increase its efficiency, a logic program interpreter is essentially a resolution theorem prover.

[4] Much of this section is abstracted from the article "Logic Programming and Prolog: A Tutorial," by R. E. Davis, published in *IEEE Software*, Volume 2, Number 5, September, 1985. ©1985 IEEE.

3.4.2.1 Horn Clauses

We have seen that every wff of Predicate Calculus is equivalent to a wff in reduced conjunctive normal form that was derived from a Skolem free variable form of the original wff. We then considered this wff as a set (understood by convention to be the conjunction) of clauses, each of which was a set (understood to be the disjunction) of literals.

DEFINITION: A ***Horn clause*** is a clause with at most one positive literal. ■

It is convenient, from a programming viewpoint, to write clauses as implications rather than disjunctions. Thus the clause

$$\neg A_1 \vee \ldots \vee \neg A_n \vee B_1 \vee \ldots \vee B_k$$

would be written

$$(A_1 \wedge \ldots \wedge A_n) \rightarrow (B_1 \vee \ldots \vee B_k)$$

And a Horn clause, such as

$$\neg A_1 \vee \ldots \vee \neg A_n \vee B$$

would be written

$$(A_1 \wedge \ldots \wedge A_n) \rightarrow B$$

So, a Horn clause is an implication whose antecedant is a conjunction of atomic formulas and whose consequent consists of at most one atomic formula. There are four types of Horn clauses: (1) those with a conclusion but no conditions; (2) those with conditions and a conclusion; (3) those with conditions, but no conclusion; and (4) the empty clause, written $\Box$, as before.

In the rest of the discussion about logic programming, we shall use Prolog syntax conventions. This will allow the use of more meaningful names for predicates, functions, constants, and variables. Predicate, function, and constant symbols will begin with lowercase letters (numbers may also be used as constant symbols), variables will begin with uppercase letters. We shall also write the Horn clause implications backwards, (i.e., the conclusion will be given first, and we will use :- instead of $\leftarrow$ to separate the conclusion from the conditions of the implications).

3.4.2.2 An Example

Programming in logic is the process of defining relationships. We program by asserting some facts and rules about individuals and their relationships. We call these programs by asking questions about individuals and their relationships. For example, suppose we wish to build a database of information about family relationships. We will represent the relationships:

F is the father of C.
M is the mother of C.

by the atomic formulas:

```
father(F, C)
mother(M, C)
```

We can then supply facts about a family tree by giving the clauses listed below. Every clause terminates with a period. If there are no conditions in the clause, we leave out the :- to the right of the conclusion. We read such a clause as an assertion of fact; the conclusion is claimed to hold unconditionally.

```
father(paul, rob).
father(rob, bev).
father(rob, theresa).
father(jeff, aaron).
mother(mary, rob).
mother(dorothy, bev).
mother(dorothy, theresa).
mother(theresa, aaron).
```

We do not want to assert every possible family relationship; there are too many, and such an approach would result in a database with an overabundance of redundant information. We have a choice of either storing assertions of specific relationships or computing relationships from general definitions. For example, if we know that two people have the same parents, then we can conclude that they are siblings. We can define the parent relationship in terms of mother and father, and the grandparent relationship in terms of parent, by the following:

```
parent(M, C) :- mother(M, C).
parent(F, C) :- father(F, C).
grandparent(Gparent, Gchild) :- parent(Gparent, X),
                                parent(X, Gchild).
```

These clauses are examples of rules with conditions. Gparent is a grandparent of Gchild if Gparent is a parent of someone who is a parent of Gchild. We let the variable X stand for the required parent of Gchild.

We can build a database of facts and rules that describe many family relationships (aunt, uncle, cousin, ancestor, etc.). We can then ask questions of the database. Using Horn clauses, queries take the form of conditions to be satisfied that yield no conclusion. Thus, they are written with the :- to the left. Some require simple yes or no answers:

Is Bev a sibling of Theresa?
`:- sibling(bev, theresa).`

Some queries require that a name be supplied as an answer; that is, they request that one or more values be computed that will satisfy the given condition(s).

Who is a grandparent of Aaron?
`:- grandparent(Gparent, aaron).`

Who are the parents of Rob?
`:- mother(M, rob), father(F, rob).`

3.4.2.3 Declarative Semantics

An atomic formula is always the expression of a relationship (named by the predicate of the formula) among the terms that are the arguments of the atomic formula. It will be true or false, depending on the values of the terms. The terms represent objects; they can be constants, variables, or complex terms constructed by function application. The value represented by a function application is an object; the value represented by a predicate application is a statement that is true or false.

A Horn clause logic program has both declarative and procedural semantics. The declarative semantics is inherited from Predicate Calculus. As mentioned above, a Horn clause is an implication. It states that for all possible values of the variables appearing in the clause, if all the conditions to the right of the :- hold, then the conclusion (to the left of :-) also holds. We mentioned that the case in which there are no conditions is interpreted as a statement that the conclusion holds unconditionally, (i.e., it is a fact). We also indicated that we interpret a clause with no conclusion as a question, or a request to find variables that satisfy the given conditions. The Predicate Calculus interpretation of such a question is actually a denial that all of the conditions can be satisfied.

$$\leftarrow B_1, \ldots, B_n \quad \equiv \quad \neg(B_1 \wedge \ldots \wedge B_n)$$

Our resolution refutation procedure establishes that the denial is false by showing it is inconsistent with the other clauses we have asserted (those defining the relationship we are asking about). Keeping track of the substitutions made while deriving $\Box$ allows us to provide a counterexample to the denial (i.e., an instantiation under which the original set of conditions is satisfied).

To determine that a program will compute only correct results, one need only consider each clause individually and determine that it produces a valid conclusion whenever the conditions are met. To determine that *all* correct results are attainable, one must ensure that enough clauses are included to cover every possible instance of the relationship (a much more difficult task).

Whether or not one chooses to use logic as an implementation language, one can benefit from the Horn clause definition as a specification of the problem at hand. If a formal verification is to be attempted, one must have a formal specification against which to verify the implementation, regardless of the implementation language. Horn clauses provide a specification language that is both formal and executable (see [15,12]).

3.4.2.4 Procedural Semantics

We can view Horn clauses as a programming language if we interpret each clause as a procedure definition. The conclusion of a clause is the procedure name, and the conditions of the clause represent the procedure body. A main program is then a procedure body with no name—that is, a set of conditions to be satisfied with no conclusion. One attempts to satisfy conditions by calling them as procedures. To execute the body of a procedure, one calls each procedure listed.

Procedures are invoked by unification. Given a set of procedure calls, one selects a call and looks for a procedure (clause) whose name (conclusion) unifies with the selected call. The selected procedure (clause) and the set of calls are, as in general resolution, standardized apart (see page 76) before unification. The unifying substitution is made throughout the current list of procedure calls and throughout the body of the selected procedure. Then, as in the familiar substitution and simplification model of computation, the original procedure call is replaced by the body of the selected procedure. Replacing a goal by the subgoals that establish it is also known as *backward chaining.*

Execution terminates when all procedures have successfully terminated. A procedure with no body terminates as soon as the unifying substitution is made (the call is replaced by the empty body).

For example, suppose we want to know whether Aaron has a grandparent. Our goal (or main program) is:

```
:- grandparent(G, aaron).
```

We look for all clauses that have grandparent in their conclusions (there is only one):

```
grandparent(Gparent, Gchild) :- parent(Gparent, X),
                                parent(X, Gchild).
```

We make the substitution [(G, Gparent), (aaron, Gchild)] and replace the call by the body of the grandparent procedure with the substitution made, yielding:

```
:- parent(G, X), parent(X, aaron).
```

Now we are left with two calls on parent. We can choose to work on either one first. Applying a heuristic that it is often more efficient to select a call in which more arguments are supplied values, we choose the second. We now need a clause defining parent. There are two:

```
parent(M, C) :- mother(M, C).
parent(F, C) :- father(F, C).
```

We can use either clause; suppose we choose the first. We make the substitution [(X, M), (aaron, C)] throughout and replace the call by the body, leaving

:- parent(G, X), mother(X, aaron).

Again choosing to work on the second call, we must find a definition of mother that will match this call. There is only one candidate; the substitution we need is [(theresa, X)]. Since the body of the chosen procedure is empty, we are left with

:- parent(G, theresa).

(Recall that the unifying substitution is made throughout both the procedure body and the current list of procedure calls, also referred to as subgoals, before the body is substituted for the selected call.) Using the first clause defining parent, this reduces to

:- mother(G, theresa).

Finally, with the substitution [(dorothy, G)], we are through. Successful termination simply means we have nothing left to do. The answer to our original query is found in the substitutions made along the way. In this example, we found that Dorothy is a grandparent of Aaron. Our computation scheme can be summarized as follows:

Backward-chaining Horn Clause Computation

Computation is initiated by a main program (or query) consisting of a set of procedure calls:

1. Select a call to execute.
2. Select a procedure to use in executing the chosen call.
3. Standardize apart — rename variables as necessary to ensure that there are no variables that occur both in the current set of calls and in the selected procedure.
4. Find a most general unifier (MGU) of the selected call and the name (conclusion) of the selected procedure.
5. Replace the selected call by the body of the procedure.
6. Apply the MGU to the new set of calls resulting from step 5.
7. a. If no calls remain, you have terminated successfully.
   b. If you found no procedure name to match the selected call, back up and redo the previous call, using a different procedure.
   c. If all options under b have been exhausted, terminate with failure.

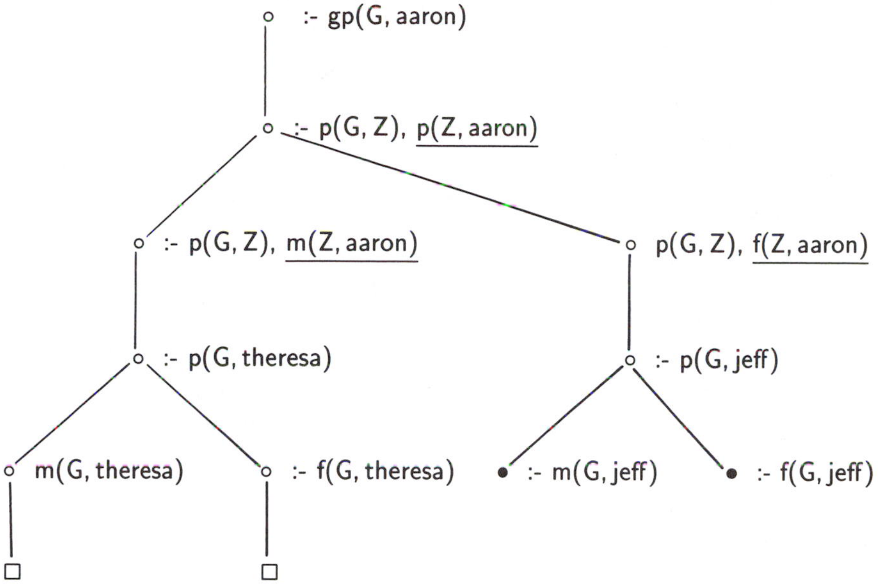

Figure 3.1 Search space for the ":- grandparent(G, aaron)" problem. (©1985 IEEE)

3.4.2.5 Nondeterminism

A logic programming language based on Horn clauses is nondeterministic in two different ways.

1. We are free to choose any order in which to execute several procedure calls in the body of a procedure.

2. When executing a selected procedure call, we are free to choose any procedure definition whose name can unify with the selected call.

The original goal and the selection of subgoals at each step in the computation (the first kind of nondeterministic choice) determine a search space containing several possible computations. A search space containing all possible answers for the problem just described is shown in Figure 3.1. In the figure, we have abbreviated all predicate names to save space and in each clause have underlined the subgoal to be attempted next. The box □, indicates successful termination. Darkened nodes represent dead ends (computationally speaking); they indicate that there is no clause whose head unifies with the selected subgoal. Any path in the search space from the original goal to a box represents a successful computation. Different paths may result in different bindings (answers) to the variables of the original goal. Along the path we took in our example, we found that Dorothy is a grandparent of Aaron; we might have chosen a different path and discovered that Rob is a grandparent of Aaron.

If we had chosen to satisfy the subgoals (execute the procedure calls) in a different order, we would have generated a different search space. For example, Figure 3.2 illustrates the search space we obtain by choosing to work on the first subgoal each time we have a choice. In this example we have abbreviated all names by their first characters. Recall that a branching occurs whenever there is more than one clause whose head can be unified with the selected subgoal. In particular, our database contains four different clauses whose heads are unifiable with mother(G, Z) (written m(G, Z) in the diagram), and four different clauses whose heads can be unified with father(G, Z) (or f(G, Z)), producing the abundance of branching in Figure 3.2.

3.4.2.6 Invertibility

Nothing about the definition of grandparent suggests we must always supply a grandchild and ask the program to find a grandparent. We could use the same definitions given above and ask for a grandchild of Mary:

```
:- grandparent(mary, Gchild).
```

Or we might supply both names and ask, for example, whether Paul is a grandparent of Bev:

```
:- grandparent(paul, bev).
```

We might even supply no values, asking whether any grandparent relationships can be derived in our database:

```
:- grandparent(Gparent, Gchild).
```

We refer to this flexibility of calling styles as the *invertibility* of logic programs. The terminology stems from the special case that the same definition can be used to compute a function and its inverse.

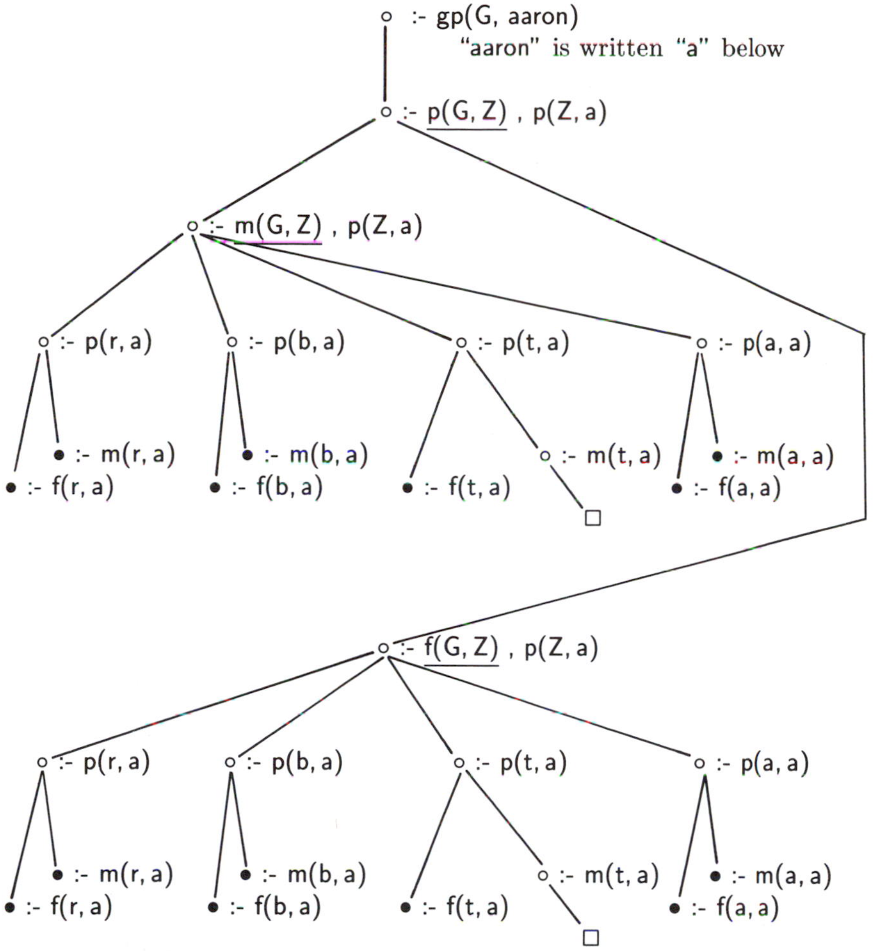

Figure 3.2 Search space obtained by changing the order of the subgoals. (©1985 IEEE)

Invertibility is not restricted to database applications. An appropriate definition of multiplication can also be used for division, or even square root. (Of course it is more efficient to make use of the arithmetic capabilities supplied as primitives in the implementation.) A program that translates English words into their French equivalents can do just as well translating French to English.

Not all relationships are invertible in all directions. For more complete discussions of invertibility see [34,33].

3.4.2.7 Computing with Partially Defined Objects

Since program evaluation is done by means of unification, one never gets an "undefined argument" error message. If a value is undetermined, it is represented by an unbound variable. An object might also be partially determined. We might not know the value we are looking for, but might know that it is a multiple of three. Or, in list applications, we may not know (or need) the entire list, but we may have determined its first four elements.

Partial information is always better than none at all, and we often prefer not to generate an entire answer before performing some other computation on it.

For example, consider the following top-level specification of a sort:

```
sort(Old, New) :- perm(Old, New), ordered(New).
```

This clause states that the list New is a sorted version of the list Old, if New is a permutation of Old and New is ordered.

This is not the kind of specification of a sort routine that we think of when writing procedural programs. We do not mean to ignore the mass of knowledge we have accumulated about efficient sorting techniques. We are simply taking a higher level approach to the original specification. See [7] for a discussion of the logic specification of several standard sorting algorithms, all derived from the ordered permutation description.

It is easy to believe that an ordered permutation is an accurate definition of the sorted version of a list, given that perm and ordered are properly defined. We can also agree that it makes sense procedurally for ordered to check the order of a proposed permutation as it is being generated, rather than wait until the list is completely determined, only to discover that it fails to be ordered in the first two elements.

We can define perm and ordered as follows. Again using Prolog syntax, we indicate the empty list by the empty brackets [] and the list whose first element is X and whose remaining elements are in the list Y by [X|Y].

```
perm([], []).
perm(L, [X|Y]) :- delete(X, L, L2), perm(L2, Y).
```

```
delete(X, [X|L], L).
delete(X, [Y|L], [Y|Z]) :- delete(X, L, Z).

ordered([]).
ordered([X|[]]).
ordered([X|[Y|L]]) :- X < Y, ordered([Y|L]).
```

Again, if we read each line as an implication, it is easy to see that if the conditions are met then the conclusion must hold.

Because of the nondeterministic nature of logic programming, while building a permutation we can delete elements from the original list in any arbitrary order. The element chosen each time depends upon which clause defining delete is used at that time. For example, if we satisfy the condition delete(X, L, L2) by using the first clause in the definition of delete (after renaming variables to avoid clashes), X is bound to the first element of L, and L2 gets bound to the rest of L. If we had chosen instead to use the second defining clause of delete, and then the first clause on the new condition thus generated, our original X would be bound to the second element of L, and L2 would get everything but the second element of L.

To illustrate this, in Figure 3.3 we show the entire search space for the problem of deleting an element from the list [a, b, c]. We ensure that our clauses are standardized apart before unification by generating a new instance of each definitional clause (generating new variables by attaching a number to each variable in the clause) each time we need to use it. In this example we show the substitution made at each step of the computation.

The element chosen to be deleted from L becomes the first element of the permutation being generated. We generate the next element of the permutation by deleting an element from what was left of the list after the first deletion. Once two elements have been generated, it makes sense to check that they are in order. This means that when we have the conditions

```
:- perm(Old, [X|[Y|L]]), ordered([X|[Y|L]]).
```

in which X and Y have been bound to specific values, we should use the partial results to check whether the permutation generated thus far is ordered, rather than continue generating a permutation of Old. If the partial permutation is ordered, then we continue with more of the

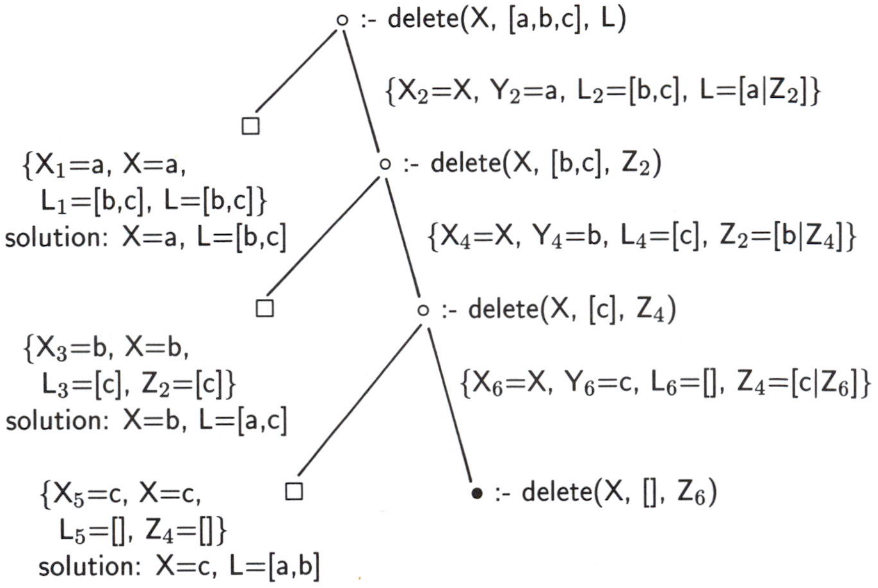

Figure 3.3 Search space for ":- delete(X, [a,b,c], L)." (©1985 IEEE)

permutation; if not, we back up and make a new choice for the first pair of elements. This swapping of control back and forth between goals is known as coroutining. (See [8] for a discussion of an implementation of coroutining in IC-Prolog.)

This example shows how partial results (permutations in which only the first two elements are known) might be used to guide the efficient execution of a program that will eventually compute the entire result. The same mechanism also allows computation with infinite objects. Although an infinite object is never fully realizable, one can compute as much of it as one desires. Thus, one might write a program involving a term that represents a list of all the positive integers. (Of course, one should never attempt to print such a term!)

Another advantage of unification is that it eliminates the need for selector functions on complex data structures. Consider the definition of ordered given above. We have no need for functions to select the head or tail of a list; nor do we need functions to test whether a list is empty, has only one element, or has at least two elements. We supply a pattern, and, if unification succeeds, we simply refer to the pieces of the structure by the names we gave them in the pattern.

3.4.2.8 Logic Programming vs. Prolog

Logic Programming has much to recommend it, whether it is used as an executable specification language or an implementation language. Separation of the logic and control aspects of a program allow a very-high-level description of the desired relationships without the overspecification that results from prescribing how they are to be computed. The declarative semantics of logical implication, the locality of reference (all variables are local to the clause in which they appear), and the unification-driven computation scheme all ensure that there can be no side effects and that each clause can be understood without reference to its position in a set of clauses. Specifying relationships rather than computations allows the same definition to be used in different ways, depending on what is supplied as input and what is expected as result. Unification, as the procedure-calling mechanism, obviates the need for selector functions and allows computation with partially defined objects.

Some, but not all, of these advantages are compromised in Prolog. Prolog is a deterministic language, and its order of evaluation is known by all Prolog programmers. In order to write more efficient programs, they depend upon the ordering of clauses and goals within clauses. Thus conditions made redundant by the positioning of clauses are left out, though they would be necessary for the program to be correct as a set of clauses.

In a Prolog program, one must usually consider together all the clauses defining a given predicate, since the correctness of a clause may depend on its position with respect to the others. It is also possible, and in some applications necessary, to "side-effect" the database within a Prolog program. The extent to which Prolog programs are invertible depends largely on one's programming style and on avoiding the extralogical features of Prolog. Prolog inherits all the advantages of unification-driven computation and the easy-to-read, high-level specification afforded by Horn clauses.

Prolog is best viewed as a first approximation to an efficient logic programming language. (For a tutorial discussion of logic programming and Prolog see [14].)

Exercises 3.4.2

1. Prove:

$$\neg A_1 \vee \cdots \vee \neg A_n \vee B_1 \vee \cdots \vee B_k \equiv (A_1 \wedge \cdots \wedge A_n) \rightarrow (B_1 \vee \cdots \vee B_k)$$

2. We have seen definitions of family relationships, some given by facts asserting that the relationship holds between specific individuals (for example, mother(theresa, aaron) and father(rob, bev)), and others given by rules describing the conditions under which the relationship holds (such as parent(Par, Child) and grandparent(Gpar, Gchild)).

   Assume that you are provided with definitions of the following relationships:

   - mother(X, Y) — X is the mother of Y
   - father(X, Y) — X is the father of Y
   - female(X) — X is female
   - male(X) — X is male
   - parent(X, Y) — X is a parent of Y
   - grandparent(X, Y) — X is a grandparent of Y
   - diff(X,Y) — X and Y are different

   a. Define some new relationships:
      - sibling(X, Y) — X is a sibling of Y
      - uncle(X, Y) — X is an uncle of Y
      - sister(X, Y) — X is a sister of Y
      - first_cousin(X, Y) — X is a first cousin of Y
      - ancestor(X, Y) — X is an ancestor of Y
      - kin(X, Y) — X and Y are related

   b. Do your definitions include half-relations? step-relations? What about "in-laws"? How might you change the definitions to include/exclude them?

3. Write logic programs to define the following utilities for dealing with list structures:

   a. insert(X, NewL, OldL) — NewL is the result of inserting X (anywhere) into OldL.

   b. delete_all(X, L, NewL) — NewL is the result of deleting all occurrences of X from the list L.

   c. append(FrontL, BackL, L) — L is the list containing all the elements of the list FrontL followed by all the elements of the list BackL.

   d. sublist(X, Y) — The list X is a sublist of the list Y (i.e., the entire list X appears contiguously in the list Y). It is *not* simply that each element of X is also an element of Y. (Try defining it with and without using append.)

      e.g., sublist([1, 2], [2, 1, 2, 3]) is true
      sublist([1, 2], [1, 1, 2]) is true
      sublist([1, 2], [2, 1, 3]) is false
      sublist([1, 2], [1, 3, 2]) is false

   e. search(X, L, P) — If X occurs in list L, then P is that sublist of L that begins with the first occurrence of X, otherwise P is the empty list.

      e.g., search(2, [1, 2, 3], [2, 3])
      search([1, 2], [1, 2, [1, 2], 3], [[1, 2], 3])

   f. max(L, X) — The maximum value in the list of numbers L is X. (Assume that you are given the relationship > (X, Y), which holds if X is greater than Y.)

3.5 Completeness Results

Now that we have described what is meant by truth, deduction, and computation in Predicate Calculus, we wish to investigate the relationships among these notions. First, we will show that $\mathcal{PC}$ is sound. Second, we will establish that if a wff is logically valid, then we can find a resolution refutation of its negation. Finally, we will show that if $\neg P \xrightarrow{*} \Box$ then $\vdash P$.

THEOREM 3.5.1 Every theorem of the Predicate Calculus is logically valid.

Proof: By property 6 of the consequences of the definition of truth (beginning page 53), the axioms **PC1**–**PC3** are logically valid. By Corollary 3.2.1.1, and property 8, **PC4** and **PC5** are logically valid.

By properties 2 and 5, the rules of inference preserve logical validity. Thus, every theorem of predicate calculus is logically valid. ■

Therefore we know that $\mathcal{PC}$ is sound (proof implies truth). Now we turn our attention to establishing that truth implies computation. Since our computation scheme is a refutation procedure, the statement of this relationship is: If $\underline{S}$ is unsatisfiable, then there exists a resolution refutation of $\underline{S}$.

Recall that $P((\underline{S}))$ is the set of all ground instances of wffs of $\underline{S}$ in which variables have been replaced by terms from the set P. $\Re(\underline{S})$ is the union of the set of wffs $\underline{S}$ and the set of all resolvents of clauses in $\underline{S}$.

LEMMA 3.5.2 Let $\mathcal{H}$ be the Herbrand domain for $\underline{S}$. If $P \subseteq \mathcal{H}$, then $\Re(P((\underline{S}))) \subseteq P((\Re(\underline{S})))$.

Proof: Suppose $C \in P((\underline{S}))$, then since $\underline{S} \subseteq \Re(\underline{S})$, $C \in P((\Re(\underline{S})))$.

If C is a resolvent, then $C = (A\alpha - L\alpha) \cup (B\beta - M\beta)$ where $A, B \in \underline{S}$, $A\alpha, B\beta \in P((\underline{S}))$, and $L\alpha$ and $M\beta$ are complementary literals. Now let $\alpha = [(s_1, u_1), \ldots, (s_k, u_k)]$ and $\beta = [(t_1, v_1), \ldots, (t_m, v_m)]$, where $u_1, \ldots, u_k$ are all the variables in A and $v_1, \ldots, v_m$ are all the variables in B. Let $\theta = [(u_{k+1}, v_1), \ldots, (u_{k+m}, v_m)]$ be the changes of variables that standardize A and B apart, and then let $\sigma = [(s_1, u_1), \ldots, (s_k, u_k), (t_1, u_{k+1}), \ldots, (t_m, u_{k+m})]$.

Then $A\sigma = A\alpha$, $B\theta\sigma = B\beta$ and $C = (A - \underline{L})\sigma \cup (B - \underline{M})\theta\sigma$, where $\underline{L}\sigma = L\alpha$ and $\underline{M}\theta\sigma = M\beta$.

Furthermore, since σ unifies the set $\underline{L} \cup \neg\underline{M}\theta$ (where $\neg\underline{M}\theta$ is the set of negated literals of $\underline{M}\theta$) there is a most general substitution σ_0 (chosen by Robinson's algorithm) and a resolvent C' of A and B, where $C' = (A - \underline{L})\sigma_0 \cup (B - \underline{M})\theta\sigma_0$.

Let $\sigma = \sigma_0\lambda$; then $C = C'\lambda$. Thus $C \in P((\Re(\underline{S})))$; that is, C is a substitution instance of a resolvent of clauses in $\underline{S}$. ■

(Loosely, the lemma above states that the set of resolvents of the instances is contained in the set of instances of the resolvents, assuming that by "resolvents" in this sentence we really mean the union of the actual resolvents and the set of clauses they came from.)

Corollary 3.5.2.1 $\Re^n(P(\!(\underline{S})\!)) \subseteq P(\!(\Re^n(\underline{S}))\!)$

Proof: This is just the generalized form of Lemma 3.5.2, which follows by induction:

Basis case: $n = 1$. See Lemma 3.5.2.

Induction step: Assume $\Re^n(P(\!(\underline{S})\!)) \subseteq P(\!(\Re^n(\underline{S}))\!)$; we must show

$$\Re^{n+1}(P(\!(\underline{S})\!)) \subseteq P(\!(\Re^{n+1}(\underline{S}))\!)$$

$$\begin{array}{rcll} \Re^{n+1}(P(\!(\underline{S})\!)) & = & \Re(\Re^n(P(\!(\underline{S})\!))) & \text{by definition of } \Re^{n+1} \\ & \subseteq & \Re(P(\!(\Re^n(\underline{S}))\!)) & \text{inductive assumption} \\ & \subseteq & P(\!(\Re(\Re^n(\underline{S})))\!) & \text{Lemma 3.5.2} \\ & = & P(\!(\Re^{n+1}(\underline{S}))\!) & \text{by definition of } \Re^{n+1} \end{array}$$

■

And now we have the ammunition we need to demonstrate the completeness of our computation scheme.

Theorem 3.5.3 If $\underline{S}$ is unsatisfiable, then $\Box \in \Re^n(\underline{S})$ for some n. (i.e., $\models \neg\underline{S}$ implies $\Box \in \Re^n(\underline{S})$)

Proof: If $\underline{S}$ is unsatisfiable, a finite subset of $\mathcal{H}(\!(\underline{S})\!)$ is inconsistent. Suppose this is $P(\!(\underline{S})\!)$. Then $\Box \in \Re^n(P(\!(\underline{S})\!))$ for some n, by Theorem 2.5.5 (since $P(\!(\underline{S})\!)$ consists of ground clauses). Therefore $\Box \in P(\!(\Re^n(\underline{S}))\!)$ by Corollary 3.5.2.1. This implies $\Box \in \Re^n(\underline{S})$, since substituting terms for variables cannot reduce a nonempty clause to the empty clause. ■

Note: Since $\underline{S}$ is in Skolem free variable form, it is equivalent to $(\forall x_1)\ldots(\forall x_n)\underline{S}$ where $x_1, \ldots, x_n$ are all the variables occurring in $\underline{S}$. Recall that $\underline{S}$ arose from a formula $\underline{S}'$ in prenex normal form (in which every variable is quantified) by replacing existentially quantified variables by functions of the universally quantified variables governing them. This leaves only universally quantified variables in the formula, eliminating the need to point them out as such.

In order to show that the existence of a refutation implies that we can prove the negation of a wff, we need to establish a correspondence between resolution and deduction in $\mathcal{PC}$. But first we establish that a universally quantified formula implies any ground instance of itself.

Lemma 3.5.4 If P is a quantifier-free wff, and $x_1, \ldots, x_n$ are all the variables occurring in P, then

$$\forall x_1 \ldots \forall x_n P(x_1, \ldots, x_n) \rightarrow P(t_1, \ldots, t_n)$$

Proof: By induction on the number of quantifiers:

Basis case: $n = 1$.

$\forall x_1 P(x_1) \rightarrow P(t_1)$ **PC4**

(Note: t_1 must be free for x_1 since there are no quantifiers in P.)

Induction step: Assume $\forall x_1 \ldots \forall x_n P(x_1, \ldots, x_n) \rightarrow P(t_1, \ldots, t_n)$ for all $n < k$; we must show:

$$\forall x_1 \ldots \forall x_k P(x_1, \ldots, x_k) \rightarrow P(t_1, \ldots, t_k)$$

1. $\forall x_1 \ldots \forall x_{k-1} P(x_1, \ldots, x_k) \rightarrow P(t_1, \ldots, t_{k-1}, x_k)$ induction hypothesis
2. $\forall x_k (\forall x_1 \ldots \forall x_{k-1} P(x_1, \ldots, x_k) \rightarrow P(t_1, \ldots, t_{k-1}, x_k))$ Gen
3. $\forall x_k (\forall x_1 \ldots \forall x_{k-1} P(x_1, \ldots, x_k) \rightarrow P(t_1, \ldots, t_{k-1}, x_k)) \rightarrow (\forall x_k \forall x_1 \ldots \forall x_{k-1} P(x_1, \ldots, x_k) \rightarrow \forall x_k P(t_1, \ldots, t_{k-1}, x_k))$ Theorem 3.3.6
4. $(\forall x_k \forall x_1 \ldots \forall x_{k-1} P(x_1, \ldots, x_k) \rightarrow \forall x_k P(t_1, \ldots, t_{k-1}, x_k))$ MP 2,3
5. $\forall x_k P(t_1, \ldots, t_{k-1}, x_k) \rightarrow P(t_1, \ldots, t_k)$ **PC4**
6. $\forall x_k \forall x_1 \ldots \forall x_{k-1} P(x_1, \ldots, x_k) \rightarrow P(t_1, \ldots, t_k)$ Lemma 2.3.4
7. $\forall x_1 \ldots \forall x_k P(x_1, \ldots, x_k) \rightarrow \forall x_k \forall x_1 \ldots \forall x_{k-1} P(x_1, \ldots, x_k)$ Exercise 1e, page 63
8. $\forall x_1 \ldots \forall x_k P(x_1, \ldots, x_k) \rightarrow P(t_1, \ldots, t_k)$ Lemma 2.3.4

■

Lemma 3.5.5 If Q is a resolvent of clauses P_1 and P_2, then

$$\vdash (P_1 \wedge P_2) \rightarrow Q$$

Proof: Q is a resolvent of P_1 and P_2 means

$$Q = (P_1 - \underline{L})\sigma_0 \cup (P_2 - \underline{M})\theta\sigma_0$$

where $\underline{L} = \{L_1, \ldots, L_k\} \subseteq P_1$, $\underline{M} = \{M_1, \ldots, M_n\} \subseteq P_2$, and θ is the substitution invoked to ensure that no variable in P_1 occurs also in

P_2. $\{L_1, \ldots, L_k, \neg M_1, \ldots, \neg M_n\}$ is unified by the chosen most general substitution σ_0 to a single literal L. Thus, $Q = (P_1\sigma_0 - L) \vee (P_2\theta\sigma_0 - (\neg L))$. Recalling that we are dealing with the Skolem free variable form, and assuming that $x_1, \ldots, x_n$ are all the variables occurring in $P_1 \wedge P_2$, we wish to show that

$$\vdash \forall x_1 \ldots \forall x_n (P_1 \wedge P_2) \rightarrow \forall x_1 \ldots \forall x_n ((P_1\sigma_0 - L) \vee (P_2\theta\sigma_0 - (\neg L)))$$

1. $\forall x_1 \ldots \forall x_n P_1 \wedge P_2$ — hypothesis

2. $\forall x_1 \ldots \forall x_n P_1 \wedge P_2 \rightarrow (P_1 \wedge P_2)\theta\sigma_0$ — Lemma 3.5.4

3. $(P_1 \wedge P_2)\theta\sigma_0$ — MP 1,2
   $\equiv (P_1'\sigma_0 \vee L) \wedge (P_2'\theta\sigma_0 \vee \neg L)$ — where:
   $\equiv (\neg P_1'\sigma_0 \rightarrow L) \wedge (L \rightarrow P_2'\theta\sigma_0)$ — P_1' is $P_1 - \underline{L}$ and P_2' is $P_2 - \underline{M}$

4. $\neg P_1'\sigma_0 \rightarrow L,\ L \rightarrow P_2'\theta\sigma_0 \vdash \neg P_1'\sigma_0 \rightarrow P_2'\theta\sigma_0$ — Lemma 2.3.4

5. $\neg P_1'\sigma_0 \rightarrow P_2'\theta\sigma_0$ — Exercise 6, page 25
   $\equiv P_1'\sigma_0 \vee P_2'\theta\sigma_0$
   $\equiv (P_1\sigma_0 - L) \vee (P_2\theta\sigma_0 - (\neg L))$

6. $\forall x_1 \ldots \forall x_n ((P_1\sigma_0 - L) \vee (P_2\theta\sigma_0 - (\neg L)))$ — n applications of Gen

7. $\forall x_1 \ldots \forall x_n (P_1 \wedge P_2) \rightarrow \forall x_1 \ldots \forall x_n ((P_1\sigma_0 - L) \vee (P_2\theta\sigma_0 - (\neg L)))$
   Deduction Theorem for $\mathcal{PC}$ 1,6

Thus, $P_1 \wedge P_2 \rightarrow Q$. ∎

Lemma 3.5.6 $\neg \underline{S} \xrightarrow{*} Q$ implies $\vdash \neg \underline{S} \rightarrow Q$

Proof: $\neg \underline{S} \xrightarrow{*} Q$ means there exists a resolution deduction of Q from $\neg \underline{S}$ — that is, there exist $P_1, \ldots, P_n = Q$ such that for all i, $1 \leq i \leq n$, P_i is either

1. a clause of $\neg \underline{S}$;

   or

2. a resolvent of two previous P_i's in the sequence

We show that for all i, $\vdash \neg \underline{S} \rightarrow P_i$, establishing the lemma by induction on i.

Basis case: $i = 1$ P_i is a clause of $\neg\underline{S}$

$\neg\underline{S} \vdash P_i$	definition of "deducible from"
$\vdash \neg\underline{S} \rightarrow P_i$	Deduction Theorem for $\mathcal{PC}$

Induction Step: Assume $\vdash \neg\underline{S} \rightarrow P_i$ for $i < k$; we must show $\vdash \neg\underline{S} \rightarrow P_k$.

1. P_k is a clause of $\neg\underline{S}$, in which case we reason as in the case $i = 1$ above.

   or

2. P_k is a resolvent of P_i and P_j, $i, j < k$

a. $\neg\underline{S} \vdash P_i$	induction hypothesis
b. $\neg\underline{S} \vdash P_j$	induction hypothesis
c. $\neg\underline{S} \vdash P_i \wedge P_j$	Exercise 2, page 25
d. $P_i \wedge P_j \rightarrow P_k$	Lemma 3.5.5
e. $\neg\underline{S} \vdash P_k$	MP c,d
f. $\vdash \neg\underline{S} \rightarrow P_k$	Deduction Theorem for $\mathcal{PC}$

Thus, for $i = n$, $\vdash \neg\underline{S} \rightarrow P_n$ — that is,
$\neg\underline{S} \xrightarrow{*} Q$ implies $\vdash \neg\underline{S} \rightarrow Q$. ■

Theorem 3.5.7 $\neg\underline{S} \xrightarrow{*} \Box$ implies $\vdash \underline{S}$

Proof: Recall that $\Box$ is just $(L \wedge \neg L)$ or, equivalently, $\neg(L \rightarrow L)$, so we have

$$\neg\underline{S} \xrightarrow{*} \neg(L \rightarrow L)$$

1. $\vdash \neg\underline{S} \rightarrow \neg(L \rightarrow L)$	Lemma 3.5.6
2. $\vdash L \rightarrow L$	Lemma 2.3.2
3. $\vdash (\neg\underline{S} \rightarrow \neg(L \rightarrow L)) \rightarrow ((L \rightarrow L) \rightarrow \underline{S})$	Lemma 2.3.5
4. $\vdash (L \rightarrow L) \rightarrow \underline{S}$	MP 1,3
5. $\vdash \underline{S}$	MP 2,4

■

Theorems 3.5.1, 3.5.3, and 3.5.7, give us the completeness results for Predicate Calculus.

Theorem 3.5.8 For Predicate Calculus the following three statements are equivalent:

1. $\vdash \underline{S}$ $\quad$ $\underline{S}$ is provable
2. $\models \underline{S}$ $\quad$ $\underline{S}$ is logically valid
3. $\neg\underline{S} \xrightarrow{*} \square$ $\quad$ there exists a resolution refutation of $\neg\underline{S}$.

Thus we have a theory that is sound, complete, and consistent, but not decidable. We have not proven that $\mathcal{PC}$ is undecidable, but we know that the computation scheme we have chosen to use does not provide a decision procedure (see the discussion on page 81). As the Horn clause proof procedure discussed in Section 3.4.2 is simply a special case of resolution, it also does not provide a decision procedure. We will see (Theorem 4.4.11) that there does not exist a decision procedure for Predicate Calculus.

CHAPTER 4

ELEMENTARY NUMBER THEORY

4.1 The Language

The language of Elementary Number Theory ($\mathcal{ENT}$) is very much like that of Predicate Calculus, with the restrictions that we allow only a single predicate symbol, a single constant symbol, and three function symbols (one unary and two binary). Of course other predicates and functions can be defined as abbreviations of expressions involving this minimal set. The formal description of the language is as follows:

Countable set of symbols:

constant symbol $\mathsf{0}$

variables a, b, c, $\ldots$, x, y, z with or without subscripts.

predicate letter A, which we will write as an infix $=$

function letters f_1^1, f_1^2, and f_2^2 which we will write as a postfix $'$, and infix $+$ and $\cdot$ respectively.[1]

logical connectives $\neg$, $\rightarrow$, and $\forall$

auxiliary symbols), (, and ,

[1]We are anticipating the standard interpretation of these function symbols as representing the successor, addition, and multiplication functions, respectively, of natural number arithmetic.

As before, a formal expression is any finite sequence of these symbols.

We define the terms and wffs of our system as follows:

term ::= "0" | variable | "(" term "+" term ")"
| "(" term "·" term ")" | term"′"
wff ::= "(" term "=" term ")" | "(" wff "→" wff ")" | "(¬" wff ")"
| "((∀" variable ")" wff ")"

The symbols ∨, ∧, and ∃ are defined as for the predicate calculus. We use the same conventions for eliminating parentheses in wffs, and we eliminate parentheses in terms by ordering our function symbols from greatest scope to least: $+$, $\cdot$, and $'$. We use A, B, C, ... as metavariables over wffs and r, s, t, ... as metavariables over terms.

4.2 Truth

Truth for elementary number theory can be formalized as for $\mathcal{PC}$, (Section 3.2), with the restriction that we force a partial interpretation of the predicate symbol $=$, the function symbols $+$, $\cdot$, and $'$, and the constant 0 (for example, $=$ is a substitutive equivalence relation). Recall that a wff A is said to be *logically valid* if and only if A is true for every interpretation. A is satisfiable if and only if there is an interpretation for which A is satisfied by at least one sequence of elements of the domain of interpretation. A is unsatisfiable if and only if $\neg A$ is logically valid (i.e., A is false for every interpretation).

However, we are no longer so concerned with every interpretation. The reason behind the definition of a formal theory for natural number arithmetic was the desire to provide a framework within which irrefutable proofs of every truth in the mathematics of natural number arithmetic could be constructed. This was part of a larger effort — starting around 1900 and headed by David Hilbert — called the "Hilbert Programme," to construct a "pure" logical formalism in which the methods of proof used to establish properties of the formalism would leave no question as to their trustworthiness, being established without having to rely on any assumptions about the truth or falsity of relationships on the domain of some interpretation. Having firmly established the validity of the logical tools, Hilbert then hoped to be able to define formal theories of mathematics (e.g., for natural number arithmetic, set theory, and real analysis) and prove them to be both sound and complete. It was thirty years before Gödel established the impossibility of the existence of such a theory for natural number arithmetic. He established that any theory powerful enough to represent all recursive functions (defined precisely in Section 4.2.1) must be either inconsistent or incomplete.

Gödel's incompleteness result is one of the greatest mathematical discoveries of all time. It has had a profound impact on the study of the foundations of mathematics as well as the foundations of computer science. Gödel also established that any theory of natural number arithmetic must be undecidable. Raphael Robinson defined a smaller (fewer axioms) example of a theory in which all recursive functions were representable; thus, his theory was also undecidable. As a result, Alonzo Church was able to show, in 1936, that $\mathcal{PC}$ is also undecidable.

In this chapter we want to move rather single-mindedly toward the incompleteness and undecidability results mentioned above. For our discussion of "truth," we will consider only the standard interpretation of Elementary Number Theory, which is Intuitive Number Theory or Recursive Function Theory, since this represents the mathematical truth system that $\mathcal{ENT}$ was intended to formalize.

4.2.1 Intuitive Number Theory (INT)

Gödel, elaborating on an idea of Herbrand, formalized the concept of total computable functions in general recursive function theory. Every total computable function can be expressed as a general recursive function. We will refer to general recursive function theory as INT, for Intuitive Number Theory, as it is a mathematical formalization of natural number arithmetic.

DEFINITION: The class of ***general recursive functions*** is defined as follows:

- The following functions are called ***initial functions***:

  I. The zero function: $\mathbf{Z}(\mathbf{x}) = \mathbf{0}$ for all $\mathbf{x}$.[2]

  II. The successor function (Next): $\mathbf{N}(\mathbf{x}) = \mathbf{x} + \mathbf{1}$ for all $\mathbf{x}$[3]

[2] In the following, we will write the constant $\mathbf{0}$ instead of the function application $\mathbf{Z}(\mathbf{x})$.

[3] We will usually write the more easily understood $\mathbf{x}+\mathbf{1}$ instead of $\mathbf{N}(\mathbf{x})$, but it should be remembered that $\mathbf{x}+\mathbf{1}$ indicates a unary successor function applied to

III. The projection functions:

$$\mathbf{U_i^n(x_1, \ldots, x_n) = x_i} \qquad \text{for all } \mathbf{x_1, \ldots, x_n}.$$

- The following are rules for obtaining new functions from given functions:

IV. Substitution: In

$$\mathbf{f(x_1, \ldots, x_n) = g(h_1(x_1, \ldots, x_n), \ldots, h_m(x_1, \ldots, x_n))}$$

$\mathbf{f}$ is said to be obtained by substution from the functions

$$\mathbf{g(y_1, \ldots, y_m), h_1(x_1, \ldots, x_n), \ldots, h_m(x_1, \ldots, x_n)}$$

V. Recursion:

$$\mathbf{f(x_1, \ldots, x_n, 0) = g(x_1, \ldots, x_n)}$$
$$\mathbf{f(x_1, \ldots, x_n, y + 1) = h(x_1, \ldots, x_n, y, f(x_1, \ldots, x_n, y))}$$

In the case where $\mathbf{n = 0}$, we have

$$\mathbf{f(0) = k} \qquad \text{(where } \mathbf{k} \text{ is a fixed integer)}$$
$$\mathbf{f(y + 1) = h(y, f(y))}$$

We say that $\mathbf{f}$ is obtained from $\mathbf{g}$ and $\mathbf{h}$ (or in the case $\mathbf{n = 0}$, from $\mathbf{h}$ alone) by recursion. The ***parameters*** of the recursion are $\mathbf{x_1, \ldots, x_n}$.

VI. μ-operator: For any relation $\mathbf{R(x_1, \ldots, x_n, y)}$, we denote by $\mu\mathbf{yR(x_1, \ldots, x_n, y)}$ the least $\mathbf{y}$ such that $\mathbf{R(x_1, \ldots, x_n, y)}$ is true, if there is any $\mathbf{y}$ at all such that $\mathbf{R(x_1, \ldots, x_n, y)}$ holds. Let $\mathbf{f(x_1, \ldots, x_n)} = \mu\mathbf{y(g(x_1, \ldots, x_n, y) = 0)}$. Then $\mathbf{f}$ is said to be obtained from $\mathbf{g}$ by means of the μ-operator, if the given assumption about $\mathbf{g}$ holds; i.e., that for any $\mathbf{x_1, \ldots, x_n}$, there is at least one $\mathbf{y}$ such that $\mathbf{g(x_1, \ldots, x_n, y) = 0}$. ■

DEFINITION: A function is said to be ***primitive recursive*** if and only if it can be obtained from the initial functions by any finite number of substitutions (IV) and recursions (V); i.e., if there is a finite sequence

---

$\mathbf{x}$, rather than a binary addition function applied to $\mathbf{x}$ and $\mathbf{1}$.

of functions $\mathbf{f_1, \ldots, f_n}$ such that $\mathbf{f = f_n}$ and for any $\mathbf{i}$, $\mathbf{0 \leq i \leq n}$, either $\mathbf{f_i}$ is an initial function or $\mathbf{f_i}$ is obtained from preceding functions in the sequence by an application of rule IV (Substitution) or rule V (Recursion). ■

For example, addition is primitive recursive. To establish this formally we show the sequence of functions $\mathbf{f_0, f_1, f_2, f_3, f_4 \equiv plus}$ that satisfies the definition. The intuitive recursive definition of **plus** is

$$\begin{aligned} \mathbf{plus(x, 0)} &= \mathbf{x} \\ \mathbf{plus(x, y + 1)} &= \mathbf{plus(x, y) + 1} \end{aligned}$$

Guided by this we generate the sequence of functions:

$$\begin{aligned} \mathbf{f_0(x, y)} &= \mathbf{U^2_1(x, y)} \\ \mathbf{f_1(x, y, z)} &= \mathbf{U^3_3(x, y, z)} \\ \mathbf{f_2(x)} &= \mathbf{N(x)} \\ \mathbf{f_3(x, y, z)} &= \mathbf{f_2(f_1(x, y, z))} \end{aligned}$$

$$\begin{aligned} \mathbf{f_4(x, 0)} &= \mathbf{f_0(x, y)} \\ \mathbf{f_4(x, y + 1)} &= \mathbf{f_3(x, y, f_4(x, y))} \end{aligned}$$

Although the above sequence of functions clearly shows that $\mathbf{f_4}$, the binary addition function, is primitive recursive, the intuition apparent in the informal definition above is lost. We will soon establish some lemmas that will support the more informal style of definition.

DEFINITION: A function is said to be ***recursive*** (or ***general recursive*** if and only if it can be obtained from the initial functions by a finite number of applications of Substitution, Recursion, and the μ-operator (VI). ■

Clearly, every primitive recursive function is recursive; it can be shown that the converse is false.

For example, Ackermann's function is a general recursive function that is not primitive recursive. (In fact, it can be shown that it grows faster than any primitive recursive function.) Ackermann's function can be defined by the following equations:

$$\begin{aligned}
\mathbf{Ack(0,y)} &= \mathbf{2\cdot y}\\
\mathbf{Ack(x,0)} &= \mathbf{0}\\
\mathbf{Ack(x,1)} &= \mathbf{2}\\
\mathbf{Ack(x+1,y+1)} &= \mathbf{Ack(x-1,Ack(x,y-1))}
\end{aligned}$$

For a discussion of recursive functions that are not primitive recursive, see [32].

DEFINITION: If $\mathbf{R(x_1,\ldots,x_n)}$ is a relation, then its ***characteristic function*** $\mathbf{C_R(x_1,\ldots,x_n)}$ is defined as follows:

$$\mathbf{C_R(x_1,\ldots,x_n)} = \begin{cases} \mathbf{0} & \text{if } \mathbf{R(x_1,\ldots,x_n)} \text{ is true} \\ \mathbf{1} & \text{if } \mathbf{R(x_1,\ldots,x_n)} \text{ is false} \end{cases}$$ ■

DEFINITION: If $\mathbf{A}$ is a set of natural numbers, then its ***characteristic function*** $\mathbf{C_A(x)}$ is defined as follows:

$$\mathbf{C_A(x)} = \begin{cases} \mathbf{0} & \text{if } \mathbf{x \in A} \\ \mathbf{1} & \text{if } \mathbf{x \notin A} \end{cases}$$ ■

DEFINITION: A ***relation*** $\mathbf{R(x_1,\ldots,x_n)}$ is said to be ***primitive recursive*** if and only if its characteristic function is primitive recursive, and it is ***recursive*** if and only if its characteristic function is recursive. Similarly, a ***set*** $\mathbf{A}$ of natural numbers is ***primitive recursive*** or ***recursive*** if and only if its characteristic function is primitive recursive or recursive, respectively. ■

The following lemma and corollary lend support to our informal intuition that a function should be primitive recursive, or recursive, if it can be defined in terms of other primitive recursive, or recursive, functions using the substitution, recursion, and μ-operator rules. The informal notion of "defined in terms of" does not involve a restriction that each function in the definition be defined on all of the same variables in the same order. We expect to be allowed the freedom to add dummy variables to and permute and identify variables in the previously defined functions. In other words, we should be able to ignore some arguments, change the order of arguments, and use the same argument more than once.

We will use this less formal style of definition, justified by Lemma 4.2.1, rather than the formal definition of a sequence of functions, to establish that functions are (primitive) recursive.

LEMMA 4.2.1 Let $\mathbf{g(y_1, \ldots, y_k)}$ be primitive recursive (or recursive). Let $\mathbf{x_1, \ldots, x_n}$ be distinct variables, and for $\mathbf{1 \le i \le k}$ let $\mathbf{z_i}$ be one of $\mathbf{x_1, \ldots, x_n}$.

Then the function $\mathbf{f(x_1, \ldots, x_n) = g(z_1, \ldots, z_k)}$ is primitive recursive (or recursive).

Proof: Let $\mathbf{z_i = x_{j_i}}$ (where $\mathbf{1 \le j_i \le n}$). Then $\mathbf{z_i = U^n_{j_i}(x_1, \ldots, x_n)}$; thus

$$\mathbf{f(x_1, \ldots, x_n) =}$$
$$\mathbf{g(U^n_{j_2}(x_1, \ldots, x_n),\ U^n_{j_2}(x_1, \ldots, x_n),\ \ldots,\ U^n_{j_k}(x_1, \ldots, x_n))}$$

and therefore $\mathbf{f}$ is PR-R,[4] since it arises from $\mathbf{g}$ and the initial functions by the substitution rule. ■

The following corollary calls out some particularly useful special cases of Lemma 4.2.1.

COROLLARY 4.2.1.1

1. Each n-ary zero function $\mathbf{Z_n(x_1, \ldots, x_n) = 0}$ is PR.

2. Each n-ary constant function $\mathbf{C^n_k(x_1, \ldots, x_n) = k}$, where $\mathbf{k}$ is some fixed integer, is PR.

3. The substitution rule (IV) can be extended to the case where each $\mathbf{h_i}$ may be a function of some but not necessarily all of the variables. Likewise, in the Recursion rule (V), the function $\mathbf{g}$ may not involve all of the variables, $\mathbf{x_1, \ldots, x_n}$; and $\mathbf{h}$ may not involve all of the variables $\mathbf{x_1, \ldots, x_n}$and $\mathbf{y}$ or $\mathbf{f(x_1, \ldots, x_n, y)}$.

---

[4]We abbreviate "primitive recursive" by PR, and "recursive" by R.

LEMMA 4.2.2 The following functions[5] are all PR:

a. $\mathbf{x} + \mathbf{y}$ b. $\delta(\mathbf{x}) = \begin{cases} x - 1 & \textbf{if } \mathbf{x} > \mathbf{0} \\ 0 & \textbf{if } \mathbf{x} = \mathbf{0} \end{cases}$ c. $\mathbf{x} \cdot \mathbf{y}$

d. $\mathbf{x}^{\mathbf{y}}$ e. $\mathbf{x} \dot{-} \mathbf{y}$ f. $|\, \mathbf{x} - \mathbf{y} \,|$

g. $\mathbf{x}!$ h. $\mathbf{min}(\mathbf{x}, \mathbf{y})$ i. $\mathbf{max}(\mathbf{x}, \mathbf{y})$

j. $\mathbf{min}(\mathbf{x_1}, \ldots, \mathbf{x_n})$ k. $\mathbf{max}(\mathbf{x_1}, \ldots, \mathbf{x_n})$

l. $\mathbf{sg}(\mathbf{x}) = \begin{cases} 0 & \textbf{if } \mathbf{x} = \mathbf{0} \\ 1 & \textbf{if } \mathbf{x} \neq \mathbf{0} \end{cases}$ m. $\mathbf{nsg}(\mathbf{x}) = \begin{cases} 1 & \textbf{if } \mathbf{x} = \mathbf{0} \\ 0 & \textbf{if } \mathbf{x} \neq \mathbf{0} \end{cases}$

n. $\mathbf{rm}(\mathbf{x}, \mathbf{y})$ = remainder upon division of $\mathbf{y}$ by $\mathbf{x}$.

o. $\mathbf{qt}(\mathbf{x}, \mathbf{y})$ = quotient upon division of $\mathbf{y}$ by $\mathbf{x}$.

Proof: The proof of part a was provided in the example on page 109. We'll provide the informal style of definition, justified by the preceding lemma and corollary, for parts b, c and n. The more formal proofs, as well as parts d–m and o, are left as exercises.

Proof of b, using the Recursion rule:

$$\delta(\mathbf{0}) = \mathbf{0}$$
$$\delta(\mathbf{y} + \mathbf{1}) = \mathbf{y}$$

Proof of c, using the Recursion rule:

$$\mathbf{x} \cdot \mathbf{0} = \mathbf{0}$$
$$\mathbf{x} \cdot (\mathbf{y} + \mathbf{1}) = (\mathbf{x} \cdot \mathbf{y}) + \mathbf{x}$$

Proof of n, using the Recursion rule:

$$\mathbf{rm}(\mathbf{x}, \mathbf{0}) = \mathbf{0}$$
$$\mathbf{rm}(\mathbf{x}, \mathbf{y} + \mathbf{1}) = \mathbf{N}(\mathbf{rm}(\mathbf{x}, \mathbf{y})) \cdot \mathbf{sg}(|\, \mathbf{x} - \mathbf{N}(\mathbf{rm}(\mathbf{x}, \mathbf{y}))\, |)$$ ■

[5]In the following we use the common infix and postfix notations for the functions rather than expressing them all in prefix notation. Thus, we write $\mathbf{x} + \mathbf{y}$ instead of $\mathbf{plus}(\mathbf{x}, \mathbf{y})$, $\mathbf{x} \cdot \mathbf{y}$ for $\mathbf{times}(\mathbf{x}, \mathbf{y})$, $\mathbf{x}^{\mathbf{y}}$ for $\mathbf{exp}(\mathbf{x}, \mathbf{y})$, $\mathbf{x} \dot{-} \mathbf{y}$ for $\mathbf{dotminus}(\mathbf{x}, \mathbf{y})$, $|\, \mathbf{x} - \mathbf{y} \,|$, for **absolute_difference(x, y)**, and x! for $\mathbf{factorial}(\mathbf{x})$. $\mathbf{x} \dot{-} \mathbf{y}$ is the familiar $\mathbf{x} - \mathbf{y}$ if $\mathbf{x} \geq \mathbf{y}$, otherwise it is $\mathbf{0}$.

Note that we have "overloaded" the symbol +. Here we are defining the binary addition operator, whereas before (page 107) we had introduced +1 as a postfix notation for the successor (Next) function, **N**. We expect no confusion to arise as both functions are primitive recursive, and where there may be ambiguity of intent, $\mathbf{x} + \mathbf{1}$ as $+(\mathbf{x}, \mathbf{1})$ or as $\mathbf{N}(\mathbf{x})$, both functions yield the same result.

In the following we further investigate the class of (primitive) recursive functions and relations.

DEFINITION: We can define ***bounded sums*** and ***bounded products*** as follows:

$$\sum_{y<z} f(x_1,\ldots,x_n,y) =$$
$$\begin{cases} 0 & \text{if } z=0 \\ f(x_1,\ldots,x_n,0)+\cdots+f(x_1,\ldots,x_n,z-1) & \text{if } z>0 \end{cases}$$

$$\sum_{y\le z} f(x_1,\ldots,x_n,y) = \sum_{y<z+1} f(x_1,\ldots,x_n,y)$$

$$\prod_{y<z} f(x_1,\ldots,x_n,y) =$$
$$\begin{cases} 1 & \text{if } z=0 \\ f(x_1,\ldots,x_n,0)\cdot \;\cdots\; \cdot f(x_1,\ldots,x_n,z-1) & \text{if } z>0 \end{cases}$$

$$\prod_{y\le z} f(x_1,\ldots,x_n,y) = \prod_{y<z+1} f(x_1,\ldots,x_n,y)$$

■

We can also define doubly bounded sums and products in terms of single bounded sums and products above. For example:

$$\begin{aligned} &\sum_{u<y<v} f(x_1,\ldots,x_n,y) \\ &\quad = f(x_1,\ldots,x_n,u+1)+\cdots+f(x_1,\ldots,x_n,v-1) \\ &\quad = \sum_{y<(v-u)-1} f(x_1,\ldots,x_n,y+u+1) \end{aligned}$$

LEMMA **4.2.3** If $f(x_1,\ldots,x_n,y)$ is PR (or R), then all the bounded sums and products defined above are also PR (or R).

Proof: Let

$$g(x_1,\ldots,x_n,z) = \sum_{y<z} f(x_1,\ldots,x_n,y)$$

Then:

$$\begin{aligned} \mathbf{g}(\mathbf{x_1}, \ldots, \mathbf{x_n}, \mathbf{0}) &= \mathbf{0} \\ \mathbf{g}(\mathbf{x_1}, \ldots, \mathbf{x_n}, \mathbf{z}+\mathbf{1}) &= \mathbf{g}(\mathbf{x_1}, \ldots, \mathbf{x_n}, \mathbf{z}) + \mathbf{f}(\mathbf{x_1}, \ldots, \mathbf{x_n}, \mathbf{z}+\mathbf{1}) \end{aligned}$$

The other proofs are quite similar. ■

We also introduce the notion of bounded quantification as well as a bounded μ-operator. Using these together with the logical connectives, we can build new number-theoretic relations from those we have already defined.

DEFINITION: We shall use $(\forall \mathbf{y})_{\mathbf{y}<\mathbf{z}}\mathbf{R}(\mathbf{x_1}, \ldots, \mathbf{x_n}, \mathbf{y})$ to express the relation: "For all $\mathbf{y}$, if $\mathbf{y}$ is less than $\mathbf{z}$, then $\mathbf{R}(\mathbf{x_1}, \ldots, \mathbf{x_n}, \mathbf{y})$ holds." We shall use $(\forall \mathbf{y})_{\mathbf{y}\leq\mathbf{z}}$, $(\exists \mathbf{y})_{\mathbf{y}<\mathbf{z}}$, and $(\exists \mathbf{y})_{\mathbf{y}\leq\mathbf{z}}$ in an analogous way. We call these ***bounded quantifiers.*** ■

DEFINITION: In addition we define a ***bounded μ-operator***:
$\mu\mathbf{y}_{\mathbf{y}<\mathbf{z}}\mathbf{R}(\mathbf{x_1}, \ldots, \mathbf{x_n}, \mathbf{y})$ = the least $\mathbf{y} < \mathbf{z}$ for which $\mathbf{R}(\mathbf{x_1}, \ldots, \mathbf{x_n}, \mathbf{y})$ holds, if there is such a $\mathbf{y}$, and $\mathbf{z}$ otherwise. ■

THEOREM 4.2.4 Relations that are obtained from PR (or R) relations by means of the propositional connectives and the bounded quantifiers are also PR (or R). Also, applications of the bounded μ-operator, $\mu\mathbf{y}_{\mathbf{y}<\mathbf{z}}$ lead from PR (or R) relations to PR (or R) relations.

Proof: Assume $\mathbf{R_1}(\mathbf{x_1}, \ldots, \mathbf{x_n})$ and $\mathbf{R_2}(\mathbf{x_1}, \ldots, \mathbf{x_n})$ are PR-R relations. By definition, the characterisic functions $\mathbf{C_{R_1}}$ and $\mathbf{C_{R_2}}$ are PR-R.

$$\mathbf{C_{\neg R_1}}(\mathbf{x_1}, \ldots, \mathbf{x_n}) = \mathbf{1} \dot{-} \mathbf{C_{R_1}}(\mathbf{x_1}, \ldots, \mathbf{x_n})$$

Hence, $\neg\mathbf{R_1}$ is PR-R. We also have

$$\begin{aligned} &\mathbf{C_{R_1 \wedge R_2}}(\mathbf{x_1}, \ldots, \mathbf{x_n}) = \\ &\qquad \mathbf{1} \dot{-} \mathbf{nsg}(\mathbf{C_{R_1}}(\mathbf{x_1}, \ldots, \mathbf{x_n}) + \mathbf{C_{R_2}}(\mathbf{x_1}, \ldots, \mathbf{x_n})) \end{aligned}$$

hence, $\mathbf{R_1} \wedge \mathbf{R_2}$ is PR-R. Since all of the propositional connectives are definable in terms of $\neg$ and $\wedge$ (see Exercise 5, page 19), this is sufficient to show that relations built from PR-R relations using any of the connectives of propositional logic are also PR-R.

Now assume $\mathbf{R}(\mathbf{x_1}, \ldots, \mathbf{x_n})$ is PR-R. Let $\mathbf{Q}(\mathbf{x_1}, \ldots, \mathbf{x_n})$ be the relation $(\exists \mathbf{y})_{\mathbf{y<z}}\mathbf{R}(\mathbf{x_1}, \ldots, \mathbf{x_n}, \mathbf{y})$. If $\mathbf{R}(\mathbf{x_1}, \ldots, \mathbf{x_n}, \mathbf{y})$ holds for some $\mathbf{y} < \mathbf{z}$ then $\mathbf{C_R}(\mathbf{x_1}, \ldots, \mathbf{x_n}, \mathbf{y}) = \mathbf{0}$, and if $\mathbf{R}(\mathbf{x_1}, \ldots, \mathbf{x_n}, \mathbf{y})$ is false for all $\mathbf{y} < \mathbf{z}$ then $\mathbf{C_R}(\mathbf{x_1}, \ldots, \mathbf{x_n}, \mathbf{y}) = \mathbf{1}$ for all $\mathbf{y} < \mathbf{z}$. Therefore,

$$\mathbf{C_Q}(\mathbf{x_1}, \ldots, \mathbf{x_n}, \mathbf{z}) = \prod_{\mathbf{y<z}} \mathbf{C_R}(\mathbf{x_1}, \ldots, \mathbf{x_n}, \mathbf{y})$$

which by Lemma 4.2.3 is PR-R.

The bounded quantifier $(\exists \mathbf{y})_{\mathbf{y \le z}}$ is equivalent to $(\exists \mathbf{y})_{\mathbf{y<z+1}}$, which is obtainable from $(\exists \mathbf{y})_{\mathbf{y<z}}$ by substitution. Also $(\forall \mathbf{y})_{\mathbf{y<z}}$ is equivalent to $\neg(\exists \mathbf{y})_{\mathbf{y<z}}\neg$, and $(\forall \mathbf{y})_{\mathbf{y\le z}}$ is equivalent to $\neg(\exists \mathbf{y})_{\mathbf{y\le z}}\neg$. Doubly bounded quantifiers such as $(\exists \mathbf{y})_{\mathbf{u<y<v}}$ can be defined by substitution in the bounded quantifiers already mentioned.

Finally, we need to show that $\mu_{\mathbf{y<z}}\mathbf{R}(\mathbf{x_1}, \ldots, \mathbf{x_n}, \mathbf{y})$ is PR-R as $\mathbf{R}$ is PR-R.

$\prod_{\mathbf{u \le y}} \mathbf{C_R}(\mathbf{x_1}, \ldots, \mathbf{x_n}, \mathbf{u})$ has the value $\mathbf{1}$ for all $\mathbf{y}$ such that the relationship $\mathbf{R}(\mathbf{x_1}, \ldots, \mathbf{x_n}, \mathbf{u})$ is false for all $\mathbf{u} \le \mathbf{y}$; it has the value $\mathbf{0}$ as soon as there is some $\mathbf{u} \le \mathbf{y}$ such that $\mathbf{R}(\mathbf{x_1}, \ldots, \mathbf{x_n}, \mathbf{u})$ holds. Hence, the number of integers from $\mathbf{0}$ up to but not including the first $\mathbf{y} < \mathbf{z}$ such that $\mathbf{R}(\mathbf{x_1}, \ldots, \mathbf{x_n}, \mathbf{y})$ holds is

$$\sum_{\mathbf{y<z}} \Big(\prod_{\mathbf{u \le y}} \mathbf{C_R}(\mathbf{x_1}, \ldots, \mathbf{x_n}, \mathbf{u}) \Big)$$

If there is no such $\mathbf{y}$, the sum is equal to $\mathbf{z}$; that is, in any case,

$$\mu\mathbf{y}_{\mathbf{y<z}}\mathbf{R}(\mathbf{x_1}, \ldots, \mathbf{x_n}, \mathbf{y}) = \sum_{\mathbf{y<z}} \Big(\prod_{\mathbf{u \le y}} \mathbf{C_R}(\mathbf{x_1}, \ldots, \mathbf{x_n}, \mathbf{u}) \Big)$$

and so the bounded μ-operator leads from PR-R relations to PR-R relations by Lemma 4.2.3. ■

The following theorem, which allows us to use definition by cases, is the basis of conditional expressions in programming languages. We will use this technique when developing the recursive functions that we need to establish the incompleteness of number theory.

Theorem 4.2.5 Let:

$$\mathbf{f}(\mathbf{x_1},\ldots,\mathbf{x_n}) = \begin{cases} \mathbf{g_1}(\mathbf{x_1},\ldots,\mathbf{x_n}) & \text{if } \mathbf{R_1}(\mathbf{x_1},\ldots,\mathbf{x_n}) \text{ holds} \\ \mathbf{g_2}(\mathbf{x_1},\ldots,\mathbf{x_n}) & \text{if } \mathbf{R_2}(\mathbf{x_1},\ldots,\mathbf{x_n}) \text{ holds} \\ \vdots & \\ \mathbf{g_k}(\mathbf{x_1},\ldots,\mathbf{x_n}) & \text{if } \mathbf{R_k}(\mathbf{x_1},\ldots,\mathbf{x_n}) \text{ holds} \end{cases}$$

If the functions $\mathbf{g_1},\ldots,\mathbf{g_k}$, and the relations $\mathbf{R_1},\ldots,\mathbf{R_k}$ are PR-R, and if, for any $\mathbf{x_1},\ldots,\mathbf{x_n}$, exactly one of the relations $\mathbf{R_1}(\mathbf{x_1},\ldots,\mathbf{x_n})$, $\ldots$, $\mathbf{R_k}(\mathbf{x_1},\ldots,\mathbf{x_n})$ is true, then $\mathbf{f}$ is PR-R.

Proof:

$$\begin{aligned} &\mathbf{f}(\mathbf{x_1},\ldots,\mathbf{x_n}) = \\ &\quad \mathbf{g_1}(\mathbf{x_1},\ldots,\mathbf{x_n}) \cdot \mathbf{nsg}(\mathbf{C_{R_1}}(\mathbf{x_1},\ldots,\mathbf{x_n})) \\ &\quad + \cdots + \mathbf{g_k}(\mathbf{x_1},\ldots,\mathbf{x_n}) \cdot \mathbf{nsg}(\mathbf{C_{R_k}}(\mathbf{x_1},\ldots,\mathbf{x_n})) \end{aligned}$$

■

A number-theoretic function is one whose arguments and values are natural numbers, and a number-theoretic relation is a relation whose arguments are natural numbers. For example, multiplication is a number-theoretic function of two arguments, and the expression $\mathbf{x} + \mathbf{y} < \mathbf{z}$ determines a number-theoretic relation of three arguments.

We have presented the groundwork for the mathematics of natural number arithmetic. As mentioned earlier, the class of recursively definable functions is the same as the class of total computable functions.

In the following section we will attempt to define a formal theory in which all and only true statements about number-theoretic functions and relations will be provable. We then investigate the relationship between the formal theory (proof) and intuitive mathematics (truth), and discover that the task we set out to accomplish is in fact impossible. There can be no consistent and complete formal theory for natural number arithmetic.

Exercises 4.2.1

1. Prove Corollary 4.2.1.1.

2. Provide formal proofs of parts b, c, and n of Lemma 4.2.2.

3. Show that parts d–m and o of Lemma 4.2.2 are primitive recursive.

4. Show that the relations $\mathbf{even(x)}$ and $\mathbf{odd(x)}$ are primitive recursive.

5. Prove that the bounded product $\prod_{\mathbf{y<z}}\mathbf{f}(\mathbf{x_1},\ldots,\mathbf{x_n},\mathbf{y})$ is primitive recursive if $\mathbf{f}$ is primitive recursive.

4.3 Deduction

We will call the formal theory of Elementary Number Theory $\mathcal{ENT}$. $\mathcal{ENT}$ is a first-order theory, as defined on page 57, in which we have only one predicate symbol, one constant symbol, and three function symbols, as described in Section 4.1, page 105. It remains to present the axioms of theory $\mathcal{ENT}$.

Axioms:

The first five axioms are the logical axioms of any first-order theory as defined on page 57.

A1: $A\to(B\to A)$

A2: $(A\to(B\to C))\to((A\to B)\to(A\to C))$

A3: $(\neg B\to\neg A)\to((\neg B\to A)\to B)$

A4: $(\forall x)A(x)\to A(t)$, if $A(x)$ is a wff and t is a term free for x in $A(x)$. Note that if t is x, we have the axioms $(\forall x)A(x)\to A(x)$.

A5: $(\forall x)(A\to B)\to(A\to(\forall x)B)$ if A is a wff containing no free occurrences of x.

We add the following set of proper axioms, consisting of eight specific axioms and one axiom schema:

A6: $(\mathsf{a}' = \mathsf{b}') \to (\mathsf{a} = \mathsf{b})$

A7: $\neg\mathsf{a}' = 0$ (we will abbreviate $\neg r = s$ as $r \neq s$, for all terms r and s)

A8: $(\mathsf{a} = \mathsf{b}) \to ((\mathsf{a} = \mathsf{c}) \to (\mathsf{b} = \mathsf{c}))$

A9: $(\mathsf{a} = \mathsf{b}) \to (\mathsf{a}' = \mathsf{b}')$

A10: $\mathsf{a} + 0 = \mathsf{a}$

A11: $\mathsf{a} + \mathsf{b}' = (\mathsf{a} + \mathsf{b})'$

A12: $a \cdot 0 = 0$

A13: $a \cdot b' = a \cdot b + a$

and one new axiom schema:

A14: For any wff $A(x)$,
$$A(0) \to ((\forall x)(A(x) \to A(x')) \to \forall x A(x))$$

Note that **A6**–**A13** are particular wffs of the theory $\mathcal{ENT}$ (they contain no metavariables), while **A14** is an axiom schema providing an infinite number of axioms.

Rules of Inference:

From the definition of first-order theory, page 57, we know that the rules of inference of $\mathcal{ENT}$ must include MP and Gen.

From **A14** and MP we can derive a new rule of inference: the Induction Rule (IR).

$$A(0),\ \forall x(A(x) \to A(x')) \ \vdash\ \forall x A(x)$$

In adding the specific axioms **A6**–**A13**, instead of eight more axiom schemata, we are again attempting to keep our formal theory as small as possible. We haven't lost any power, as we can immediately prove as theorems the form we need of any of the axioms.

Lemma 4.3.1 For any terms t, s, and r, the following wffs are theorems of $\mathcal{ENT}$:

$$\begin{aligned}
\mathbf{A6'}&: \quad t' = r' \to t = r \\
\mathbf{A7'}&: \quad t' \neq 0 \\
\mathbf{A8'}&: \quad t = r \to (t = s \to r = s) \\
\mathbf{A9'}&: \quad t = r \to t' = r' \\
\mathbf{A10'}&: \quad t + 0 = t \\
\mathbf{A11'}&: \quad t + r' = (t + r)' \\
\mathbf{A12'}&: \quad t \cdot 0 = 0 \\
\mathbf{A13'}&: \quad t \cdot r' = (t \cdot r) + t
\end{aligned}$$

Proof: These follow from the axioms **A6**–**A13**, respectively, by first forming the closure by means of Gen, and then applying **A4** and

MP with the appropriate terms t, s, and r. As an example we exhibit the proof of **A10′**.

1. $\mathsf{a}+0=\mathsf{a}$ **A10**
2. $\forall\mathsf{a}(\mathsf{a}+0=\mathsf{a})$ Gen 1
3. $\forall\mathsf{a}(\mathsf{a}+0=\mathsf{a})\rightarrow(t+0=t)$ **A4**
4. $t+0=t$ MP 2,3

■

The following lemma establishes several properties we know to be true of natural number arithmetic and thus hoped would be provable in $\mathcal{ENT}$. For example, $=$ is a substitutive equivalence relation and $+$ and $\cdot$ are commutative operations.

Lemma 4.3.2 For any terms t, r, and s, the following wffs are theorems.

a. $t=t$
b. $t=r\rightarrow r=t$
c. $t=r\rightarrow(r=s\rightarrow t=s)$
d. $r=t\rightarrow(s=t\rightarrow r=s)$
e. $t=r\rightarrow t+s=r+s$
f. $t=0+t$
g. $t'+r=(t+r)'$
h. $t+r=r+t$
i. $t=r\rightarrow s+t=s+r$
j. $t\cdot r=r\cdot t$
k. $t=r\rightarrow t\cdot s=r\cdot s$
l. $0\cdot t=0$
m. $t\neq 0\rightarrow(s\cdot t=0\rightarrow s=0)$

Proof: of parts a, b, c, and f.

Part a:

1. $t+0=t$ **A10′** Lemma 4.3.1
2. $t+0=t\rightarrow(t+0=t\rightarrow t=t)$ **A8′** Lemma 4.3.1
3. $t+0=t\rightarrow t=t$ MP 1,2
4. $t=t$ MP 1,3

Part b:

1. $t = r$ hypothesis
2. $t = t$ part a
3. $t = r \rightarrow (t = t \rightarrow r = t)$ **A8′** Lemma 4.3.1
4. $t = t \rightarrow r = t$ MP 1,3
5. $r = t$ MP 2,4
6. $t = r \rightarrow r = t$ Deduction Theorem[6] 1,5

Part c:

1. $t = r \rightarrow r = t$ part b
2. $r = t \rightarrow (r = s \rightarrow t = s)$ **A8′** Lemma 4.3.1
3. $t = r \rightarrow (r = s \rightarrow t = s)$ Lemma 2.3.4, page 24

Part f: First, we use the Induction Rule (IR), derived above, to show that $\forall x(x = 0 + x)$, then **A4** and MP to get $t = 0 + t$

1. $0 + 0 = 0$ **A10′** Lemma 4.3.1
2. $0 + 0 = 0 \rightarrow 0 = 0 + 0$ part b
3. $0 = 0 + 0$ MP 1,2
4. $x = 0 + x$ hypothesis
5. $x = 0 + x \rightarrow x' = (0 + x)'$ **A9′** Lemma 4.3.1
6. $x' = (0 + x)' \rightarrow ((0 + x)' = 0 + x' \rightarrow x' = 0 + x')$ part c
7. $x' = (0 + x)'$ MP 4,5
8. $(0 + x)' = 0 + x' \rightarrow x' = 0 + x'$ MP 6,7
9. $0 + x' = (0 + x)'$ **A11′** Lemma 4.3.1

[6]The Deduction Theorem referred to here is Theorem 3.3.5, originally stated on page 61 as the Deduction Theorem for $\mathcal{PC}$. It would have been more accurate to describe it as the Deduction Theorem for First-Order Theories, as it holds in any first-order theory. (One can be convinced of this by reviewing the proof.)

10. $0 + x' = (0 + x)' \to (0 + x)' = 0 + x'$ part b

11. $(0 + x)' = 0 + x'$ MP 9,10

12. $x' = 0 + x'$ MP 8,11

13. $x = 0 + x \to x' = 0 + x'$ Deduction Theorem 4,12

14. $\forall x(x = 0 + x \to x' = 0 + x')$ Gen 13

15. $\forall x(x = 0 + x)$ Induction Rule 3,14

16. $\forall x(x = 0 + x) \to t = 0 + t$ **A4**

17. $t = 0 + t$ MP 15,16

(The proofs of the other parts are left as exercises.) ■

DEFINITION: Let $\mathcal{K}$ be a first-order theory containing a binary predicate symbol, which we will write as =. $\mathcal{K}$ is called a ***first-order theory with equality*** if the following are theorems of $\mathcal{K}$.

1. $(\forall \mathsf{x}_1)(\mathsf{x}_1 = \mathsf{x}_1)$
2. $\mathsf{x} = \mathsf{y} \to (A(\mathsf{x},\mathsf{x}) \to A(\mathsf{x},\mathsf{y}))$
where x and y are any variables, $A(\mathsf{x},\mathsf{x})$ is any wff, and $A(\mathsf{x},\mathsf{y})$ is the result of replacing some free occurrences of x in $A(\mathsf{x},\mathsf{x})$ by y, provided that y is free for each occurrence of x that it replaces. ■

THEOREM 4.3.3 $\mathcal{ENT}$ is a first-order theory with equality.

It can be shown that item 2 (= is substitutive) of the definition of a first-order theory with equality will hold for all wffs if and only if it holds for all atomic formulas. It can also be shown that the general statement of item 2 can be derived from the result that it holds for exactly one replacement of x by y. Given these results, the proof that $\mathcal{ENT}$ is a first-order theory with equality follows from Lemma 4.3.2. For a complete proof see [28].

DEFINITION: We may often refer to the ***numeral*** n as an abbreviation for $0''^{\cdots\prime}$, where $'$ appears n times.[7] ■

[7] A reference to the *numeral* n, is distinguished from the *number* n by font. For example, 1, 2, 3 represent numerals; and **1**, **2**, **3** represent numbers.

There are many theorems that can be proved about the properties of $\cdot$ and $+$ (properties such as commutativity, associativity and distributivity, that we know hold of multiplication and addition). However, they are not particularly relevant to our discussion. Again, our goal is to establish *in*completeness; that is, we want to show that *any* attempt to formalize Intuitive Number Theory is doomed to failure in that it cannot completely characterize all true statements about natural number arithmetic. We are not nearly so interested in what facts we may be able to prove in a particular theory that attempts such a formalization, so we do not investigate it in depth. For these reasons, such proofs are omitted here. For examples of such proofs see [28], [20], or [26].

4.3.1 Consistency of $\mathcal{ENT}$

If we recognize the standard interpretation, INT, to be a model for $\mathcal{ENT}$ (i.e., everything that is provable in $\mathcal{ENT}$ is true in INT), then of course $\mathcal{ENT}$ is consistent (since no statement can be both true and false). However, this semantic approach, relying on our understanding of truth in the model, is less rigorous than a formal proof of consistency. (The goal of Hilbert's program, see page 106, was to eliminate such informal intuitive arguments.) Thus, when the consistency of $\mathcal{ENT}$ enters into the argument of a proof, we take the statement of consistency as an explicit, unproved assumption. Although we will not prove the truth of the axioms and rules of inference of $\mathcal{ENT}$ in INT, we expect that the reader is comfortable with the assumption that they are true, given an intuitive understanding of natural number arithmetic.

There is an alternative definition of the consistency of a theory that is useful to introduce at this point.

DEFINITION: A theory $\mathcal{T}$ is consistent if there is an unprovable well-formed formula in $\mathcal{T}$. ∎

This definition is equivalent to our initial definition — i.e., that $\mathcal{T}$ is consistent iff there is no A such that $\vdash A$ and $\vdash \neg A$ — in any theory in which axioms **A1** and **A3** and Modus Ponens are included (either given or derivable from what is given).

Theorem 4.3.4 The two definitions of consistency (def1 and def2) are equivalent in any theory in which axioms **A1** and **A3**, and Modus Ponens can be used.

def1 there is no A such that $\vdash A$ and $\vdash \neg A$

def2 there is an unprovable well-formed formula

Proof:

def1 $\Rightarrow$ def2: $\vdash$ **A1**. Therefore, by def1 we know that $\neg$**A1** is not provable, thus def2 also holds.

def2 $\Rightarrow$ def1: Assume that a theory is consistent by def2 and not consistent by def1. Then there is a wff A, such that $\vdash A$ and $\vdash \neg A$; therefore,

1.	$(\neg B\rightarrow\neg A)\rightarrow((\neg B\rightarrow A)\rightarrow B))$	**A3**
2.	$A\rightarrow(\neg B\rightarrow A)$	**A1**
3.	A	assumption
4.	$\neg B\rightarrow A$	MP 2,3
5.	$\neg A\rightarrow(\neg B\rightarrow\neg A)$	**A1**
6.	$\neg A$	assumption
7.	$\neg B\rightarrow\neg A$	MP 5,6
8.	$(\neg B\rightarrow A)\rightarrow B$	MP 1,7
9.	B	MP 4,8

Thus everything is provable, contradicting the assumption that the theory was consistent by def2. ■

Definition: Any first order theory $\mathcal{K}$ is said to be ***ω-consistent*** if and only if, for every wff $A(x)$ of $\mathcal{K}$, if $\vdash A(\mathsf{n})$ for every natural number n, then it is not the case that $\vdash (\exists x)\neg A(x)$. ■

Clearly, ω-consistency only makes sense for theories in which we can represent the mathematical notion of natural numbers. As with consistency, if we choose to accept the standard interpretation as a model of $\mathcal{ENT}$, then $\mathcal{ENT}$ is ω-consistent; but rather than concern ourselves with a proof of ω-consistency for $\mathcal{ENT}$, we shall always explicitly state the assumption that $\mathcal{ENT}$ is ω-consistent whenever it is used in a proof. In fact, this is a stronger restriction than simple consistency, as the following lemma shows.

Lemma 4.3.5 Let $\mathcal{K}$ be any first order theory with the same symbols as $\mathcal{ENT}$. If $\mathcal{K}$ is ω-consistent, then $\mathcal{K}$ is consistent.

Proof: Assume $\mathcal{K}$ is ω-consistent. Consider any wff $A(\mathsf{x})$, with free variable x, that is provable in $\mathcal{K}$, (for example $\mathsf{x} = \mathsf{x} \rightarrow \mathsf{x} = \mathsf{x}$). Then, for all natural numbers n, $\vdash A(\mathsf{n})$, as follows:

1. $A(\mathsf{x})$	assumption
2. $\forall \mathsf{x} A(\mathsf{x})$	Gen 1
3. $\forall \mathsf{x} A(\mathsf{x}) \rightarrow A(\mathsf{n})$	**A4**
4. $A(\mathsf{n})$	MP 2,3

Hence, by ω-consistency, $(\exists \mathsf{x})\neg A(\mathsf{x})$ is not provable in $\mathcal{K}$. Therefore, $\mathcal{K}$ is consistent (by def2 given above). ■

A proof of consistency can be found in the appendix to [28].

4.4 Undecidability and Incompleteness

We have not described a computation scheme for $\mathcal{ENT}$. We could have extended general resolution by adding the appropriate clausal form of the new axioms as "resident" clauses. That is, they would be assumed to be included in every set of clauses we attempted resolution on. Alternatively, we could have described Turing machines as a computation mechanism. However, we are less interested in investigating a given computation scheme than in establishing that *any* computation scheme must be incomplete with respect to both proof and truth.

In describing a process of computation for a theory, what we are attempting to do is establish a decision procedure. We want an algorithm that, given any wff of the theory, will tell us whether or not that wff is provable. For propositional logic we described an algorithm in terms of complementary literal elimination. We could instead have described an algorithm for constructing truth tables with the same result. We had both completeness and decibability.

In the case of predicate logic we again established completeness, but our algorithm was only a partial decision procedure. Given a theorem, it would indeed tell us we had a theorem, but given a nontheorem it might let us know (by closing out) or the computation might continue infinitely. We have not shown that there does not exist a decision procedure for $\mathcal{PC}$; we have only established that resolution is not one.

We shall prove that there is no decision procedure for determining whether an arbitrary wff of $\mathcal{ENT}$ is a theorem. Undecidability for $\mathcal{PC}$ will follow from a related result showing that a finite extension of $\mathcal{PC}$ is undecidable, together with the fact that any finite extension of a decidable theory must be decidable.

If there did exist a decision procedure ϕ for $\mathcal{ENT}$, it would have to be a total computable function over all wffs of $\mathcal{ENT}$, whose value $\phi(A)$, for any A, would tell us whether or not A is provable in $\mathcal{ENT}$. For example,

$$\begin{aligned} \phi(A) &= 0 \quad \text{if } A \text{ is provable} \\ \phi(A) &= 1 \quad \text{if } A \text{ is not provable} \end{aligned}$$

We'd like to know more about the structure of ϕ. We know that it must be an effective procedure; given input it carries out a precise sequence of steps to compute output. In other words, it must be a total computable function (i.e., a general recursive function). "Effectively computable" is an intuitive idea. The equivalence between the notions of "effectively computable" and "general recursive" is known as *Church's thesis.* We take Church's thesis as an assumption. Thus, when speaking of decidability, we equate the terms "effectively decidable" and "recursively decidable" and speak only of "decidable." Before attempting to prove the undecidability and incompleteness of $\mathcal{ENT}$, we investigate the relationship between the mathematical theory of general recursive functions and the formal theory $\mathcal{ENT}$. In particular, we define what it means for number-theoretic relations and functions (INT) to be expressible and representable, respectively, in $\mathcal{ENT}$.

DEFINITION: A number-theoretic relation $\mathbf{R}(\mathbf{x_1}, \ldots, \mathbf{x_n})$ is said to be ***expressible*** in $\mathcal{ENT}$ if and only if there is a wff $A(\mathsf{x}_1, \ldots, \mathsf{x}_n)$ of $\mathcal{ENT}$ with $\mathbf{n}$ free variables such that for any natural numbers $\mathbf{k_1}, \ldots, \mathbf{k_n}$:

1. If $\mathbf{R}(\mathbf{k_1}, \ldots, \mathbf{k_n})$ is true, then $\vdash A(\mathsf{k}_1, \ldots, \mathsf{k}_n)$.
2. If $\mathbf{R}(\mathbf{k_1}, \ldots, \mathbf{k_n})$ is false, then $\vdash \neg A(\mathsf{k}_1, \ldots, \mathsf{k}_n)$.

   where $\mathsf{k}_i = 0'' \cdots '$ (the $\mathbf{k_i}$th successor of $\mathbf{0}$), or simply the numeral representing $\mathbf{k_i}$ if we let the numerals 1, 2, 3, ... represent respectively the 1st, 2nd, 3rd, etc., successors of $\mathbf{0}$. ■

Examples:

1. The equality relation is expressed in $\mathcal{ENT}$ by the wff $\mathsf{x}_1 = \mathsf{x}_2$. If $\mathbf{k_1} = \mathbf{k_2}$ then $\mathbf{k_1}$ is the same term as $\mathbf{k_2}$, and so by Lemma 4.3.2 a, page 119, $\vdash \mathsf{k}_1 = \mathsf{k}_2$. Also, if $\mathbf{k_1} \neq \mathbf{k_2}$, then $\vdash \mathsf{k}_1 \neq \mathsf{k}_2$. (Proof left to the reader.)
2. The less-than relation is expressed in $\mathcal{ENT}$ by the wff $\mathsf{x}_1 < \mathsf{x}_2$. If $\mathbf{k_1} < \mathbf{k_2}$, then there must exist some positive number $\mathbf{n}$ such that $\mathbf{k_2} = \mathbf{k_1} + \mathbf{n}$. Thus, since we know that equality is expressible, we have $\vdash \mathsf{k}_2 = \mathsf{k}_1 + \mathsf{n}$, and $\vdash \mathsf{n} \neq 0$ (by the proof of the previous example). So it is possible to prove in $\mathcal{ENT}$ the wff $(\exists \mathsf{w})(\mathsf{k}_2 = \mathsf{k}_1 + \mathsf{w} \wedge \mathsf{w} \neq 0)$ — i.e., $\mathsf{k}_1 < \mathsf{k}_2$.

   We must also show that if $\mathbf{k_1} \not< \mathbf{k_2}$ then $\vdash \neg(\mathsf{k}_1 < \mathsf{k}_2)$. If $\mathbf{k_1} \not< \mathbf{k_2}$, then $\mathbf{k_1} = \mathbf{k_2}$ or $\mathbf{k_2} < \mathbf{k_1}$, thus $\vdash \mathsf{k}_1 = \mathsf{k}_2$ or $\vdash \mathsf{k}_2 < \mathsf{k}_1$. To complete the proof that the less-than relation is expressed by $\mathsf{x}_1 < \mathsf{x}_2$, we need to show that for all terms s and t: $\vdash \neg(\mathsf{t} < \mathsf{t})$ and $\vdash (\mathsf{s} < \mathsf{t}) \rightarrow \neg(\mathsf{t} < \mathsf{s})$. Again, these diversions are left to the interested reader.[8]

It can also be shown that the negation, conjunction, and disjunction of expressible relations are also expressible.

[8]In order to build sufficiently powerful theorems to formally prove the expressibility (representability) of each relation (function) we wish to use, we should have to divert our attention to deriving many (intuitively obvious) lemmas. Since our goal is to drive toward the incompleteness and undecidability results, we state that many wffs are provable without explicitly deriving them in the theory. The complete proofs may be found in textbooks on mathematical logic (such as [28]), but are outside the scope of this text.

Before we can define the conditions under which a number-theoretic function is representable, we must introduce some new notation. The modified quantification $(\exists! x)A(x)$ is read "there exists a *unique* x such that $A(x)$." It is an abbreviation for the wff:

$$(\exists x)A(x) \wedge (\forall x)(\forall y)(A(x) \wedge A(y) \rightarrow x = y)$$

DEFINITION: A number-theoretic function $\mathbf{f}(\mathbf{x_1}, \ldots, \mathbf{x_n})$ is said to be ***representable*** in $\mathcal{ENT}$ if there is a wff $A(\mathsf{x_1}, \ldots, \mathsf{x_n}, \mathsf{x_{n+1}})$ of $\mathcal{ENT}$ with the free variables $\mathsf{x_1}, \ldots, \mathsf{x_n}, \mathsf{x_{n+1}}$, such that for any numbers $\mathbf{k_1}, \ldots, \mathbf{k_n}, \mathbf{k_{n+1}}$:

1. If $\mathbf{f}(\mathbf{k_1}, \ldots, \mathbf{k_n}) = \mathbf{k_{n+1}}$ then $\vdash A(\mathsf{k_1}, \ldots, \mathsf{k_n}, \mathsf{k_{n+1}})$.
2. $\vdash (\exists! \mathsf{x_{n+1}})A(\mathsf{k_1}, \ldots, \mathsf{k_n}, \mathsf{x_{n+1}})$.

If, in this definition, we change 2 to

1′. $\vdash (\exists! \mathsf{x_{n+1}})A(\mathsf{x_1}, \ldots, \mathsf{x_n}, \mathsf{x_{n+1}})$.

then the function $\mathbf{f}$ is said to be ***strongly representable*** (in $\mathcal{ENT}$). It can be shown that a function is representable iff it is strongly representable. Therefore we can use either 2 or 2′ to determine representability. ■

Examples:

1. The zero function, $\mathbf{Z}(\mathbf{x}) = \mathbf{0}$, is representable by the wff

$$(\mathsf{x_1} = \mathsf{x_1}) \wedge (\mathsf{x_2} = 0)$$

2. The successor function, $\mathbf{N}(\mathbf{x}) = \mathbf{x} + \mathbf{1}$, is representable by the wff

$$\mathsf{x_2} = \mathsf{x_1}'$$

3. The projection function, $\mathbf{U_i^n}(\mathbf{x_1}, \ldots, \mathbf{x_n}) = \mathbf{x_i}$, is representable by the wff

$$(\mathsf{x_1} = \mathsf{x_1}) \wedge (\mathsf{x_2} = \mathsf{x_2}) \wedge \cdots \wedge (\mathsf{x_n} = \mathsf{x_n}) \wedge (\mathsf{x_{n+1}} = \mathsf{x_i})$$

4. Assume that the functions $\mathbf{g}(\mathbf{x_1}, \ldots, \mathbf{x_m})$, $\mathbf{h_1}(\mathbf{x_1}, \ldots, \mathbf{x_n})$, ..., $\mathbf{h_m}(\mathbf{x_1}, \ldots, \mathbf{x_n})$ are representable by the wffs $B(\mathsf{x}_1, \ldots, \mathsf{x}_{m+1})$, $A_1(\mathsf{x}_1, \ldots, \mathsf{x}_{n+1})$, ..., $A_m(\mathsf{x}_1, \ldots, \mathsf{x}_{n+1})$, respectively. Define $\mathbf{f}$ by the equation

$$\mathbf{f}(\mathbf{x_1}, \ldots, \mathbf{x_n}) = \mathbf{g}(\mathbf{h_1}(\mathbf{x_1}, \ldots, \mathbf{x_n}), \ldots, \mathbf{h_m}(\mathbf{x_1}, \ldots, \mathbf{x_n}))$$

i.e., $\mathbf{f}$ is obtained from $\mathbf{g}$, $\mathbf{h_1}$, ..., $\mathbf{h_m}$, by substitution. Then $\mathbf{f}$ is also representable by the wff:

$$\begin{aligned} A(\mathsf{x}_1, \ldots, \mathsf{x}_{n+1}) \colon (\exists \mathsf{y}_1) \ldots (\exists \mathsf{y}_m)\ & (A_1(\mathsf{x}_1, \ldots, \mathsf{x}_n, \mathsf{y}_1) \\ & \wedge \cdots \wedge A_m(\mathsf{x}_1, \ldots, \mathsf{x}_n, \mathsf{y}_m) \\ & \wedge B(\mathsf{y}_1, \ldots, \mathsf{y}_m, \mathsf{x}_{n+1})) \end{aligned}$$

For proofs of the above and the next three lemmas, see [28].

Lemma 4.4.1 $\mathbf{R}(\mathbf{x_1}, \ldots, \mathbf{x_n})$ is expressible in $\mathcal{ENT}$ if and only if its characteristic function $\mathbf{C_R}(\mathbf{x_1}, \ldots, \mathbf{x_n})$ is representable in $\mathcal{ENT}$.

We now introduce the β function to show that we can express statements about finite sequences of natural numbers in $\mathcal{ENT}$. We use this to establish that functions defined using the recursion rule of INT are representable in $\mathcal{ENT}$.

Lemma 4.4.2 Let $\beta(\mathbf{x_1}, \mathbf{x_2}, \mathbf{x_3}) = \mathbf{rm}(\mathbf{1} + (\mathbf{x_3} + \mathbf{1}) \cdot \mathbf{x_2}, \mathbf{x_1})$ (the remainder upon division of $\mathbf{x_1}$ by $\mathbf{1} + (\mathbf{x_3} + \mathbf{1}) \cdot \mathbf{x_2}$). Then β is primitive recursive. Also, $\beta(\mathbf{x_1}, \mathbf{x_2}, \mathbf{x_3})$ is representable in $\mathcal{ENT}$ by the wff:

$$\begin{aligned} & \mathsf{B_t}(\mathsf{x}_1, \mathsf{x}_2, \mathsf{x}_3, \mathsf{x}_4) : \\ & \quad (\exists \mathsf{y})(\mathsf{x}_1 = (1 + (\mathsf{x}_3 + 1) \cdot \mathsf{x}_2) \cdot \mathsf{y} + \mathsf{x}_4 \wedge \mathsf{x}_4 < 1 + (\mathsf{x}_3 + 1) \cdot \mathsf{x}_2) \end{aligned}$$

Lemma 4.4.3 For any sequence of natural numbers $\mathbf{k_0}, \mathbf{k_1}, \ldots, \mathbf{k_n}$, there exist natural numbers $\mathbf{b}$, and $\mathbf{c}$, such that $\beta(\mathbf{b}, \mathbf{c}, \mathbf{i}) = \mathbf{k_i}$ for $\mathbf{0} \leq \mathbf{i} \leq \mathbf{n}$.

Theorem 4.4.4 Every recursive function is representable in $\mathcal{ENT}$.

Sketch of proof: We exhibit without proof the well-formed formulas that represent functions defined in terms of the initial functions using the Substitution, Recursion, and μ-operator rules. For the proofs that the given wffs do indeed correctly represent the functions, see [28].

The initial functions $\mathbf{Z}$, $\mathbf{N}$, $\mathbf{U_i^n}$ are representable in $\mathcal{ENT}$ by the wffs given in examples 1–3 page 127. Functions created by using the Substitution rule are represented as described in example 4.

The Recursion rule: Assume that the functions $\mathbf{g}(\mathbf{x_1}, \ldots, \mathbf{x_n})$ and $\mathbf{h}(\mathbf{x_1}, \ldots, \mathbf{x_n}, \mathbf{y}, \mathbf{z})$ are representable by the wffs $A(\mathsf{x_1}, \ldots, \mathsf{x_{n+1}})$ and $B(\mathsf{x_1}, \ldots, \mathsf{x_{n+3}})$, respectively, and let

$$\begin{aligned} \mathbf{f}(\mathbf{x_1}, \ldots, \mathbf{x_n}, \mathbf{0}) &= \mathbf{g}(\mathbf{x_1}, \ldots, \mathbf{x_n}) \\ \mathbf{f}(\mathbf{x_1}, \ldots, \mathbf{x_n}, \mathbf{y} + \mathbf{1}) &= \mathbf{h}(\mathbf{x_1}, \ldots, \mathbf{x_n}, \mathbf{y}, \mathbf{f}(\mathbf{x_1}, \ldots, \mathbf{x_n}, \mathbf{y})) \end{aligned}$$

Now $\mathbf{f}(\mathbf{x_1}, \ldots, \mathbf{x_n}, \mathbf{y}) = \mathbf{z}$ if and only if there exists a finite sequence of numbers $\mathbf{b_0}, \ldots, \mathbf{b_y}$, such that for $\mathbf{w} + \mathbf{1} \leq \mathbf{y}$ and $\mathbf{b_y} = \mathbf{z}$, we have $\mathbf{b_0} = \mathbf{g}(\mathbf{x_1}, \ldots, \mathbf{x_n})$, and $\mathbf{b_{w+1}} = \mathbf{h}(\mathbf{x_1}, \ldots, \mathbf{x_n}, \mathbf{w}, \mathbf{b_w})$. We know by Lemma 4.4.3 that reference to finite sequences can be paraphrased in terms of the function β, and by Lemma 4.4.2, β is representable. Thus, the function $\mathbf{f}(\mathbf{x_1}, \ldots, \mathbf{x_n}, \mathbf{x_{n+1}})$ is representable in $\mathcal{ENT}$ by the wff:

$$\begin{aligned} &\mathsf{C}(\mathsf{x_1}, \ldots, \mathsf{x_{n+2}}): \\ &(\exists \mathsf{u})(\exists \mathsf{v})[((\exists \mathsf{w})(\mathsf{B_t}(\mathsf{u}, \mathsf{v}, 0, \mathsf{w}) \wedge A(\mathsf{x_1}, \ldots, \mathsf{x_n}, \mathsf{w}))) \\ &\qquad \wedge \mathsf{B_t}(\mathsf{u}, \mathsf{v}, \mathsf{x_{n+1}}, \mathsf{x_{n+2}}) \wedge \\ &\qquad (\forall \mathsf{w})(\mathsf{w} < \mathsf{x_{n+1}} \rightarrow (\exists \mathsf{y})(\exists \mathsf{z})(\mathsf{B_t}(\mathsf{u}, \mathsf{v}, \mathsf{w}', \mathsf{y}) \wedge \\ &\qquad\qquad\qquad\qquad \mathsf{B_t}(\mathsf{u}, \mathsf{v}, \mathsf{w}, \mathsf{z}) \wedge \\ &\qquad\qquad\qquad\qquad B(\mathsf{x_1}, \ldots, \mathsf{x_n}, \mathsf{w}, \mathsf{y}, \mathsf{z}))))] \end{aligned}$$

The μ-operator: Assume that for any $\mathbf{x_1}, \ldots, \mathbf{x_n}$, there is some $\mathbf{y}$ such that $\mathbf{g}(\mathbf{x_1}, \ldots, \mathbf{x_n}, \mathbf{y}) = \mathbf{0}$, and that $\mathbf{g}$ is representable by a wff $D(\mathsf{x_1}, \ldots, \mathsf{x_{n+2}})$.

Let $\mathbf{f}(\mathbf{x_1}, \ldots, \mathbf{x_n}) = \mu\mathbf{y}(\mathbf{g}(\mathbf{x_1}, \ldots, \mathbf{x_n}, \mathbf{y}) = \mathbf{0})$. Then $\mathbf{f}$ is representable by the wff:

$$\begin{aligned} &\mathsf{E}(\mathsf{x_1}, \ldots, \mathsf{x_{n+1}}): \\ &\quad D(\mathsf{x_1}, \ldots, \mathsf{x_{n+1}}, 0) \wedge (\forall \mathsf{y})(\mathsf{y} < \mathsf{x_{n+1}} \rightarrow \neg D(\mathsf{x_1}, \ldots, \mathsf{x_n}, \mathsf{y}, 0)) \end{aligned}$$

■

Corollary 4.4.4.1 Every recursive relation (and set) is expressible in $\mathcal{ENT}$.

Proof: Let $\mathbf{R}(\mathbf{x_1}, \ldots, \mathbf{x_n})$ be a recursive relation. Then its characteristic function $\mathbf{C_R}$ is recursive, and by Theorem 4.4.4, $\mathbf{C_R}$ is representable in $\mathcal{ENT}$. Thus, by Lemma 4.4.1, $\mathbf{R}$ is expressible in $\mathcal{ENT}$. ■

We are now going to see that anything that can be expressed in $\mathcal{ENT}$ can be mapped onto a unique positive integer. This mapping of symbols, expressions, and sequences of expressions from the formal theory into positive integers was originally devised by Gödel in order to arithmetize metamathematics. He used this technique to replace assertions about the formal system by equivalent number-theoretic statements, and then represented these statements back inside the formal system.

Definition: An ***arithmetization*** of a first-order theory $\mathcal{K}$ is a one-to-one function $\mathcal{G}$ from the set of symbols of $\mathcal{K}$, expressions of $\mathcal{K}$, and finite sequences of expressions of $\mathcal{K}$, into the set of positive integers, such that the following conditions are satisfied:

1. $\mathcal{G}$ is effectively computable.
2. There is an effective procedure that determines whether any given positive integer $\mathbf{m}$ is in the range of $\mathcal{G}$, and if $\mathbf{m}$ is in the range of $\mathcal{G}$, the procedure finds the object x such that $\mathcal{G}(x) = \mathbf{m}$. ■

This idea was the key to a great number of significant problems in mathematical logic. The mapping of a language onto the objects of discussion in the language allows one to speak *of* the language *in* the language. This in turn makes it possible to construct self-referential statements (a prime source of logical paradoxes). We will soon see how this enabled the construction of a statement that made it clear that $\mathcal{ENT}$ is not complete.

The function $\mathcal{G}$ defined here is not unique. It is taken, with minor modifications, from [28]; other functions are defined elsewhere (for example, in [19,20,5,39]). What is imperative is that the function $\mathcal{G}$ and its inverse function be effectively computable.

Definition: We correlate with each symbol u of a first-order theory $\mathcal{K}$ a positive integer $\mathcal{G}(u)$, called the ***Gödel number*** of u, in the following way:

$$
\begin{array}{lll}
\mathcal{G}(() = 3; & \mathcal{G}()) = 5; & \mathcal{G}(,) = 7; \\
\mathcal{G}(\neg) = 9; & \mathcal{G}(\rightarrow) = 11; & \mathcal{G}(\forall) = 13; \\
\mathcal{G}(x_k) = 7 + 8k & & \text{for } k = 1,\ 2,\ \ldots \\
\mathcal{G}(a_k) = 9 + 8k & & \text{for } k = 1,\ 2,\ \ldots \\
\mathcal{G}(f_k^n) = 11 + 8(2^n 3^k) & & \text{for } k,\ n \geq 1 \\
\mathcal{G}(A_k^n) = 13 + 8(2^n 3^k) & & \text{for } k,\ n \geq 1
\end{array}
$$
■

Thus different symbols have different Gödel numbers, and every Gödel number of a symbol is an odd positive integer. This numbering is applicable to *any* first-order theory. For $\mathcal{ENT}$ we have only one constant, one predicate, and three function symbols, rather than a denumerable number of each. By the above definition we can compute that:

$$
\begin{array}{lllllll}
\mathcal{G}(0) & = & \mathbf{17} & & & & \\
\mathcal{G}(') & = & \mathbf{11 + 8(2 \cdot 3)} & = & \mathbf{11 + 48} & = & \mathbf{59} \\
\mathcal{G}(+) & = & \mathbf{11 + 8(2^2 \cdot 3)} & = & \mathbf{11 + 96} & = & \mathbf{107} \\
\mathcal{G}(\cdot) & = & \mathbf{11 + 8(2^2 \cdot 3^2)} & = & \mathbf{11 + 288} & = & \mathbf{299} \\
\mathcal{G}(=) & = & \mathbf{13 + 8(2^2 \cdot 3)} & = & \mathbf{13 + 96} & = & \mathbf{109}
\end{array}
$$

Having mapped all the symbols of the theory into natural numbers, we extend the mapping to expressions and sequences of expressions as follows.

DEFINITION: Given an expression (i.e., a sequence of symbols) $u_1 u_2 \ldots u_r$, we define its Gödel number to be

$$\mathcal{G}(u_1 u_2 \ldots u_r) = \mathbf{2}^{\mathcal{G}(u_1)} \cdot \mathbf{3}^{\mathcal{G}(u_2)} \cdot \ldots \cdot \mathbf{p}_r^{\mathcal{G}(u_r)}$$

where $\mathbf{p}_i$ is the ith prime. ■

For example,

$$
\begin{aligned}
\mathcal{G}(\mathsf{A}_1^2(\mathsf{x}_1,\ \mathsf{x}_2)) &= \mathbf{2}^{\mathcal{G}(\mathsf{A}_1^2)} \cdot \mathbf{3}^{\mathcal{G}(()} \cdot \mathbf{5}^{\mathcal{G}(\mathsf{x}_1)} \cdot \mathbf{7}^{\mathcal{G}(,)} \cdot \mathbf{11}^{\mathcal{G}(\mathsf{x}_2)} \cdot \mathbf{13}^{\mathcal{G}())} \\
&= \mathbf{2^{109} \cdot 3^3 \cdot 5^{15} \cdot 7^7 \cdot 11^{23} \cdot 13^5}
\end{aligned}
$$

By the unique factorization of the integers into primes we know that different expressions have different Gödel numbers. Furthermore, every expression has an even Gödel number while every symbol is assigned an odd number. Thus symbols and expressions have different numbers. A single symbol considered as an expression has a number that differs from its number as a symbol.

DEFINITION: If we have an arbitrary finite sequence of expressions $e_1, \ldots, e_r$ we can assign a Gödel number to this sequence by setting

$$\mathcal{G}(e_1 \ldots e_r) = \mathbf{2}^{\mathcal{G}(e_1)} \cdot \mathbf{3}^{\mathcal{G}(e_2)} \cdot \ \ldots \ \cdot \mathbf{p}_r^{\mathcal{G}(e_r)} \qquad \blacksquare$$

Again, by the uniqueness of the prime factorization of a number, we know different sequences of expressions will have different Gödel numbers. Since the Gödel number of a sequence of expressions has an even exponent of **2** in its prime factorization, we know it differs from Gödel numbers of symbols and expressions. Thus, $\mathcal{G}$ is a one-to-one function from the set of symbols, expressions, and finite sequences of expressions of $\mathcal{ENT}$, into the set of positive integers. The range of $\mathcal{G}$ is not the entire set of positive integers; for example, **14** is not a Gödel number. To determine whether a number **n** is in the range of $\mathcal{G}$, and if so, recover its pre-image in $\mathcal{ENT}$, we proceed as follows:

If* n *is odd: It is the Gödel number of a symbol if it is an element of the set $\{\mathbf{3}, \mathbf{5}, \mathbf{7}, \mathbf{9}, \mathbf{11}, \mathbf{13}, \mathbf{17}, \mathbf{59}, \mathbf{61}, \mathbf{107}, \mathbf{299}\}$ or if $\mathbf{n} - \mathbf{7}$ is divisible by **8**. The symbols represented by the numbers in the set can be looked up. If $\mathbf{n} = \mathbf{7} + \mathbf{8k}$ then the symbol mapped into **n** is x_k.

Otherwise, sem n is not in the range of $\mathcal{G}$.

If* n *is even: If the prime factorization of **n** consists of a product of consecutive primes and the exponent of **2** is odd, then **n** is the Gödel number of an expression (a sequence of symbols) if and only if each of the exponents is the Gödel number of a symbol (which can be recovered as described above).

If the prime factorization of **n** consists of a product of consecutive primes and the exponent of **2** is even, then **n** is the Gödel number of a sequence of expressions if and only if each of the exponents is the Gödel number of an expression (which can be recovered as described above).

Otherwise, **n** is not in the range of $\mathcal{G}$.

To facilitate definitions (and avoid trying to think up too many consecutive primes) we define a juxtaposition function $\star$.

DEFINITION: If we say $x = \mathbf{2^{a_0}3^{a_1} \cdot \ldots \cdot p_k^{a_k}}$ represents the sequence of positive integers $\mathbf{a_0, a_1, \ldots, a_k}$, and $y = \mathbf{2^{b_0}3^{b_1} \cdot \ldots \cdot p_m^{b_m}}$ represents the sequence $\mathbf{b_0, b_1, \ldots, b_m}$, then the number

$$x \star y = \mathbf{2^{a_0}3^{a_1} \cdot \ldots \cdot p_k^{a_k} p_{k+1}^{b_0} p_{k+2}^{b_1} \cdot \ldots \cdot p_{k+m+1}^{b_m}}$$

represents the new sequence $\mathbf{a_0, a_1, \ldots, a_k, b_0, b_1, \ldots, b_m}$ obtained by juxtaposing the two original sequences. (For a proof that $\star$ is both primitive recursive and associative, see [28].)

We also define the selector function $(\ )_i$ as follows: With y as defined above, $(y)_i = \mathbf{b_i}$. ∎

THEOREM 4.4.5 For $\mathcal{ENT}$, the following relations and functions (1–10) are recursive. (Actually, this holds for any first-order theory, but we show it for $\mathcal{ENT}$ — i.e., assuming only one constant symbol, one predicate symbol, and three function symbols.)

1. **Is_symbol(x)**: **x** is the Gödel number of a symbol of $\mathcal{ENT}$. This can be defined in terms of the following, together with a check for logical and auxiliary symbols.

   a. **Is_zero(x)**: **x** is the Gödel number of the symbol 0.

   $$\mathbf{x = 17}$$

   b. **Is_fcn(x)**: **x** is the Gödel number of a function letter.

   $$\mathbf{x = 59} \ \vee \ \mathbf{x = 107} \ \vee \ \mathbf{x = 299}$$

   By Theorem 4.2.4 this relation is primitive recursive.

   c. **Is_pred(x)**: **x** is the Gödel number of a predicate letter.

   $$\mathbf{x = 61}$$

   d. **Is_var(x)**: **x** is the Gödel number of a variable.

   $$(\exists \mathbf{z})_{\mathbf{z<x}} \mathbf{x = 7 + 8z}$$

Note that our numbering system allows us to put a bound on our search for $\mathbf{z}$, since the number of any expression must be larger than that of any part of it (exponent, addend, multiplier).

2. An expression consisting of a single symbol has a different Gödel number from its number as a symbol.

   a. **EZero(x)**: $\mathbf{x}$ is the Gödel number of the expression consisting of the constant symbol 0.

$$\mathbf{x} = \mathbf{2^{17}}$$

   b. **EVbl(x)**: $\mathbf{x}$ is the number of an expression consisting of a variable symbol.

$$(\exists \mathbf{z})_{\mathbf{z}<\mathbf{x}}(\mathbf{1} \leq \mathbf{z} \land \mathbf{x} = \mathbf{2^{7+8z}})$$

3. **Term(x)**: $\mathbf{x}$ is the Gödel number of a term.

$$\begin{aligned}&\mathbf{EZero(x)} \lor \mathbf{EVbl(x)}\\ &\quad \lor (\exists \mathbf{y})_{\mathbf{y}<\mathbf{x}}(\mathbf{Term(y)} \land \mathbf{x} = \mathbf{2^{59}} \star \mathbf{2^3} \star \mathbf{y} \star \mathbf{2^5})\\ &\quad \lor (\exists \mathbf{y})_{\mathbf{y}<\mathbf{x}}(\exists \mathbf{z})_{\mathbf{z}<\mathbf{x}}(\mathbf{Term(y)} \land \mathbf{Term(z)}\\ &\qquad\qquad \land \mathbf{x} = \mathbf{2^w} \star \mathbf{2^3} \star \mathbf{y} \star \mathbf{2^7} \star \mathbf{z} \star \mathbf{2^5}\\ &\qquad\qquad \land (\mathbf{w} = \mathbf{107} \lor \mathbf{w} = \mathbf{299}))\end{aligned}$$

Note that we've taken advantage of the fact that there are only three different function symbols in $\mathcal{ENT}$. Several of these definitions become more complex when considering an arbitrary first-order theory.

4. **Atfml(x)**: $\mathbf{x}$ is the Gödel number of an atomic formula.

$$\begin{aligned}&(\exists \mathbf{y})_{\mathbf{y}<\mathbf{x}}(\exists \mathbf{z})_{\mathbf{z}<\mathbf{x}}(\mathbf{Term(y)} \land \mathbf{Term(z)}\\ &\qquad\qquad \land \mathbf{x} = \mathbf{2^61} \star \mathbf{2^3} \star \mathbf{y} \star \mathbf{2^7} \star \mathbf{z} \star \mathbf{2^5})\end{aligned}$$

5. **MP(x, y, z)**: The expression with Gödel number $\mathbf{z}$ is a direct consequence of the expressions with Gödel numbers $\mathbf{x}$ and $\mathbf{y}$ by modus ponens.

$$\mathbf{y} = \mathbf{2^3} \star \mathbf{x} \star \mathbf{2^{11}} \star \mathbf{z} \star \mathbf{2^5}$$

Running back and forth to see which symbols are represented by which numbers, we can decode the above to find **y** is the Gödel number of (x→z), where $\mathcal{G}(\mathsf{x}) = \mathbf{x}$ and $\mathcal{G}(\mathsf{z}) = \mathbf{z}$.

Matters get worse quickly, and it is easy to get lost in the numbers. Having been convinced of the correctness of the numbering, we can dispose of the concrete syntax in favor of an abstract syntax that is more readable than strings of exponents. For example, we could represent $\mathbf{MP}(\mathbf{x}, \mathbf{y}, \mathbf{z})$ as:

$$\mathbf{is\_Imp}(\mathbf{y}) \wedge \mathbf{is\_Ant}(\mathbf{x}, \mathbf{y}) \wedge \mathbf{is\_Cons}(\mathbf{z}, \mathbf{y})$$

where:

$\mathbf{is\_Imp}(\mathbf{y})$ means "**y** is (the Gödel number of)[9] an implication"

$\mathbf{is\_Ant}(\mathbf{x}, \mathbf{y})$ means "**x** is the antecedent of **y**"

$\mathbf{is\_Cons}(\mathbf{z}, \mathbf{y})$ means "**z** is the consequent of **y**"

6. $\mathbf{is\_Fml}(\mathbf{y})$: **y** is the Gödel number of a wff.

$$\begin{aligned}&\mathbf{is\_Atfml}(\mathbf{y})\\ &\quad \vee\ \mathbf{is\_Imp}(\mathbf{y}) \wedge \mathbf{is\_Fml}(\mathbf{Ant}(\mathbf{y})) \wedge \mathbf{is\_Fml}(\mathbf{Cons}(\mathbf{y}))\\ &\quad \vee\ \mathbf{is\_Neg}(\mathbf{y}) \wedge \mathbf{is\_Fml}(\mathbf{Body}(\mathbf{y}))\\ &\quad \vee\ \mathbf{is\_Forall}(\mathbf{y}) \wedge \mathbf{is\_Fml}(\mathbf{Body}(\mathbf{y}))\end{aligned}$$

Now, **y** is a wff if and only if it is an atomic formula, an implication, a negation, or a generalization of some formula. The selectors **Ant** and **Cons** pick out the antecedent and consequent parts of an implication, $\mathbf{Body}(\mathbf{y})$ will strip a negation or generalization off of (the wff whose Gödel number is) **y**, leaving the part negated or generalized. And so we bid farewell to concrete syntax. We will instead describe abstractly what recognizers and selectors we may need and how they work.

7. a. $\mathbf{Pf}(\mathbf{y}, \mathbf{x})$ is a recognizer; it will utilize another recognizer that tells us whether or not **y** is the Gödel number of a sequence of wffs obeying the formation rules for a proof, and a selector

[9] We will not continue to say "the Gödel number of" a "whatever" in the following, although it is implicitly assumed. Thus when we say "**x** is the antecedent of **y**" we really mean "**x** is the Gödel number of the antecedent of the implication whose Gödel number is **y**."

that picks off the last wff of the sequence, which can then be compared with the wff with Gödel number **x** to see if we have a proof of the formula we want.

b. Let $A(\mathsf{x}_1, \ldots, \mathsf{x}_n)$ be a fixed wff of $\mathcal{ENT}$ containing $\mathsf{x}_1, \ldots, \mathsf{x}_n$ as its only free variables. We define the relation

$$\mathbf{Bw_A}(\mathbf{u_1}, \ldots, \mathbf{u_n}, \mathbf{y})$$

which means that: **y** is the Gödel number of a proof of $A(\mathsf{u}_1, \mathsf{u}_2, \ldots, \mathsf{u}_n)$.

8. $\mathbf{Sub(y, u, v)}$ is the Gödel number of the result of substituting the term with Gödel number **u** for all free occurrences of the variable with Gödel number **v** in the expression with Gödel number **y**.

9. $\mathbf{W_1(u, y)}$: **u** is the Gödel number of a wff $A(\mathsf{x}_1)$ containing the free variable x_1, and **y** is the Gödel number of a proof of $A(\mathsf{u})$. This is equivalent to:

$$\mathbf{is\_Fml(u)} \wedge \mathbf{is\_FreeVar(u, 2^{15})} \wedge \mathbf{Bw_A(u, y)}$$

or

$$\mathbf{is\_Fml(u)} \wedge \mathbf{is\_FreeVar(u, 2^{15})} \wedge \mathbf{Pf(y, Sub(u, Num(u), 2^{15})}$$

where $\mathbf{Num(u)}$ is the Gödel number of the term (numeral) u (recall that the numeral u refers to the term $0''^{\cdots\prime}$, where $'$ appears **u** times). Note that substituting u into A for x_1 makes $A(\mathsf{u})$ a formula that states something about itself.

10. We define a function $\mathbf{D(u)}$ such that, if **u** is the Gödel number of a wff $A(\mathsf{x}_1)$ with free variable x_1, then $\mathbf{D(u)}$ is the Gödel number of $A(\mathsf{u})$. So,

$$\mathbf{D(u)} = \mathbf{Sub(u, Num(u), 2^{15})}$$

If the conditions described above are not met, we can define $\mathbf{D(u)}$ to be **0**. Similarly, to ensure that **Sub** is totally defined, we should give it a value (say **0**) for the cases in which the conditions on the arguments are not met.

For proofs that the functions and relations given above are recursive, see [28].

Theorem 4.4.6 Any function $\mathbf{f}(\mathbf{x_1}, \ldots, \mathbf{x_n})$ that is representable in $\mathcal{ENT}$ is recursive.

Proof: Let $A(\mathsf{x_1}, \ldots, \mathsf{x_n}, \mathsf{z})$ be a wff representing $\mathbf{f}$. Consider the natural numbers $\mathbf{k_1}, \ldots, \mathbf{k_n}$. Let $\mathbf{f}(\mathbf{k_1}, \ldots, \mathbf{k_n}) = \mathbf{m}$. Then we know that $\vdash A(\mathsf{k_1}, \ldots, \mathsf{k_n}, \mathsf{m})$. Let $\mathbf{j}$ be the Gödel number of a proof in $\mathcal{ENT}$ of $A(\mathsf{k_1}, \ldots, \mathsf{k_n}, \mathsf{m})$. Then $\mathbf{B_{W_A}}(\mathbf{k_1}, \ldots, \mathbf{k_n}, \mathbf{m}, \mathbf{j})$. So, for any $\mathbf{x_1}, \ldots, \mathbf{x_n}$ there is some $\mathbf{y}$ such that $\mathbf{B_{W_A}}(\mathbf{x_1}, \ldots, \mathbf{x_n}, (\mathbf{y})_\mathbf{0}, (\mathbf{y})_\mathbf{1})$.[10]
Then

$$\mathbf{f}(\mathbf{x_1}, \ldots, \mathbf{x_n}) = (\mu\mathbf{y}(\mathbf{B_{W_A}}(\mathbf{x_1}, \ldots, \mathbf{x_n},\ (\mathbf{y})_\mathbf{0},\ (\mathbf{y})_\mathbf{1})))_\mathbf{0}$$

$\mathbf{B_{W_A}}$ is recursive. Hence, by the μ-operator rule (VI), $\mu\mathbf{y}(\mathbf{B_{W_A}}(\mathbf{x_1}, \ldots, \mathbf{x_n},\ (\mathbf{y})_\mathbf{0},\ (\mathbf{y})_\mathbf{1}))$ is recursive, and therefore so is $\mathbf{f}$. ∎

Thus, by Theorems 4.4.4 and 4.4.6, a number-theoretic function is recursive if and only if it is representable in $\mathcal{ENT}$.

Corollary 4.4.6.1 A number-theoretic relation $\mathbf{R}(\mathbf{x_1}, \ldots, \mathbf{x_n})$ is recursive if and only if $\mathbf{R}(\mathbf{x_1}, \ldots, \mathbf{x_n})$ is expressible in $\mathcal{ENT}$. (And, of course, a set is recursive if and only if it is expressible.)

We've taken a slight side trip on our way to showing the nonexistence of a decision procedure ϕ for provability in $\mathcal{ENT}$. We did not need the result that any function representable in $\mathcal{ENT}$ is recursive to show undecidability, but we will need it shortly when we look at completeness. Now let's get back to the decision problem.

We would like to be able to extend the undecidability results to theories other than $\mathcal{ENT}$, so we state the theorems in a slightly more general setting. In particular, we let $\mathcal{K}$ be any first-order theory with equality (defined on page 121) that has the same symbols as $\mathcal{ENT}$. Recall the definition of $\mathbf{D(u)}$ (page 136) and that $\mathbf{D}$ is recursive. Let $\mathcal{T}_\phi$ be the set of Gödel numbers of theorems of $\mathcal{K}$. If $\mathcal{K}$ is decidable, then the set of Gödel numbers of theorems of $\mathcal{K}$, $\mathcal{T}_\phi$ (whose characteristic function is the decision procedure) is recursive. We show that $\mathcal{ENT}$ is undecidable by establishing that $\mathcal{T}_\phi$ is not expressible in $\mathcal{K}$.

[10] The selectors $(\ )_i$ were defined on page 133.

THEOREM 4.4.7 If $\mathcal{K}$ is consistent and the function D is representable in $\mathcal{K}$, then $\mathcal{T}_\phi$ is not expressible in $\mathcal{K}$.

Proof: Assume **D** is representable and $\mathcal{T}_\phi$ is expressible in $\mathcal{K}$. Then, by the definitions of representable and expressible, respectively, there are wffs $D(\mathsf{x}_1, \mathsf{x}_2)$ and $T(\mathsf{x}_2)$ such that:

1. If $\mathbf{D}(\mathbf{k}) = \mathbf{j}$ then $\vdash D(\mathsf{k}, \mathsf{j})$.
2. $(\exists! \mathsf{x}_2) D(\mathsf{k}, \mathsf{x}_2)$.
   (i.e., $(\exists \mathsf{x}_2) D(\mathsf{k}, \mathsf{x}_2) \wedge (D(\mathsf{k}, \mathsf{x}_3) \rightarrow (\mathsf{x}_2 = \mathsf{x}_3))$)
3. If $\mathbf{k}$ is in $\mathcal{T}_\phi$ then $\vdash T(\mathsf{k})$.
4. If $\mathbf{k}$ is not in $\mathcal{T}_\phi$ then $\vdash \neg T(\mathsf{k})$.

Consider the formula

$$A(\mathsf{x}_1) : (\forall \mathsf{x}_2)(D(\mathsf{x}_1, \mathsf{x}_2) \rightarrow \neg T(\mathsf{x}_2))$$

Let $\mathbf{p}$ be the Gödel number of this wff. Construct the wff:

$$A(\mathsf{p}) : (\forall \mathsf{x}_2)(D(\mathsf{p}, \mathsf{x}_2) \rightarrow \neg T(\mathsf{x}_2))$$

Let $\mathbf{q}$ be the Gödel number of $A(\mathsf{p})$. Hence $\mathbf{D}(\mathbf{p}) = \mathbf{q}$. Therefore, by 1, $\vdash D(\mathsf{p}, \mathsf{q})$.

Now, either $\vdash A(\mathsf{p})$, or not $\vdash A(\mathsf{p})$. If not $\vdash A(\mathsf{p})$, then q is not in $\mathcal{T}_\phi$, and so, by 4, $\vdash \neg T(\mathsf{q})$. On the other hand, if $\vdash A(\mathsf{p})$, then

$$\vdash (\forall \mathsf{x}_2)(D(\mathsf{p}, \mathsf{x}_2) \rightarrow \neg T(\mathsf{x}_2))$$

Hence, by axiom 4, and MP $\vdash D(\mathsf{p}, \mathsf{q}) \rightarrow \neg T(\mathsf{q})$; since $\vdash D(\mathsf{p}, \mathsf{q})$, by MP we get $\vdash \neg T(\mathsf{x}_2)$. Thus, in either case we know $\vdash \neg T(\mathsf{q})$.

a. $D(\mathsf{p}, \mathsf{x}_2) \rightarrow (\mathsf{q} = \mathsf{x}_2)$ — by MP, given $\vdash D(\mathsf{p}, \mathsf{q})$ and 2

b. $(\mathsf{q} = \mathsf{x}_2) \rightarrow (\neg T(\mathsf{q}) \rightarrow \neg T(\mathsf{x}_2))$ — Theorem 4.3.3

c. $((\mathsf{q} = \mathsf{x}_2) \rightarrow (\neg T(\mathsf{q}) \rightarrow \neg T(\mathsf{x}_2)))$
   $\rightarrow (((\mathsf{q} = \mathsf{x}_2) \rightarrow \neg T(\mathsf{q})) \rightarrow ((\mathsf{q} = \mathsf{x}_2) \rightarrow \neg T(\mathsf{x}_2)))$ — **A2**

d. $((\mathsf{q} = \mathsf{x}_2) \rightarrow \neg T(\mathsf{q})) \rightarrow ((\mathsf{q} = \mathsf{x}_2) \rightarrow \neg T(\mathsf{x}_2))$ — MP b,c

e. $\neg T(\mathsf{q}) \rightarrow ((\mathsf{q} = \mathsf{x}_2) \rightarrow \neg T(\mathsf{q}))$ — **A1**

f. $(\mathsf{q} = \mathsf{x}_2) \rightarrow \neg T(\mathsf{q})$ — by MP, given $\vdash \neg T(\mathsf{q})$ and e

g. $(\mathsf{q} = \mathsf{x}_2) \rightarrow \neg T(\mathsf{x}_2)$ — MP f,d

h. $D(\mathsf{p}, \mathsf{x}_2) \rightarrow \neg T(\mathsf{x}_2)$ — Lemma 2.3.4 a,g

i. $(\forall \mathsf{x}_2) D(\mathsf{p}, \mathsf{x}_2) \rightarrow \neg T(\mathsf{x}_2)$ — Gen h

that is, $\vdash A(\mathsf{p})$. Therefore, **q** is in $\mathcal{T}_\phi$ and by 3, $\vdash T(\mathsf{q})$.

Since we have already determined that $\vdash \neg T(\mathsf{q})$, this implies $\mathcal{K}$ is inconsistent — a contradiction. Therefore, under the given hypotheses, $\mathcal{T}_\phi$ is not expressible. ■

Corollary 4.4.7.1 If $\mathcal{K}$ is consistent and every recursive function is representable in $\mathcal{K}$, then $\mathcal{T}_\phi$ is not recursive, hence $\mathcal{K}$ is not decidable.

Proof: D is recursive, and therefore representable. By Theorem 4.4.7, $\mathcal{T}_\phi$ is not expressible. By Lemma 4.4.1 (page 128), the characteristic function ϕ is not recursive, and so, $\mathcal{T}_\phi$ is not recursive.

We chose the notation $\mathcal{T}_\phi$ for our set of theorems because ϕ is the characteristic function of $\mathcal{T}_\phi$. That is,

$$\phi(A) = \begin{cases} 0 & \text{if } A \in \mathcal{T}_\phi \\ 1 & \text{if } A \notin \mathcal{T}_\phi \end{cases}$$

We knew, by the definition of decidable, that if such a ϕ existed it would be effectively computable, which by Gödel's work means that it would be recursive. We have shown that it is not recursive, thus we must conclude that no decision procedure for $\mathcal{K}$ can exist. ■

Corollary 4.4.7.2 If $\mathcal{ENT}$ is consistent then $\mathcal{ENT}$ is undecidable.

4.4.1 Extending Undecidability Results

As mentioned earlier, we have not yet shown that $\mathcal{PC}$ is undecidable, only that resolution does not provide a decision procedure. Now we would like to establish that it is impossible to extend resolution (or even invent a new algorithm) in such a way as to provide a decision procedure for $\mathcal{PC}$.

DEFINITION: Let $\mathcal{K}_1$ and $\mathcal{K}_2$ be two first-order theories having the same symbols. $\mathcal{K}_2$ is called a ***finite extension*** of $\mathcal{K}_1$ if and only if there is a set $\mathcal{A}$ of wffs and a *finite* set $\mathcal{B}$ of wffs such that:

1. The theorems of $\mathcal{K}_1$ are precisely the wffs derivable from $\mathcal{A}$.

2. The theorems of $\mathcal{K}_2$ are precisely the wffs derivable from $\mathcal{A} \cup \mathcal{B}$. ■

THEOREM 4.4.8 Let $\mathcal{K}_1$ and $\mathcal{K}_2$ be first-order theories having the same symbols as $\mathcal{ENT}$. If $\mathcal{K}_2$ is a finite extension of $\mathcal{K}_1$, and $\mathcal{K}_2$ is undecidable, then $\mathcal{K}_1$ is also undecidable.

Proof: Let $\mathcal{A}$ be the set of axioms of $\mathcal{K}_1$ and $\mathcal{A} \cup \{A_1, \ldots, A_n\}$ be the set of axioms of $\mathcal{K}_2$. We may assume $A_1, \ldots, A_n$ are closed wffs. By the Deduction Theorem, a wff B is provable in $\mathcal{K}_2$ if and only if $(A_1 \wedge A_2 \wedge \cdots \wedge A_n) \rightarrow B$ is provable in $\mathcal{K}_1$. Therefore, if $\mathcal{K}_1$ were decidable, $\mathcal{K}_2$ would also be decidable. Thus, $\mathcal{K}_1$ is undecidable. ■

Unfortunately, $\mathcal{ENT}$ is not a finite extension of $\mathcal{PC}$, since the set of symbols is different and **A14**is an axiom schema by which we have added an infinite number of axioms. An infinite number of axioms are not needed in the proof of undecidability. What we need are enough axioms to ensure that every recursive function is representable in the theory.

Let $\mathcal{PC}_{\mathcal{ENT}}$ be $\mathcal{PC}$ with its language restricted to the same symbols as $\mathcal{ENT}$. We will exhibit a finite extension of $\mathcal{PC}_{\mathcal{ENT}}$ that is undecidable, thus establishing that $\mathcal{PC}_{\mathcal{ENT}}$ is undecidable. We then consider the full theory $\mathcal{PC}$ and show that it is undecidable as well.

Raphael Robinson came up with a first-order theory with equality, called "Robinson's system," which we shall call $\mathcal{RR}$. $\mathcal{RR}$ is a first-order theory with equality, with the same symbols as $\mathcal{ENT}$, and having the following finite number of proper axioms:

1. $x_1 = x_1$

2. $x_1 = x_2 \rightarrow x_2 = x_1$

3. $x_1 = x_2 \rightarrow (x_2 = x_3 \rightarrow x_1 = x_3)$

4. $x_1 = x_2 \rightarrow x_1' = x_2'$

5. $x_1 = x_2 \rightarrow (x_1 + x_3 = x_2 + x_3 \wedge x_3 + x_1 = x_3 + x_2)$

6. $x_1 = x_2 \rightarrow (x_1 \cdot x_3 = x_2 \cdot x_3 \wedge x_3 \cdot x_1 = x_3 \cdot x_2)$

7. $x_1' = x_2' \rightarrow x_1 + x_2$

8. $0 \neq x_1'$

9. $x_1 \neq 0 \rightarrow (\exists x_2)(x_1 = x_2')$

10. $x_1 + 0 = x_1$

11. $x_1 + x_2' = (x_1 + x_2)'$

12. $x_1 \cdot 0 = 0$

13. $x_1 \cdot x_2' = (x_1 \cdot x_2) + x_1$

Lemma 4.4.9 $\mathcal{RR}$ is undecidable.

Proof: We take for granted that $\mathcal{RR}$ is consistent. It can be shown that every recursive function is representable in $\mathcal{RR}$, therefore, by Corollary 4.4.7.1, $\mathcal{RR}$ is undecidable. ∎

Theorem 4.4.10 $\mathcal{PC}_{\mathcal{ENT}}$ is undecidable.

Proof: $\mathcal{RR}$ is a finite extension of $\mathcal{PC}_{\mathcal{ENT}}$. In the definition of finite extension, the set $\mathcal{A}$ is the set of axioms for $\mathcal{PC}_{\mathcal{ENT}}$ (**PC1**–**PC5**) and the set $\mathcal{B}$ is the set of axioms 1–13 above. Since $\mathcal{RR}$ is undecidable, by Theorem 4.4.8 $\mathcal{PC}_{\mathcal{ENT}}$ must also be undecidable. ∎

Theorem 4.4.11 $\mathcal{PC}$ is undecidable.

Proof: A wff A of $\mathcal{PC}_{\mathcal{ENT}}$ is provable in $\mathcal{PC}_{\mathcal{ENT}}$ if and only if it is logically valid. (The theorems establishing the soundness and completeness of $\mathcal{PC}$ actually hold for *any* first-order predicate calculus.) It is also the case that the wff A is provable in $\mathcal{PC}$ if and only if it is logically valid. Thus, $\vdash_{\mathcal{PC}_{\mathcal{ENT}}} A$ if and only if $\vdash_{\mathcal{PC}} A$.

Now, $\mathbf{Fml}_{\mathcal{PC}_{\mathcal{ENT}}}$, the set of Gödel numbers of wffs of $\mathcal{PC}_{\mathcal{ENT}}$, is recursive, by Theorem 4.4.5 part 6. So, let $\mathcal{T}_{\mathcal{PC}_{\mathcal{ENT}}}$ and $\mathcal{T}_{\mathcal{PC}}$ be the sets of Gödel numbers of theorems of $\mathcal{PC}_{\mathcal{ENT}}$ and $\mathcal{PC}$, respectively. Then

$$\mathcal{T}_{\mathcal{PC}_{\mathcal{ENT}}} = \mathcal{T}_{\mathcal{PC}} \cap \mathbf{Fml}_{\mathcal{PC}_{\mathcal{ENT}}}$$

If $\mathcal{T}_{\mathcal{PC}}$ were recursive, then $\mathcal{T}_{\mathcal{PC}} \cap \mathbf{Fml}_{\mathcal{PC}_{\mathcal{ENT}}}$ would be recursive, contradicting Theorem 4.4.10. Therefore, $\mathcal{T}_{\mathcal{PC}}$ is not recursive (i.e., $\mathcal{PC}$ is not decidable). ■

These results can be further generalized as follows:

DEFINITION: We say $\mathcal{K}$ is ***essentially undecidable*** if and only if $\mathcal{K}$ and every consistent extension of $\mathcal{K}$ is undecidable. ■

THEOREM 4.4.12 If $\mathcal{K}$ is consistent and every recursive function is representable in $\mathcal{K}$, then $\mathcal{K}$ is essentially undecidable.

Proof: Let $\mathcal{T}$ be any consistent extension of $\mathcal{K}$. Since every recursive function is representable in $\mathcal{K}$, the same holds for $\mathcal{T}$. Therefore, by Corollary 4.4.7.1, $\mathcal{T}$ is undecidable. ■

4.4.2 Incompleteness of $\mathcal{ENT}$

We have established that $\mathcal{ENT}$ is undecidable, but have yet to show that it is also incomplete. We will demonstrate the incompleteness of $\mathcal{ENT}$ by constructing a wff that, interpreted, is a statement of its own unprovability. The statement is closed, and thus either it or its negation must be true in the standard interpretation. However, we will show that neither formula is provable, thus establishing the existence of a wff that is true (in INT) but not provable in the formal theory ($\mathcal{ENT}$).

Recall the definition of $\mathbf{W_1(u, y)}$ on page 136. $\mathbf{W_1(u, y)}$ is primitive recursive and so, by Corollary 4.4.4.1, $\mathbf{W_1}$ is expressible in $\mathcal{ENT}$ by a wff $W_1(\mathsf{x}_1, \mathsf{x}_2)$ with two free variables, x_1, x_2 — i.e., if $\mathbf{W_1(k_1, k_2)}$, then we know $\vdash W_1(\mathsf{k}_1, \mathsf{k}_2)$, and if $\mathbf{W_1(k_1, k_2)}$ does not hold, then we know $\vdash \neg W_1(\mathsf{k}_1, \mathsf{k}_2)$. Consider the wff

$$(\forall \mathsf{x}_2)\neg W_1(\mathsf{x}_1, \mathsf{x}_2) \tag{4.1}$$

Let $\mathbf{m}$ be the Gödel number of the wff (4.1). Substitute m for x_1 in (4.1) to obtain the closed wff:

$$(\forall \mathsf{x}_2)\neg W_1(\mathsf{m}, \mathsf{x}_2) \tag{4.2}$$

By definition, we know that $\mathbf{W_1(u, y)}$ means $\mathbf{u}$ is the Gödel number of a wff $A(\mathsf{x}_1)$ containing the free variable x_1, and $\mathbf{y}$ is the Gödel number of a proof in $\mathcal{ENT}$ of $A(\mathsf{u})$. Since $\mathbf{m}$ is the Gödel number of (4.1), and (4.2) comes from (4.1) by substituting m for the variable x_1, we know

$\mathbf{W_1}(\mathbf{m}, \mathbf{y})$ holds if and only if $\mathbf{y}$ is the Gödel number of a proof in $\mathcal{ENT}$ of (4.2). (4.3)

We will now show that neither (4.2) nor its negation is provable in $\mathcal{ENT}$. Recall the definition of ω-consistency: For every wff $A(x)$, if $\vdash A(\mathsf{n})$ for every natural number n, then it is not the case that $\vdash (\exists \mathsf{x})\neg A(\mathsf{x})$. As mentioned earlier, we state the consistency of $\mathcal{ENT}$ as an explicit assumption (even though we have great confidence in its truth).

THEOREM 4.4.13 (Gödel's incompleteness theorem for $\mathcal{ENT}$)

1. If $\mathcal{ENT}$ is consistent, then

$$(4.2): \qquad (\forall \mathsf{x}_2)\neg W_1(\mathsf{m}, \mathsf{x}_2)$$

   is not provable in $\mathcal{ENT}$.

2. If $\mathcal{ENT}$ is ω-consistent, then

$$\neg(4.2): \qquad \neg(\forall \mathsf{x}_2)\neg W_1(\mathsf{m}, \mathsf{x}_2)$$

   is not provable in $\mathcal{ENT}$.

Proof:

1. Assume $\mathcal{ENT}$ is consistent, and assume that

$$\vdash (\forall \mathsf{x}_2)\neg W_1(\mathsf{m}, \mathsf{x}_2)$$

   Let $\mathbf{k}$ be the Gödel number of a proof of this wff. By (4.3) above, $\mathbf{W_1}(\mathbf{m}, \mathbf{k})$. Since W_1 expresses $\mathbf{W_1}$ in $\mathcal{ENT}$, we have $\vdash W_1(\mathsf{m}, \mathsf{k})$.

   From $\vdash (\forall \mathsf{x}_2)\neg W_1(\mathsf{m}, \mathsf{x}_2)$ and **A4**, by MP we can deduce the wff $\neg W_1(\mathsf{m}, \mathsf{k})$.

   Thus, $\neg W_1(\mathsf{m}, \mathsf{k})$ and $W_1(\mathsf{m}, \mathsf{k})$ are both provable. This obviously contradicts the consistency of $\mathcal{ENT}$, so it cannot be the case that $\vdash (\forall \mathsf{x}_2)\neg W_1(\mathsf{m}, \mathsf{x}_2)$.

2. Assume $\mathcal{ENT}$ is ω-consistent, and assume that

$$\vdash \neg(\forall x_2)\neg W_1(m, x_2)$$

that is, $\vdash \neg(4.2)$. By Lemma 4.3.5, page 124, $\mathcal{ENT}$ is consistent, so we know it is not the case that $\vdash(4.2)$. If there does not exist a proof of (4.2), then no number can be the Gödel number of a proof of (4.2). In other words, for every $\mathbf{n}$, $\mathbf{W_1(m, n)}$ is false. Thus, by the expressibility of $\mathbf{W_1}$, for every $\mathbf{n}$, we have $\vdash \neg W_1(m, n)$.

Let $A(x_2)$ be $\neg W_1(m, x_2)$, then, since $\mathcal{ENT}$ is ω-consistent, we know that it is not the case that $\vdash (\exists x_2)\neg\neg W_1(m, x_2)$, and therefore it cannot be the case that $\vdash (\exists x_2)W_1(m, x_2)$. But this is in contradiction with our assumption that $\vdash \neg(\forall x_2)\neg W_1(m, x_2)$ — i.e., $\vdash (\exists x_2)W_1(m, x_2)$. ■

Hence, if $\mathcal{ENT}$ is ω-consistent, the closed wff (4.2) is neither provable nor disprovable in $\mathcal{ENT}$. Such a closed wff is said to be an *undecidable sentence* of $\mathcal{ENT}$. The standard interpretation of the undecidable sentence (4.2): $(\forall x_2)\neg W_1(m, x_2)$ is worth mentioning. (4.2) is a statement that $\mathbf{W_1(m, x_2)}$ is false for every natural number $\mathbf{x_2}$, in other words, no number is the Gödel number of a proof of (4.2). Thus (4.2) states that (4.2) is unprovable. By Theorem 4.4.13, if $\mathcal{ENT}$ is consistent, then (4.2) is, in fact, unprovable, and therefore is a true statement under the standard interpretation.

One might be tempted to simply add (4.2) as an axiom, thereby rendering it provable. However, such an approach is futile. We will still be able to construct an undecidable sentence in the larger theory — in fact, in much the same way.

It is possible to prove that every consistent extension of $\mathcal{ENT}$, whose set of proper axioms is recursive, is incomplete. Such an exercise is beyond the scope of this book. For those who are interested in pursuing these and related issues, we highly recommend study of [12], an excellent collection of the fundamental papers on undecidability and unsolvability.

Exercises 4.4.2

1. Summarize the arguments leading to the establishment of the undecidability and incompleteness of $\mathcal{ENT}$. Don't try to prove

every preliminary result, but state what you must believe, and why, in order to believe the proof.

2. Why was the arithmetization of number theory (Gödel numbering) so important to the formulation of the proof of incompleteness of $\mathcal{ENT}$?

CHAPTER 5

LAMBDA CALCULUS

5.1 Introduction

Wadsworth's analysis of Scott's λ-calculus model provides a good illustration of the dangers of confusing computation with deduction. In his thesis he studies various properties of β-reduction with the aim of showing that "what we would expect and hope for computationally" is indeed true in the model. One such hope was that because of "the close analogy between programs which terminate and well-formed expressions with normal forms," well-formed expressions which have normal forms should be distinguishable semantically from those which don't. Unfortunately this turns out not to be the case in $\mathcal{D}_\infty$. Initially this fact caused Wadsworth to reject $\mathcal{D}_\infty$ as an adequate model. However later on he realized that having a normal form — a notion based on the λ-conversion INFERENCE rules — shouldn't be crudely equated with the COMPUTATIONAL notion of nontermination. In fact his stuff on head normal forms is a (successful) attempt to distinguish computational and deductive aspects of β-conversion, i.e., to separate those conversions which are computations from those which aren't.

M. J. C. Gordon

We can well imagine the dangers of equating truth and proof. As we have seen, these notions describe two different worlds, semantic and syntactic. While we hope to construct formal syntactic systems that accurately reflect semantic domains, we have seen that it is impossible to do so completely. Any sufficiently expressive system will contain true statements that are not provable.

In studying the lambda calculus we will see a useful distinction between deduction and computation. We tend to think of computation as a "guided" deduction, and thus somehow subsumed in it — but here, by extracting information from partial computations we can get more information than is possible when we are restricted to the deductive notion of "provable."

The lambda calculus was introduced as a notation for representing and studying functions. We wish to study functions as objects that may be used in the same ways as any other data objects. In a programming context this means, at a minimum, that they may be values assigned (or bound) to variables, they may be passed as arguments to functions (or procedures), and they may be returned as results of function applications.

Traditional mathematical notation is too cumbersome. For example, if we wish to discuss the unary function that triples its argument, we introduce a name for it, *triple*, along with a definition: For any x, $triple(x) = 3 * x$. We can then talk of applying *triple* to arguments and evaluating the result.

We denote the application of *triple* to 4 by $triple(4)$. Given the definition of *triple* (and of $*$) we are able to evaluate $triple(4)$ by substituting 4 for x in the definition and evaluating the result. Thus

$$triple(4) = 3 * 4 = 12$$

We then define new functions in terms of those already defined. For example, *newfun* where

$$newfun(x, y) = triple(triple(x) + triple(y))$$

The application of *newfun* to arguments 2 and 3 is denoted by the expression $newfun(2, 3)$, and evaluated by substitution and simplification as before.

$$
\begin{aligned}
\mathit{newfun}(2,3) &= \mathit{triple}(\mathit{triple}(2) + \mathit{triple}(3)) \\
&= 3 * (3 * 2 + 3 * 3) \\
&= 3 * (6 + 9) = 3 * 15 = 45
\end{aligned}
$$

Although it is easy to write down applications of a function denoted in this way, we cannot understand what is meant by the function without reference to its definition. That is, to understand (or be able to evaluate) the function application *newfun*(2, 3), we need to know:

$$
\begin{aligned}
\mathit{newfun}(x,y) &= \mathit{triple}(\mathit{triple}(x) + \mathit{triple}(y)) \\
\mathit{triple}(x) &= 3 * x \\
\text{where} \quad & * \quad \text{is multiplication} \\
& + \quad \text{is addition}
\end{aligned}
$$

Instead of carrying around this extra information defining the functions we've named, we'd like a notation for functions that is self-contained. The definition of a function consists of a specification of a formal parameter list and an expression representing the application of the function to the formal parameters. (We call this expression the *body* of the function.) The lambda calculus offers a concise notation for providing this information.

Using the λ-notation, the function *triple* would be written:

$$\lambda x.3 * x$$

which can be read as: The function that for argument x has value $3*x$. Thus the λ-expression tells us all we need to know about the function. In particular, the function does not need to be named, since we can use the λ-expression itself whenever we wish to reference the function it denotes. Thus,

$$(\lambda x.3 * x)(2)$$

makes sense wherever *triple*(2) does. To evaluate *triple*(2), we need to look up the definition of *triple*, then apply it to the argument 2. To evaluate the expression above, we substitute the argument 2 for the bound variable x throughout the body $3 * x$ so that

$$(\lambda x.3 * x)(2) = 3 * 2 = 6$$

This operation of replacing a function application with the result of substituting the argument in the body is known as β-reduction.

From mathematics we know that f, where $f(x) = x^2$ and f, where $f(y) = y^2$ denote the same function. Similarly, the λ-expressions $\lambda x.x^2$ and $\lambda y.y^2$ denote the same function. This systematic change of bound variable name in a λ-expression is known as α-conversion.

We have only shown unary functions using the λ-notation. It would be easy to extend the λ-notation to n-ary functions — for example, we might write $\lambda(x, y).2 * x + y$. However, for simplicity of syntax the formal λ-calculus allows only functions of one argument. A multi-argument function is treated as a function of the first argument that yields a function of its remaining arguments. For example, f, where $f(x, y) = 2 * x + y$ could be thought of as f, where $f(x) = g_x$ and $g_x(y) = 2 * x + y$. In λ-notation, instead of $\lambda(x, y).(2 * x + y)$, we write $\lambda x.(\lambda y.2 * x + y)$. Thus, $f(2, 3)$ would be denoted (and evaluated) as follows:

$$\begin{aligned} (\lambda x.(\lambda y.2 * x + y))(2)(3) &= (\lambda y.2 * 2 + y)(3) \\ &= 2 * 2 + 3 = 7 \end{aligned}$$

This technique for representing multiargument functions as unary functions is known as *Currying* (since the notation was popularized by the logician H. B. Curry, although it was originally suggested by Schönfinkel). In the above example it is shown that a function may have a function as value; a function might also take a function as argument. For example, *twice* is a function that given a function g as argument, returns the composition of g with itself as value. Thus *twice* is denoted by $\lambda g.(\lambda y.g(g(y)))$. And if we apply *twice* to the *triple* function defined above, we get:

$$twice(triple) = \lambda y.triple(triple(y))$$

Thus, in a functional programming language based upon the λ-calculus, there is no separation of program and data objects; the distinction between program and data is based on the context in which the objects are currently being used. An object may be produced (data) as the result of one program and then the same object may be applied (program) to other objects.

5.2 The Language

Informally, we used some of the notation of the λ-calculus above to give a flavor of the language. We mixed in notations from mathematics — for example, multiplication and addition. Two points are worth noting when we set up the λ-calculus as a formal system:

1. No type restrictions are placed on the formation of function applications. For any two expressions M and N, the application $M(N)$ is well-formed. Thus all expressions of the system may be regarded either as functions or as arguments to functions, as the context in which they appear demands.

2. We deal with the pure λ-calculus, which does not include symbols for constants (such as numbers or primitive operations such as multiplication and addition); that is, we allow only functions definable from identifiers by means of the combination and abstraction operations defined below.

As always, in order to specify the language we need to define a countable set of symbols, indicate which sequences of symbols make up the class of well-formed expressions (terms), and describe how the terms may be combined to construct well-formed formulas.

DEFINITION: The formal language of the λ-calculus is defined by the following.

1. A countable set of symbols:
   identifiers (variables) $a,\ b,\ \ldots,\ z,\ a_1,\ b_1,\ \ldots,\ z_1,\ a_2,\ \ldots$
   predicate symbol $=$
   auxiliary symbols λ, ., (,)

   We use "$\equiv$" as a metasymbol indicating that two terms are syntactically identical.

2. The well-formed formulas of the λ-calculus consist of equations between terms. Thus, if M and N are terms, then $M = N$ is a well-formed formula. The set of terms, or well-formed expressions (wfes) is defined as follows:

   a. Every identifier is a term.

b. If M and N are terms, then the ***combination*** (MN) is a term; M is called the ***rator*** of the combination and N is called the ***rand*** (from "operator" and "operand").

c. If x is an ***identifier*** and M is a term, then the ***abstraction*** $(\lambda x.M)$ is a term, x its ***bv*** (for bound variable) and M is its ***body***. ■

A combination represents a function application. Note that we indicate function application by juxtaposition of terms inside parentheses, rather than by the more familiar juxtaposition of the function term with the argument term enclosed in parentheses — i.e., $(F\ A)$ instead of $F(A)$. This can all be summarized by the following context-free grammar:

wff ::= term "=" term
term ::= identifier | combination | abstraction
combination ::= "(" term term ")"
abstraction ::= "(λ" identifier "." term ")"
identifier ::= "a" | "b" | ... | "z"
| $\text{identifier}_{\text{subscript}}$
subscript ::= "1" | "2" | ... | "9" | "0" | subscript subscript

According to the grammar above, every term more complicated than a single identifier must be surrounded by parentheses. To avoid the visual clutter this entails we omit parentheses from terms according to the following conventions:

1. Association to the left:

$$M_0 M_1 M_2 \ldots M_n \qquad \text{stands for } ((\ldots((M_0 M_1) M_2) \ldots) M_n)$$

2. The scope of the . in abstractions extends as far to the right as possible — i.e., to the first unmatched) or to the end of the term, whichever occurs first.

$$\lambda x.yx\lambda z.xz \qquad \text{stands for } (\lambda x.yx(\lambda z.xz))$$

3. Consecutive λ's may be collapsed to a single λ.

$$\lambda x_0 x_1 \ldots x_n.M \qquad \text{stands for } (\lambda x_0.(\lambda x_1.(\ldots(\lambda x_n.M)\ldots)))$$

For example,

$$\lambda y.x(\lambda x.xy)$$

is an abstraction. Fully parenthesized, it is

$$(\lambda y.(x(\lambda x.xy)))$$

Its bv (bound variable) is y, and its body is the combination $(x(\lambda x.xy))$, whose rator is x, and whose rand is the abstraction $(\lambda x.xy)$. The abstraction $(\lambda x.xy)$ has bv x and body xy, a combination with rator x and rand y.

$$(\lambda y.x)\lambda x.xy$$

is a combination. Fully parenthesized, it is

$$((\lambda y.x)(\lambda x.(xy)))$$

Its rator is the abstraction $(\lambda y.x)$, with bv y and body x, and its rand is the abstraction $(\lambda x.(xy))$, whose bv is x and body is the combination (xy), with rator x and rand y.

DEFINITION: An occurrence of a variable x in a term M is ***bound*** if it is within the scope of an abstraction whose bv is x; all other occurrences of x in M are ***free***. ■

We shall write $\mathcal{FV}(M)$ and $\mathcal{BV}(M)$ for the sets of variables occurring free and bound, respectively, in M. Note that the same variable may occur both free and bound in a term.

For example, in $\lambda y.x(\lambda x.xy)$, the leftmost occurrence of x is free while the others are bound, and y is bound in both occurrences.

The definitions of free and bound are similar to those in Section 3.1. The only difference is that variables are now bound by λ's instead of by quantifiers. We also have to be concerned about a term being *free for* a variable when defining substitution. As in $\mathcal{PC}$, trouble can only arise when substituting a term with a free variable into a context where that variable is bound. This case is addressed by clause 3c of the definition of substitution.

DEFINITION: We write $[N/x]M$ for the ***substitution*** of N for the free occurrences of x in M. We define substitution recursively, following the inductive definition of a term, as follows:

1. If M is an identifier, it is either the identifier x or a different identifier.

   a. If $M \equiv x$, then $[N/x]M \equiv [N/x]x = N$.

   b. If $M \equiv y \not\equiv x$, then $[N/x]M \equiv [N/x]y = y$.

2. If M is a combination M_0M_1, then make the substitution independently in the rator and rand of the combination.

$$[N/x](M_0M_1) = ([N/x]M_0)([N/x]M_1)$$

3. If M is an abstraction $(\lambda y.M_0)$, there are three cases to consider: (a) x is not free in M; (b) N does not contain any free occurrences of the bv of M; and (c) x is free in M, and N does contain a free occurrence of the bv of M.

   a. If $x \equiv y$, or if $x \notin \mathcal{FV}(M_0)$, then $[N/x](\lambda y.M_0) = \lambda y.M_0$.

   b. If $y \notin \mathcal{FV}(N)$, then $[N/x](\lambda y.M_0) = \lambda y.[N/x]M_0$.

   c. Otherwise, $x \in \mathcal{FV}(M_0)$, $y \in \mathcal{FV}(N)$, and $x \not\equiv y$, thus,

$$[N/x](\lambda y.M_0) = \lambda w.[N/x]([w/y]M_0)$$

   where w is the first (or any other we wish to specify) identifier in a lexical ordering of identifiers that does not occur free in N or M_0. ■

As expected, the substitution of N for x in a term M with no free occurrences of x has no effect on M (clauses 1b and 3a). Another way of describing the third clause of the definition of substitution is to say that if N is free for x "at the first level" in $(\lambda y.M_0)$, then $[N/x](\lambda y.M_0) = \lambda y.[N/x]M_0$. Otherwise, change all occurrences of the bound variable y to a new identifier not appearing in M_0 or N, then substitute $[N/x]$ in this new term. The free for check at the next level is performed when making the substitution into the body of M.

5.3 Deductive System

To familiarize ourselves with the language of the λ-calculus, we consider the formal theory (deduction) of the λ-calculus before the mathematical models (truth), departing from the truth then deduction then computation sequence we had set up earlier.

We have defined the language of the λ-calculus above, having given: (1) the countable set of symbols; and (2) the well-formed formulas of the theory. To specify the formal theory of the λ-calculus, we must also provide the axioms and rules of inference.

It is convenient to list the axioms and rules of inference for the λ-calculus together. (In fact, an axiom is really just an inference rule with an empty set of hypotheses.)

Axioms and Rules of Inference:

1. $=$ is an equivalence relation.

   (ρ) $M = M$ for all terms M (reflexivity)

   (σ) $M = N \vdash N = M$ (symmetry)

   (τ) $M = N,\ N = L \vdash M = L$ (transitivity)

2. $=$ is substitutive. (Following the inductive definition of a term, we see that if two terms are equal, then replacing one by the other in any part of a term X results in a term equal to X.)

   (μ) $N = N' \vdash MN = MN'$ (replace rand)

   (ν) $M = M' \vdash MN = M'N$ (replace rator)

   (ξ) $M = N \vdash \lambda x.M = \lambda x.N$ (replace body of an abstraction)

3. conversion rules:

   (α) $\lambda x.M = \lambda y.[y/x]M$, provided $y \notin \mathcal{FV}(M)$ (renaming of bound variable)

   (β) $(\lambda x.M)N = [N/x]M$ (function application)

   (η) $\lambda x.Mx = M$, provided $x \notin \mathcal{FV}(M)$

The formal theory defined above is called the $\lambda\beta\eta$-calculus. Rules (α) and (β) formalize the operations of renaming bound variables and function application by substitution of actual arguments into the body of the function. Adding the rule (η) is equivalent to adding the rule of functional extensionality:

(Ext) From $Mx = Nx$ for all x such that $x \notin \mathcal{FV}(M)$ and $x \notin \mathcal{FV}(N)$, infer $M = N$.

To see that (Ext) implies (η), notice that if x is not an element of $\mathcal{FV}(M)$, then, by β-conversion, $(\lambda x.Mx)N = MN$ for *all* terms N — i.e., the terms $\lambda x.Mx$ and M are equivalent as functions; they yield the same thing when applied to any argument. Thus, by (Ext), $\lambda x.Mx = M$ (if $x \notin \mathcal{FV}(M)$). Using (ξ) and (η) one can show that (Ext) is derivable (left as an exercise).

The (η) rule shows how we can consider any term of the λ-calculus as a function.

DEFINITION: A term is an identifier, a combination, or an abstraction. We say that the rator and rand of a combination, and the body of an abstraction, are ***subterms*** of the term of which they are a part. We extend the terminology to arbitrary depth by saying that M is a ***subterm*** of N if M is the rator, rand, or body of N, or M is a subterm of the rator, rand, or body of N. ■

DEFINITION: A ***context*** is the opposite of a subterm. A context $C[\,]$ consists of all of a term except for one subterm. We use empty brackets $[\,]$ to indicate the missing subterm. For example,

$$C[\,] \equiv \lambda x.xy([\,]x)$$ ■

The result of filling the missing subterm in $C[\,]$ with a term M is denoted $C[M]$. For any other term N, $C[N]$ denotes the same term as $C[M]$ except that the indicated occurrence of M is replaced by N. For the example above, we have $C[yx] \equiv \lambda x.xy(yxx)$.

A context can be used to state a result that holds no matter what term we choose to supply for the missing subterm. For example, given the context $C[\,] \equiv (\lambda x.y)[\,]$, we can state that for all terms M, $C[M] = y$ is provable in the λ-calculus (using the (β) rule and the definition of substitution).

We evaluate terms by eliminating abstractions — that is, we replace terms of the form on the left of the rules (β) and (η) by the terms on the right. More precisely, we define the notion of reduction as follows.

DEFINITION: A term of the form $R \equiv (\lambda x.M)N$ is called a ***β-redex*** and $R' \equiv [N/x]M$ is called its ***contractum***. If X is a term containing a β-redex R (i.e., $X \equiv C[R]$ for some context $C[\,]$), the operation of replacing R by R' to yield $X' \equiv C[R']$ is called a ***β-contraction***. Since the (β) rule is an equation, we can also replace a term in the form of the right hand side by the form on the left. The operation of replacing R' by R is called a ***β-expansion***. A finite sequence of (0 or more) β-contractions is called a ***β-reduction***, and is denoted:

$$X \ \beta\text{-}red \ \ X'.$$

A ***β-conversion*** is a finite sequence of 0 or more β-contractions and/or β-expansions. ■

DEFINITION: A term of the form $P \equiv (\lambda x.Mx)$ is called an ***η-redex*** if $x \notin \mathcal{FV}(M)$, and M is called its ***contractum***. The terms ***η-contraction***, ***η-expansion***, ***η-reduction*** and ***η-conversion*** are defined similarly to the corresponding terms for the (β) rule. ■

DEFINITION: We say that X *red* X' if there is a sequence of terms $X_1, \ldots, X_n = X'$, $n \geq 1$, such that $X_1 = X$ and for each $i > 1$, X_{i-1} η-*red* X_i, or X_{i-1} β-*red* X_i, or $X_{i-1} = X_i$ is an instance of the (α) rule.[1] ■

The relation *red* is reflexive, transitive, and substitutive, but not symmetric. (Neither, in general, is it antisymmetric; see Exercise 1 page 166.)

DEFINITION: M is ***convertible*** to N, written M *cnv* N, if $M = N$ is a theorem of the λ-calculus.[2] ■

If in a proof of $M = N$ we use only the (β) rule, we say M β-*cnv* N; similarly for α-*cnv* and η-*cnv* . Rather than exhibit formal proofs, we

[1]Since a change of bound variable name is clearly a symmetric operation, it is difficult to justify a distinction between α-contraction and α-expansion. Thus we refer only to α-conversion, abbreviated α-*cnv* .

[2]To be precise we should be referring throughout to the $\lambda\beta\eta$-calculus, since it is possible to treat the subject without including the rule (η). However, since we will always be referring to the above formal system, no confusion should arise from the terminology λ-calculus.

will usually show conversion sequences. For example, informally

$$\begin{array}{lll}(\lambda x.\lambda y.\lambda z.xy)(\lambda z.z) & cnv & \lambda y.\lambda z.(\lambda z.z)y \\ & cnv & \lambda y.\lambda z.y\end{array}$$

Formally, a proof that the first term is equal to the last would proceed as follows. (See page 155 for the definitions of the rules referred to in the proof.)

1. $(\lambda x.\lambda y.\lambda z.xy)(\lambda z.z) = [(\lambda z.z)/x](\lambda x.\lambda y.\lambda z.xy)$ by (β)
   $= \lambda y.\lambda z.(\lambda z.z)y$ def. of substitution
2. $(\lambda z.z)y = [y/z]z = y$ by (β) and substitution
3. $\lambda z.(\lambda z.z)y = \lambda z.y$ (ξ) from 2
4. $\lambda y.\lambda z.(\lambda z.z)y = \lambda y.\lambda z.y$ (ξ) from 3
5. $(\lambda x.\lambda y.\lambda z.xy)(\lambda z.z) = \lambda y.\lambda z.y$ (τ) 1,4

■

DEFINITION: A term containing no free variables is called a ***closed*** term. Closed terms are also sometimes called ***combinators*** (see [9]).

■

We are most interested in the properties of closed terms; however, in proving general results we need to consider terms with free variables. For example, when proving some property holds of all terms we usually proceed by structural induction, and all terms have subterms containing free variables.

We are often interested in the behavior of terms as functions. A closed term M is *I-solvable* if it can be applied as a function (to 0 or more arguments) to yield the identity function

$$I \equiv \lambda x.x$$

DEFINITION: A closed term M is ***I-solvable*** if there exist terms $A_0, \ldots, A_k$, $(k \geq 0)$ such that

$$M A_0 \ldots A_k \ cnv \ I \tag{5.1}$$

■

If M has free variables, we say it is I-solvable if there exists a substitution of closed terms for the free variables such that the resulting closed term is I-solvable.

DEFINITION: A term M with free variables $x_0, \ldots, x_n$ is said to be ***I-solvable*** if there exist closed terms $N_0, \ldots, N_n$ and terms $A_0, \ldots, A_k$, such that

$$([N_0, \ldots, N_n / x_0, \ldots, x_n]M)A_0 \ldots A_k \ cnv \ I \tag{5.2}$$

where $[N_0, \ldots, N_n / x_0, \ldots, x_n]$ denotes the multiple substitution defined in the obvious way from the single case $[N/x]$, assuming $x_0, \ldots, x_n$ are distinct variables.[3] ■

We can say that *any* term M is I-solvable if and only if there exists some context $C[\,]$, such that $C[M]\ cnv\ I$. The contexts for closed terms, from (5.1), is of the form

$$[\,]A_0 \ldots A_k$$

and the context for terms with free variables, from (5.2), would be of the form

$$(\lambda x_0 \ldots x_n.[\,])N_0 \ldots N_n A_0 \ldots A_k$$

Both of these contexts are examples of what we call a head context.

DEFINITION: A ***head context*** is a context of the form

$$(\lambda x_1 \ldots x_n.[\,])X_1 \ldots X_m \qquad n \geq 0,\ m \geq 0$$

for variables $x_1, \ldots, x_n$ and terms $X_1, \ldots, X_m$. ■

Thus, for *any* term M (closed or not), M is I-solvable if and only if there is a head context $C[\,]$ such that $C[M]\ cnv\ I$.

As mentioned earlier, in studying functions and function application in the λ-calculus we are usually concerned with the evaluation of terms rather than with the proofs of wffs (equations between terms).

---

[3]Note that this multiple substitution meets the restrictions required in Section 3.4.1, page 65, for independent substitution components (since each N_i is closed we know it contains no free occurrences of any x_i) and thus the order in which the substitutions are made makes no difference in the resulting term

We perform reductions informally; however, if the reductions were performed correctly, we could always prove the equality between the term we started with and the evaluated term. If a reduction sequence produces a term that cannot be further reduced, we say that we have found a normal form of the term.

DEFINITION: A term M is said to be in ***normal form*** if it does not contain a (β- or η-) redex as a subterm. If M *cnv* N and N is in normal form, then N is said to be a ***normal form of*** M. ∎

Not all terms have a normal form. Two such terms are

$$(\lambda x.xx)(\lambda x.xx)$$

which β-reduces to itself, and the ***paradoxical combinator***:

$$Y_\lambda \equiv \lambda f.(\lambda x.f(xx))(\lambda x.f(xx))$$

which we shall see again when considering the definition of recursive functions. Since, in general, a term may contain more than one redex, there are several possible reduction sequences, depending upon which redex is chosen at each step. These correspond to different orders of evaluation. How important is this ordering? Can we get different normal forms from one term; are we guaranteed to find the right one, if it exists?

There are terms for which evaluation order is critical. For example, consider

$$(\lambda w.z)((\lambda x.xx)(\lambda x.xx))$$

which contains two β-redexes; the term itself is a β-redex whose rand is also a β-redex. When the outer redex is contracted, we obtain the normal form z; if we choose to reduce the argument first, the reduction fails to terminate since $(\lambda x.xx)(\lambda x.xx)$ repeatedly reduces to itself.

Reducing the argument first, then substituting the result into the body to be reduced later, is known as *applicative order* evaluation, or, more commonly, *call-by-value*. Making the substitution of the unreduced argument into the body of the function is known as *normal order* reduction or *call-by-name*.

Usually, applicative order evaluation is more efficient, since an argument is evaluated only once and its value may be used several times in the body of a function. Normal order evaluation would require that the term be evaluated each time it is needed in the body of the function. However, it is possible that the value of an argument may never be needed in a particular function application. (For example, consider an IF-THEN-ELSE expression. On a given application only one of the THEN and ELSE expressions will be needed.) Thus, in some cases applicative order may unnecessarily result in a nonterminating computation.

The Church–Rosser Theorem assures us that any two reduction sequences that terminate will do so with the same result. (A proof of the Church–Rosser Theorem may be found in [9].)

THEOREM 5.3.1 (Church–Rosser Theorem) If X *cnv* Y, there is a Z such that X *red* Z and Y *red* Z. Diagrammatically:

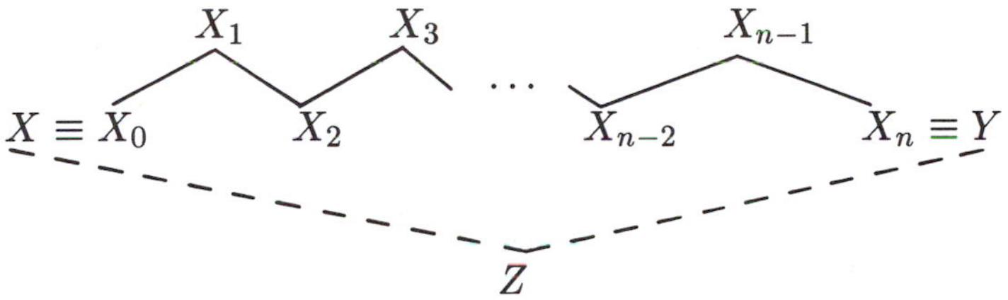

The descending lines represent contractions; ascending lines represent expansions (reversed contractions). Conversion between terms is a sequence of contractions and/or expansions — that is, X *cnv* Y iff there is a sequence $X \equiv X_0, \ldots, X_n \equiv Y$ such that, for each i, $0 \le i \le n-1$, either X_i *red* X_{i+1} or X_{i+1} *red* X_i.

The solid lines in the diagram indicate the hypothesis of the theorem, the dashed lines indicate the conclusion.

COROLLARY 5.3.1.1 If M reduces to both X and Y, there is a Z such that X *red* Z and Y *red* Z.

Proof: If M reduces to X and M reduces to Y, then X *cnv* Y. Thus we have a special case of Theorem 5.3.1. ■

COROLLARY 5.3.1.2 If a term M has two normal forms X and Y, then X α-*cnv* Y.

Proof: Since X and Y are normal forms of M, we know that M *red* X and M *red* Y. Thus by Corollary 5.3.1.1 there is a Z such that X *red* Z and Y *red* Z. Since X and Y are in normal form we know they contain no β-redexes or η-redexes; thus, the only reduction that is possible is α-conversion. So, X α-*cnv* Z and Y α-*cnv* Z, and therefore X α-*cnv* Y. ■

Corollary 5.3.1.2 assures us that if a term has a normal form, it is unique up to a change of its bound variables. That is, if we have found a normal form, we need not be concerned with the evaluation order that produced it.

As we shall see, the Church–Rosser Theorem also establishes the consistency of the λ-calculus.

Our old definition of consistent makes no sense here, as there is no negation in the λ-calculus. Another definition of consistency of a theory, equivalent in most contexts, follows.

DEFINITION: A theory $\mathcal{T}$ is consistent if there is an unprovable well-formed formula in $\mathcal{T}$. ■

This definition is equivalent to our initial definition — that $\mathcal{T}$ is consistent iff there does not exist A such that $\vdash A$ and $\vdash \neg A$, in any theory in which axioms **L1** and **L3** and Modus Ponens are included (either given or derivable from what is given).

THEOREM 5.3.2 In any theory in which axioms **L1** and **L3** , and Modus Ponens can be used, the following two definitions of consistency are equivalent.

def1 There does not exist A such that $\vdash A$ and $\vdash \neg A$.

def2 There is an unprovable well-formed formula.

Proof:

def1 $\Rightarrow$ def2: $\vdash$ **L1**, by assumption of the theorem
$\nvdash \neg$**L1** by def1, thus def2 also holds.

$\neg$def1 $\Rightarrow$ $\neg$def2: If the theory is not consistent by def1, then there exists a wff A such that $\vdash A$ and $\vdash \neg A$. Then

1. $(\neg B \rightarrow \neg A) \rightarrow ((\neg B \rightarrow A) \rightarrow B)$ **L3**
2. $A \rightarrow (\neg B \rightarrow A)$ **L1**

3. $\neg B \rightarrow A$ MP 2, given $\vdash A$
4. $\neg A \rightarrow (\neg B \rightarrow \neg A)$ **L1**
5. $\neg B \rightarrow \neg A$ MP 4, given $\vdash \neg A$
6. $(\neg B \rightarrow A) \rightarrow B$ MP 1,5
7. B MP 3,6

Thus, everything is provable, so the theory is not consistent by def2. ■

COROLLARY 5.3.2.1 The λ-calculus is consistent.

Proof: Assume that the λ-calculus is not consistent. Then $M = N$ is a theorem — i.e., M *cnv* N — for all terms M and N. In particular, since $\lambda x.\lambda y.x = \lambda x.\lambda y.y$ is a theorem, it must be the case that $\lambda x.\lambda y.x$ *cnv* $\lambda x.\lambda y.y$. However, these two terms are both in normal form and they are not α-convertible, which contradicts Corollary 5.3.1.2. ■

Now that we know the normal form of a term is unique (up to α-conversion), we turn our attention to the problem of finding such normal forms. We would like to have a method for producing normal forms that will always terminate on terms having normal forms.

DEFINITION: If at each stage in a reduction we reduce the leftmost redex in the term, we are said to be reducing the term by ***normal order reduction***. By the leftmost redex, we mean the one whose left-hand end is furthest to the left. (It sometimes helps to think of it as the leftmost outermost redex.) ■

The Standardization Theorem guarantees that normal order reduction of a term always terminates with a normal form when such a form exists. One can see that the leftmost outermost redex is in some sense essential, in that it can never be disposed of by another reduction. That is, if $(\lambda x.M)N$ is the leftmost redex of a term, any other redex can only be: (1) inside M, (2) inside N, or (3) entirely to the right of this redex in the term. No matter how many reductions are performed in each of these three categories, the redex $(\lambda x.M)N$ still remains, is still leftmost, and must eventually be reduced (unlike a redex appearing, for example, inside N, which may never need to be reduced if M

contains no free occurences of x). Since the leftmost redex must appear somewhere in a reduction to normal form, it makes sense that choosing to reduce it first will lead to a normal form whenever one exists.

Theorem 5.3.3 (Standardization Theorem) If a term X has a normal form, then X reduces to normal form by normal order reduction. (Proof ommitted.)

Remark: The class $\mathcal{N}$ of all terms in normal form can be defined inductively by the following:

1. If z is an identifier, then $z \in \mathcal{N}$.
2. If $N_0, \ldots, N_n$ are elements of $\mathcal{N}$, with $n \geq 0$, and z an identifier, then $zN_0 \ldots N_n \in \mathcal{N}$.
3. if $M \in \mathcal{N}$, then $(\lambda x.M) \in \mathcal{N}$, provided that M is not of the form $M_1 x$ with $x \notin \mathcal{FV}(M_1)$.

All variables are terms and we get new terms by combination or abstraction. Since we want only terms in normal form, an abstraction cannot appear as a rator in a combination. Thus, terms in normal form have the structure

$$\lambda x_1 \ldots x_n.zN_1 \ldots N_m$$

where $n \geq 0$, $m \geq 0$, z is an identifier, and each N_i is in normal form, for $1 \leq i \leq m$.

We define the following abbreviations for specific closed terms that are standard in the study of the λ-calculus:

$$I \equiv \lambda x.x$$

$$K \equiv \lambda x.\lambda y.x$$

$$B \equiv \lambda f.\lambda g.\lambda x.f(gx)$$

I is interpreted as the identity function. Note that a function application is a combination where the function is rator and the argument is rand. Thus $IX = X$ for any term X. The combination of terms is *not* commutative. The identity function operating on any argument returns that argument. The result of applying a function to the identity as argument, as in XI, depends on the structure of X.

K is the function that, for an argument M, yields the constant function $\lambda y.M$, which has value M for all arguments y.

The combinator B is used to create the composition of two unary functions; for functions f and g we have

$$Bfg = \lambda x.f(gx)$$

So Bfg represents $f \circ g$, the composition of f and g. If F is any term, we write F^n for the composition of F with itself n times. Note that F composed with itself is *not* F combined with itself. We define F^n as follows:

$$\begin{array}{lllll} F^0 & \equiv & I & & \\ F^{n+1} & \equiv & F \circ F^n & \equiv & BFF^n \end{array}$$

Recall that our conventions for eliminating parentheses determine that $F^{n+1} \equiv (BF)F^n$. As an example of composition, consider the following powers of K.

$$\begin{array}{rll} BKI = (\lambda f.\lambda g.\lambda x.f(gx))KI & \beta\text{-}red & (\lambda g.\lambda x.K(gx))I \\ & \beta\text{-}red & \lambda x.K(Ix) \\ & \beta\text{-}red & \lambda x.Kx \\ & \eta\text{-}red & K = \lambda x.\lambda y.x \end{array}$$

$$\begin{array}{rll} (BK)K = (\lambda f.\lambda g.\lambda x.f(gx))KK & \beta\text{-}red & (\lambda g.\lambda x.K(gx))K \\ & \beta\text{-}red & \lambda x.K(Kx) \\ & \equiv & \lambda x.K((\lambda x.\lambda y.x)x) \\ & \beta\text{-}red & \lambda x.K(\lambda y.x) \\ & \equiv & \lambda x.(\lambda x.\lambda y.x)(\lambda y.x) \\ & \beta\text{-}red & \lambda x.\lambda y.\lambda y.x \end{array}$$

Note that in the reduction sequences above, several terms contained more than one variable of the same name. By the α-conversion rule we know that the *name* of a bound variable is unimportant; however, it is very important that we recognize occurrences of the same variable and distinguish occurrences of different variables that may have the same name.

In the term $\lambda x.(\lambda x.\lambda y.x)(\lambda y.x)$ are four distinct variables — two named x and two named y. There is no confusion, since the scoping rules tell us that the first and last occurrences of x are the same variable while the middle two occurrences represent a different variable, also named x. Similarly, each occurrence of the name y stands for a different variable. Although it is unnecessary, it may be informative to reinforce the distinction between variables at times by renaming them. Thus $\lambda x.(\lambda x.\lambda y.x)(\lambda y.x)$ could be α-converted to $\lambda x.(\lambda w.\lambda y.w)(\lambda z.x)$ and β-reduced to $\lambda x.\lambda y.\lambda z.x$. Investigating further powers of K, the reader should be able to establish the following:

$$
\begin{array}{lllll}
K^0 & = & I & = & \lambda x.x \\
K^1 & = & BKI & \textit{red} & \lambda x.\lambda y.x \\
K^2 & = & (BK)K & \textit{red} & \lambda x.\lambda y.\lambda z.x \\
K^3 & = & (BK)K^2 & \textit{red} & \lambda x.\lambda y.\lambda z.\lambda w.x \\
 & \vdots & & & \\
K^n & = & (BK)K^{n-1} & \textit{red} & \lambda x_1.\lambda x_2.\ldots\lambda x_{n+1}.x_1
\end{array}
$$

Thus, K^n is a function of $n+1$ arguments that returns its first argument as value.

Exercises 5.3

1. Show that it is possible that A *red* B and B *red* A and $A \not\equiv B$ — (i.e., that *red* is not antisymmetric).

2. Show that (Ext), the rule of functional extensionality, can be derived in the λ-calculus.

3. Show the necessity of the restriction that $x \notin \mathcal{FV}(M)$ in the (η) rule, by showing that without this restriction the λ-calculus would be inconsistent (all terms A and B could be proved equal).

4. Reduce each of the following to normal form if one exists; if not, then state that no normal form exists.

   a. $\lambda y.(\lambda x.\lambda y.yx)(\lambda z.yz)$

   b. $(\lambda x.\lambda y.xy)((\lambda y.yy)(\lambda y.yy))$

   c. $(\lambda x.xx)(\lambda x.\lambda y.xy)$

   d. $(\lambda y.y(\lambda x.xx))(\lambda x.\lambda y.yx)$

e. $\lambda x.\lambda y.x(\lambda z.y(\lambda w.zw))$

5. We know that $(\lambda x.x)$ behaves as an identity function, when applied to any argument the value is always that argument. Is there a lambda expression that behaves as an "identity argument"? That is, an expression M, such that FM=F for all functions F.

5.4 Computation

Due to the Church–Rosser Theorem and a more recent result of Böhm (Theorem 5.6.2) we know that terms with different normal forms are, in an appropriate sense, separable (defined on page 194) or discretely distinguishable.

We know how to compute normal forms when they exist (just use normal order reduction), but we have not yet discussed how to deal with terms lacking normal forms. It is tempting to consider all terms without normal forms equivalent, in that they all represent nonterminating computations. When we try to relate computation with the world we are attempting to model, this approach would lead one to conclude that:

1. Terms with normal forms represent objects that are different from those represented by terms without normal forms.

2. Terms without normal forms represent objects that are indistinguishable.

3. Computation terminates if and only if a normal form is produced.

However this characterization of computation is inadequate. There are some pairs of terms that represent the same object in the models (truth), yet one has a normal form while the other does not. We shall also see that there are ways of distinguishing some terms although they have no normal form. In fact, it would be inconsistent to equate all terms not having a normal form. Consider the following example:

$$\begin{array}{rcl} M & \equiv & \lambda x.x(\lambda x.\lambda y.x)A \; = \; \lambda x.xKA \\ N & \equiv & \lambda x.x(\lambda y.\lambda x.x)A \; = \; \lambda x.x(KI)A \end{array}$$

where A is any term without a normal form, so that both M and N fail to have a normal form. But MK *β-red* K and NK *β-red* KI, so if M and N are equal, then $K = KI$; but then we would have a term with two normal forms that are not α-convertible, which contradicts Corollary 5.3.1.2. We exhibit the reductions of MK and NK to K and KI below.

$$\begin{array}{lcl} MK & \equiv & (\lambda x.x(\lambda x.\lambda y.x)A)(\lambda x.\lambda y.x) \\ & \mathit{red} & (\lambda x.\lambda y.x)(\lambda x.\lambda y.x)([\lambda x.\lambda y.x/x]A) \\ & \mathit{red} & (\lambda y_1.\lambda x.\lambda y.x)([\lambda x.\lambda y.x/x]A) \\ & \mathit{red} & \lambda x.\lambda y.x \\ & \equiv & K \end{array}$$

$$\begin{array}{lcl} NK & \equiv & (\lambda x.x(\lambda y.\lambda x.x)A)(\lambda x.\lambda y.x) \\ & \mathit{red} & (\lambda x.\lambda y.x)(\lambda y.\lambda x.x)([\lambda x.\lambda y.x/x]A) \\ & \mathit{red} & (\lambda y_1.\lambda y.\lambda x.x)([\lambda x.\lambda y.x/x]A) \\ & \mathit{red} & \lambda y.\lambda x.x \\ & \mathit{cnv} & KI \end{array}$$

So we see that in some cases it is possible to find a context in which two terms without normal forms will behave differently, and are thus distinguishable. We would like to be able to characterize the class of terms that are distinguishable even though some may not have normal forms. For this purpose we investigate the notions of solvability and head normal form.

First, we consider closed terms and how they behave as functions. Let

$$\begin{array}{lcl} \Delta & \equiv & \lambda x.xx \\ M_1 & \equiv & \Delta\Delta \\ M_2 & \equiv & \Delta(\lambda x.xxx) \end{array}$$

None of these terms has a normal form, and they are hereditarily undefined in the sense that, no matter how they are applied as functions, they never yield normal forms as results. That is, for all integers $k \geq 0$ and all terms $X_1, \ldots, X_k$ the applications $M_i X_1 \ldots X_k$ fail to have a normal form for $i = 1$ or $i = 2$.

However, as we saw in the example M and N above, not all terms without normal forms have this property. The difference is one of solvability.

DEFINITION: A closed term M is ***solvable*** if an integer $k \geq 0$ and terms $X_1, \ldots, X_k$ exist such that $MX_1 \ldots X_k$ has a normal form. Otherwise, M is ***unsolvable.*** ■

This definition has several immediate consequences and alternative statements. First, a term having a normal form is always solvable (let $k = 0$). Perhaps more surprisingly, any closed term with a normal form can be applied to suitable arguments to obtain any term (not just a normal form) as result.

LEMMA 5.4.1 If M is a (closed) term having a normal form N, and if X is a any term, then for some integer $k \geq 0$, there exist terms $X_1, \ldots, X_k$, such that

$$MX_1 \ldots X_k \ \beta\text{-}red \ X$$

Proof: Recalling the remark on page 164, we know that N, the normal form of M, can be written

$$N \equiv \lambda x_1 \ldots x_n . z N_1 \ldots N_m$$

with $z \equiv x_i$, for some i (since M is a closed term, N must also be a closed term). Now choose $k = n$, and for $j = 1, 2, \ldots, k$ define

$$X_j \equiv \begin{cases} I & \text{if } j \neq i \\ K^m X & \text{if } j = i \end{cases}$$

Then:

$$\begin{aligned} & MX_1 \ldots X_n \\ red \quad & (\lambda x_1 \ldots x_n . z N_1 \ldots N_m) X_1 \ldots X_n \\ \equiv \quad & (\lambda x_1 \ldots x_i \ldots x_n . z N_1 \ldots N_m) I \ldots K^m X \ldots I \\ \beta\text{-}red \quad & K^m X[I \ldots K^m X \ldots I / x_1 \ldots x_i \ldots x_n] N_1 \ldots N_m \end{aligned}$$

but $(K^m X) N_1 \ldots N_m$ *β-red* X for *any* terms $N_1, \ldots, N_m$, since by previous remarks (page 166) we know that K^m is a function of $m + 1$ arguments that returns its first argument as value.[4] ■

Thus the term "solvability" is apropos. Given a closed term M, an equation of the form $MX_1 \ldots X_k = X$ can be solved for all terms X if

[4]Note that we do not care what the terms $N_1, \ldots, N_m$ look like; in particular, they need not be in normal form.

and only if M is solvable. We define a term with free variables to be solvable if there is a substitution of closed terms for its free variables such that the resulting closed term is solvable.

DEFINITION: A term M is ***solvable*** if and only if there is a head context[5] $C[\,]$ such that $C[M]$ has a normal form. ■

In order to characterize the notion of solvability syntactically, we investigate the concept of *head normal form.* First, we consider some unsolvable terms and their reductions. Again, we let $\Delta \equiv (\lambda x.xx)$.

1. $M_1 \equiv \Delta\Delta$ reduces only to itself.

2. $M_2 \equiv \Delta(\lambda x.xxx)$. Let $T \equiv (\lambda x.xxx)$, then every term to which M_2 reduces is of the form

$$((\lambda x.xxx)TT)T\ldots T$$

where T appears some finite number of times (≥ 1).

3. $$\begin{array}{lll} M_3 & \equiv & \Delta(\lambda x.\lambda y.xx) \\ & \equiv & (\lambda x.xx)(\lambda x.\lambda y.xx) \\ & \mathit{red} & (\lambda x.\lambda y.xx)(\lambda x.\lambda y.xx) \\ & \mathit{red} & \lambda y.(\lambda x.\lambda y.xx)(\lambda x.\lambda y.xx) \\ & \mathit{red} & \lambda y.\lambda y_1.(\lambda x.\lambda y.xx)(\lambda x.\lambda y.xx)^6 \\ & \mathit{red} & \lambda y.\lambda y_1.\lambda y_2.(\lambda x.\lambda y.xx)(\lambda x.\lambda y.xx) \end{array}$$

and so on — that is, every term to which M_3 reduces is of the form (after α-conversion):

$$\lambda y.\lambda y_1.\lambda y_2.\ \ldots \lambda y_n.(\lambda x.\lambda y.xx)(\lambda x.\lambda y.xx)$$

4. $M_4 \equiv \Delta(\lambda x.\lambda y.xxx)$. Letting T' denote $(\lambda x.\lambda y.xxx)$, we have

$$\begin{array}{lll} M_4 & \equiv & \Delta(\lambda x.\lambda y.xxx) \\ & \mathit{red} & T'T' \\ & \mathit{red} & \lambda y.(\lambda x.\lambda y.xxx)T'T' \\ & \mathit{red} & \lambda y.(\lambda y_1.(\lambda x.\lambda y.xxx)T'T')T' \\ & \vdots & \end{array}$$

[5] Head context is defined on page 159.

[6] We've renamed the second bound variable y to y_1 for clarity.

Every term to which M_4 reduces is of the form (after α-conversion)

$$\lambda x_1.(\lambda x_2.(\ldots(\lambda x_n.(\lambda x.\lambda y.xxx)T'T')\ldots)T')T'$$

These reduced forms of M_1, M_2, M_3, and M_4 all consist of a single β-redex (M_1), a β-redex followed by a finite number of arguments (M_2), or a finite number of abstractions on one of the two (M_3 and M_4). That is, they are of the form:

$$\lambda x_1 \ldots x_n.((\lambda x.M)N)X_1 \ldots X_m \qquad n \geq 0,\ m \geq 0 \tag{5.3}$$

DEFINITION: A term of the form of (5.3) is called a term ***not in head normal form*** and the redex $(\lambda x.M)N$ is called its ***head redex***. ■

The paradoxical combinator $Y_\lambda \equiv \lambda f.(\lambda x.(f(xx))(\lambda x.f(xx))$ is of the form of (5.3), but can be β-reduced to $\lambda f.f((\lambda x.f(xx))(\lambda x.f(xx)))$, which is not of the form (5.3). Also the terms:

$$M \equiv \lambda x.x(K)(A)$$

$$N \equiv \lambda x.x(KI)(A)$$

where A is any term without a normal form, are terms that have no normal forms, and are not of form 5.3. These three terms are not in normal form, but they are in *head normal form (h.n.f.)*.

DEFINITION: A term of the general form

$$\lambda x_1 \ldots x_n.zX_1 \ldots X_k \tag{5.4}$$

where $n \geq 0$, $k \geq 0$, z is a variable, and X_i are arbitrary terms is said to be in ***head normal form***. ■

Every term of the calculus can be written in one of the forms (5.3) or (5.4) for suitable n, k, X_i.

DEFINITION: In (5.4) the variable z is known as the ***head variable***, and the term X_i as its ***ith main argument***. Two head normal forms are said to be ***similar*** if they have the same head variable, the same number of main arguments, and the same number of initial bound variables. A term H in h.n.f. is said to be a ***head normal form of*** M if M *cnv* H. ■

DEFINITION: The reduction of M that always reduces the head redex is called the ***head reduction***. ■

Analogously to normal order reduction of terms to normal form, it can be shown that a term has a head normal form if and only if its head reduction terminates, and all head normal forms of a term are similar. Note that the head redex is also the leftmost redex, so head reduction will proceed in the same way as normal order reduction. However, head reduction will terminate as soon as a head normal form is produced whereas normal order reduction would continue searching for a normal form. Thus we use head reduction as our computation scheme, being interested only in whether or not a term has h.n.f. and not caring about a normal form.

We shall see that it is consistent to equate all terms not having h.n.f. We know that computation will terminate precisely for those terms having a h.n.f.; however, we have no decision procedure for recognizing whether or not an arbitrary term has a h.n.f. That is, for a given term we may or may not be able to predict whether its head reduction will terminate.

Comparing (5.4) with the structure of normal forms discussed earlier (page 164), we can see that in a head normal form the main arguments $X_1, \ldots, X_m$ can be arbitrary terms, whereas a normal form requires that these subterms also be in normal form. Thus a head normal form is a weak kind of normal form in that it is in normal form only at the top (outermost) level of the term.

Terms having a head normal form are solvable.[7] The converse can also be shown by syntactic means though we shall see a much easier proof using Scott's lattice models (Theorem 5.6.9).

Using head reduction as our computation method, nontermination is equivalent to unsolvability of a term. This is more satisfying than an approach that insists on production of the normal form of a term, for, as we have seen, there are ways to (finitely) distinguish some terms without normal forms. On the other hand, terms without head normal

[7]The proof of Lemma 5.4.1 requires only that M have a head normal form.

forms — unsolvable terms — behave the same in any context. In particular, if U is unsolvable then so are UX and $U \circ X$ for all X, which is as we would expect for nonterminating programs. That is, if we have no information about a function then we cannot gain information by applying it to an argument; and if a program P fails to terminate then performing it in sequence with another program P_2 will also fail to terminate. However, the property of not having a normal form is not preserved by application or by composition.

It was first shown by Barendregt that it is consistent to consider all unsolvable terms[8] equal. From a computational point of view it is certainly desirable to do so since they behave alike.

We have considered what happens when solvable terms are applied as functions. What happens when unsolvable terms appear as rand in combinations, that is, when functions are applied to these terms? We can always obtain a normal form as result of an application (combination) by using a constant function. For example, if U is unsolvable, then

$$(KI)U \ \mathit{red} \ I$$

However, the result in this case was completely independent of the argument U, since $(KI)M \ \mathit{red} \ I$ for all terms M. In fact, we can make a stronger statement.

Lemma 5.4.2 If U is unsolvable, then, for all contexts $C[\,]$

1. If $C[U]$ has a normal form, then $C[M]$ has the same normal form for all M.
2. If $C[U]$ has a head normal form, then $C[M]$ has a similar head normal form for all M.

So the interpretation of unsolvable terms as being "totally undefined" or "least defined" and as "containing no information" is a good one. It should not be suprising, therefore, when we find that the unsolvable terms are exactly the terms with value $\perp$ in Scott's model.

So we interpret the unsolvable terms in a programming context as representing nonterminating programs that never provide any output while running (for example, a GO SELF loop). Note that not all nonterminating programs fall into this category. Many useful programs

[8] We can show this using Scott's models.

are intended to be nonterminating. For example the information that an operating system provides while running is analogous to the information we get from a head normal form of a term. We shall pursue this notion of partial normal forms in Section 5.6.1.

When we look at the mathematical (denotational) semantics of the lambda calculus we are interested in what functions are represented by terms. The unsolvable terms represent totally undefined functions. If we look at functions as sets of ordered pairs (argument, value), as is typical in mathematics, then an unsolvable term represents the empty set.

Exercise 5.4

1. As further examples of its expressiveness, consider how we might begin to represent number theory in the lambda calculus. The general scheme for representing the nonnegative integers is as follows:

   Represent **0** by $\overline{0} \equiv \lambda x.\lambda y.y$
   1 by $\overline{1} \equiv \lambda x.\lambda y.xy$
   2 by $\overline{2} \equiv \lambda x.\lambda y.x(xy)$
   3 by $\overline{3} \equiv \lambda x.\lambda y.x(x(xy))$
   $\vdots \quad \vdots$
   n by $\overline{n} \equiv \lambda x.\lambda y.\underbrace{x(x \ldots (x}_{n \text{ times}}\, y) \ldots)$

   We can represent the successor function as the λ-expression

   $$\lambda x.\lambda y.\lambda z.y(xyz)$$

   a. Prove that the lambda expression just given for the successor function will yield a term reducible to the representation for $\mathbf{n+1}$ when applied to the representation of the integer **n**.

   b. Find a λ-expression representing the addition function. That is, find *Add*, such that *Add X Y cnv* the representation for the sum of **x** and **y**, where X is the representation for **x** and Y is the representation for **y**.

   c. Find a λ-expression representing multiplication.

   d. Find a λ-expression representing exponentiation.

e. Find a λ-expression representing the projection function, $\mathbf{U_i^n}$, taking n arguments and returning the ith one as value.

5.5 Truth

5.5.1 Some background on lattices

> The natural numbers were created by God, all others are the invention of man.
>
> *Kronecker*

> The lord did not create "all" natural numbers, just a lot of them, plenty.
>
> *E. W. Dijkstra*

When looking for a denotational semantics for programs, we are interested in finding, for example, what mathematical function is being computed by a program. It is necessary to say "being" computed, since a mathematical function is an infinite set of ordered pairs whenever its domain is infinite, and thus cannot be computed completely. However, we don't need to know everything about a function in order to use it, we only need to know enough about it to be able to determine its value, given specific arguments.

For example, we cannot represent the entirety of the factorial function in any machine. However, we can represent a method for computing the factorial function that is capable of producing the factorial of any given argument up to the finite limits of the machine's ability to represent numbers.

Thus the behavior of infinite objects (e.g., functions) must be determined by their finite approximations, (e.g., subsets of the infinite set of ordered pairs) in order to have an effective way of carrying out a computation involving such objects.

To summarize, we have claimed that in order to provide a satisfactory mathematical semantics for computation:

1. We must be able to deal with (some) infinite objects.

2. Although we can never completely compute infinite objects in finite time, we can determine approximations to what they really are.

3. Approximations are partial objects, because they give only some of the information about the infinite object.

4. In order to deal with an infinite object computationally, it must be possible to compute better and better approximations to it that eventually produce enough of the object to enable us to deal with it in any given context. That is, the object must contain no information over and above that which is computable from its finite (i.e., finitely representable) approximations.

Thus we are led to consider the enumeration model of computation.

DEFINITION: In the ***enumeration model*** of computation a data object $\mathbf{x}$ can be computed by any program that enumerates a sequence of approximations whose total "information content" is $\mathbf{x}$. ■

For example, the program:

```
NNI⇐ begin
        n:=0;
        while true
          do begin
               print(n);
               n:= n+1
             end
     end
```

NNI is a program that computes the set of nonnegative integers. It does so incrementally, one number at a time. It never completely produces the set of nonnegative integers, but each nonnegative integer will be produced by the program in a finite amount of time.

Let S_n be the set of nonnegative integers produced by the program after n iterations of the while loop. Then

$$\begin{aligned} S_0 &= \{\} \\ S_1 &= \{0\} \\ S_2 &= \{0,1\} \\ S_3 &= \{0,1,2\} \\ &\vdots \\ S_k &= \{0,1,2,\ldots,k-1\} \end{aligned}$$

We consider the result of a finite number of iterations of the while loop to be an approximation to the set of nonnegative integers — the more iterations allowed, the better the approximation. Each S_n is an approximation of S, the set of all nonnegative integers, in that it contains some of the information that S contains and no information not contained in S. We consider S to be the limit of these approximations because there is nothing in S that is not also in S_n for some n (and in fact in every S_k where $k \geq n$).

Consider another example:

```
F(n) ⇐ if n=0 then 1
```

We recognize F as a program to compute factorials; but consider how we could determine this mechanically. The program F is a rule for computing some function, call it **f**. Without any prior knowledge of **f**, we can determine from the definition of F that **f** is a function that maps 0 to 1, by calling F with n=0. We say that the partial (since it is only partially defined) function

$$\mathbf{f}_0(\mathbf{n}) = \begin{cases} \mathbf{1} & \text{if } \mathbf{n} = \mathbf{0} \\ \text{undefined} & \text{if } \mathbf{n} > \mathbf{0} \end{cases}$$

is an approximation to **f** (in much the same way that S_n is an approximation to S in the previous example). We can generate a sequence of approximations to **f** by applying it to successively larger integers and making use of what we already know about **f** from previously generated approximations, since all approximations must agree on values of **f** for arguments on which they are defined. That is, we know that $\mathbf{f(0) = 1}$, and all approximations to **f** that specify a value for **0** must agree. Thus,

$$\mathbf{f}_1(\mathbf{n}) = \begin{cases} \mathbf{f}_0(\mathbf{0}) = \mathbf{1} & \text{if } \mathbf{n} = \mathbf{0} \\ \mathbf{1} \cdot \mathbf{f}_0(\mathbf{0}) = \mathbf{1} \cdot \mathbf{1} = \mathbf{1} & \text{if } \mathbf{n} = \mathbf{1} \\ \text{undefined} & \text{if } \mathbf{n} > \mathbf{1} \end{cases}$$

$$\mathbf{f}_2(\mathbf{n}) = \begin{cases} \mathbf{f}_1(\mathbf{0}) = \mathbf{1} & \text{if } \mathbf{n} = \mathbf{0} \\ \mathbf{f}_1(\mathbf{1}) = \mathbf{1} & \text{if } \mathbf{n} = \mathbf{1} \\ \mathbf{2} \cdot \mathbf{f}_1(\mathbf{1}) = \mathbf{2} \cdot \mathbf{1} = \mathbf{2} & \text{if } \mathbf{n} = \mathbf{2} \\ \text{undefined} & \text{if } \mathbf{n} > \mathbf{2} \end{cases}$$

$$\mathbf{f_3(n)} = \begin{cases} \mathbf{f_2(0) = 1} & \text{if } \mathbf{n = 0} \\ \mathbf{f_2(1) = 1} & \text{if } \mathbf{n = 1} \\ \mathbf{f_2(2) = 2} & \text{if } \mathbf{n = 2} \\ \mathbf{3 \cdot f_2(2) = 3 \cdot 2 = 6} & \text{if } \mathbf{n = 3} \\ \text{undefined} & \text{if } \mathbf{n > 3} \end{cases}$$

$$\vdots$$

$$\mathbf{f_k(n)} = \begin{cases} \mathbf{f_{k-1}(n)} & \text{if } \mathbf{n < k} \\ \mathbf{n \cdot f_{k-1}(n-1)} & \text{if } \mathbf{n = k} \\ \text{undefined} & \text{if } \mathbf{n > k} \end{cases}$$

As **k** increases we get better and better approximations to **f**, "better" in that each contains more information than the previous one. The total information content of the infinite sequence of $\mathbf{f_k}$'s is the factorial function.

These examples lead us to consider domains of interpretation for the lambda calculus that contain partial (partially defined) objects and infinite objects as well as the more conventional completely defined finite objects — characters, integers, strings, etc. We have a relation of approximation defined on these domains.

DEFINITION: We say that **x** ***approximates*** **y**, or **x** is less or equally defined as **y**, written

$$\mathbf{x} \sqsubseteq \mathbf{y}$$

if **y** contains all the information that **x** does (and possibly more). ■

DEFINITION: A ***partial order*** is a binary relation, **R**, on a domain **D**, that is

1. Reflexive: **xRx**

2. Transitive: If **xRy** and **yRz** then **xRz**

3. Antisymmetric: If **xRy** and **yRx** then **x=y**

for all elements **x, y, z** $\in$ **D.** ■

Clearly, approximates ($\sqsubseteq$) is reflexive, transitive, and antisymmetric, and thus is a partial order on our domain.

To combine the information given by a set **X** of approximations we introduce the join operation on a set **X**.

DEFINITION: $\bigsqcup \mathbf{X}$, the ***join*** of the set **X**, is the least upper bound of **X** under the partial ordering. It must contain the information of all elements of **X** (i.e., it must be an upper bound), and it should not contain any further information (i.e., it must be the least upper bound). ■

DEFINITION: A ***complete lattice*** is a domain with a partial order defined on its elements, such that $\bigsqcup \mathbf{X} \in \mathbf{D}$ for all subsets **X** of **D**. ■

All domains we shall consider are complete lattices under the partial ordering $\sqsubseteq$; thus, whenever we refer to a domain, assume that it is a complete lattice unless explicitly stated otherwise.

Lattice equality, defined as $\mathbf{x} = \mathbf{y}$ if and only if $\mathbf{x} \sqsubseteq \mathbf{y}$ and $\mathbf{y} \sqsubseteq \mathbf{x}$, is a substitutive equivalence relation. We can define some other lattice-theoretic concepts in terms of $\bigsqcup$ as follows.

DEFINITION: The ***meet*** of a set $\mathbf{X} \subset \mathbf{D}$, is the greatest lower bound of the elements of **X**:

$$\bigsqcap \mathbf{X} = \bigsqcup \{\mathbf{w} \mid \mathbf{w} \sqsubseteq \mathbf{x} \text{ for all } \mathbf{x} \in \mathbf{X}\}$$ ■

The meet of the set **X**, contains the information that is common to all of the elements of **X**.

DEFINITION: ***Bottom***, written $\bot$, gives no information. It is the totally undefined element.

$$\bot = \bigsqcup\{\} = \bigsqcap \mathbf{D}$$ ■

DEFINITION: ***Top***, written $\top$, gives too much information, it is overdefined to the point of being inconsistent in most domains.

$$\top = \bigsqcup \mathbf{D} = \bigsqcap\{\}$$ ■

DEFINITION: Two elements $\mathbf{x}$ and $\mathbf{y}$ of the domain $\mathbf{D}$ are said to be ***incomparable*** if neither approximates the other. That is, it is not the case that $\mathbf{x} \sqsubseteq \mathbf{y}$ and it is not the case that $\mathbf{y} \sqsubseteq \mathbf{x}$. ■

When taking the join or meet of a set of two elements we can use a binary infix join or meet operator defined as follows:

$$\mathbf{x} \sqcup \mathbf{y} = \bigsqcup\{\mathbf{x}, \mathbf{y}\}$$

$$\mathbf{x} \sqcap \mathbf{y} = \bigsqcap\{\mathbf{x}, \mathbf{y}\}$$

It is easy to see that $\forall \mathbf{x} \in \mathbf{X}, \mathbf{x} \sqsubseteq \top$ and $\bot \sqsubseteq \mathbf{x}$, and therefore

$$\mathbf{x} \sqcup \mathbf{y} = \top \qquad \text{if and only if } \mathbf{x} \text{ and } \mathbf{y} \text{ are incomparable}$$

and

$$\mathbf{x} \sqcap \mathbf{y} = \bot \qquad \text{if and only if } \mathbf{x} \text{ and } \mathbf{y} \text{ are incomparable.}$$

Let us consider some example domains of interest. First we consider domains of conventional, completely defined elements, such as integers and truth values.

Let $\mathcal{Z}$ be the domain of integers. We can diagram the partial order relation, *approximates*, by providing a directed graph in which nodes represent elements of the domain and directed arcs indicate the approximates relation. (The direction of the arcs will be implicitly provided by the positioning of the nodes; i.e., $\mathbf{x} \sqsubseteq \mathbf{y}$ if $\mathbf{x}$ is below $\mathbf{y}$ in the diagram and there is an edge connecting $\mathbf{x}$ and $\mathbf{y}$.) Thus the domain $\mathcal{Z}$ with $\top$ and $\bot$ added to make it a complete lattice looks like:

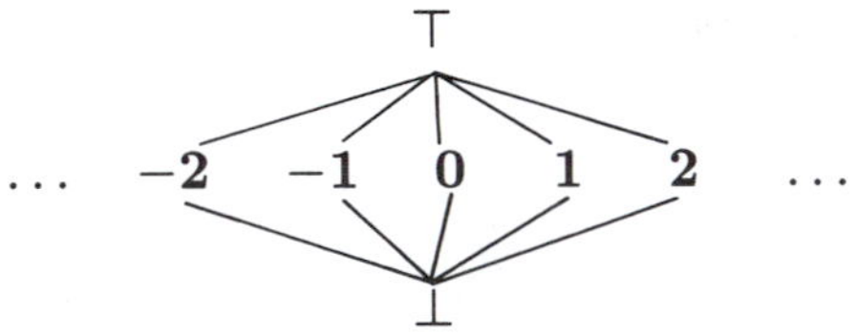

Remember that our partial order is approximates, in the sense of information content, not the numeric $\leq$. For example, 1 is no less defined than 2, and so does not approximate it.

If we were to consider the integers with $\leq$ as the partial order, the diagram of the domain would be vertical:

In this case we could think of the $\top$ and $\bot$ elements as representations of ∞ and $-\infty$, respectively.

As another example, consider $\mathcal{T}$, the domain of truth values.

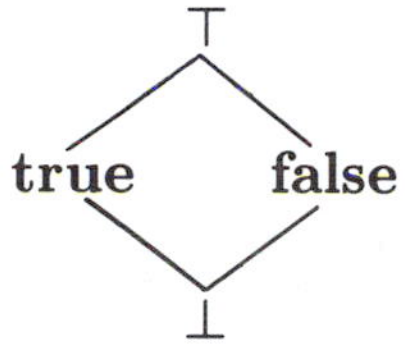

$\mathcal{T}$ and $\mathcal{Z}$ are examples of flat lattices. Their proper elements (i.e., all elements other than $\top$ and $\bot$) are discrete in the sense that none can be said to approximate another.

DEFINITION: A ***flat lattice*** is a complete lattice of elements $\mathbf{S} \cup \{\top, \bot\}$ with the partial order $\sqsubseteq$ defined by $\bot \sqsubseteq \mathbf{x} \sqsubseteq \mathbf{x} \sqsubseteq \top$ for all elements $\mathbf{x}$ of $\mathbf{S}$.

In thinking about these domains as providing interpretations of programs, we need to address what meaning is intended by the elements. If a program to compute an integer value, terminates and produces an integer, it is easily interpreted as having the value of the integer produced. We can interpret the program as $\bot$ if it never terminates and never gives any information about the integer it was expected to produce. The inclusion of $\top$ in our domain is not quite as natural, and because of controversy over its inclusion, denotational semantics has also been developed using complete partial orders rather than complete lattices, thereby eliminating the need for a top element. However, we can rationalize our inclusion of $\top$ as representing the meaning of programs that provide conflicting information about the intended output. Thus incorrect programs as well as correct ones can be assigned a meaning in the interpretation.

We've seen two example flat domains, $\mathcal{Z}$ and $\mathcal{T}$, but of course not all domains of interest are flat. Consider, for example, the set of all subsets of elements of a flat domain such as $\mathcal{Z}$. Rather than look at another infinite example, we will diagram the domain consisting of all subsets of the set $\{\mathbf{1,\ 2,\ 3}\}$, with $\sqsubseteq$ defined as the ordinary set containment (subset) relation.

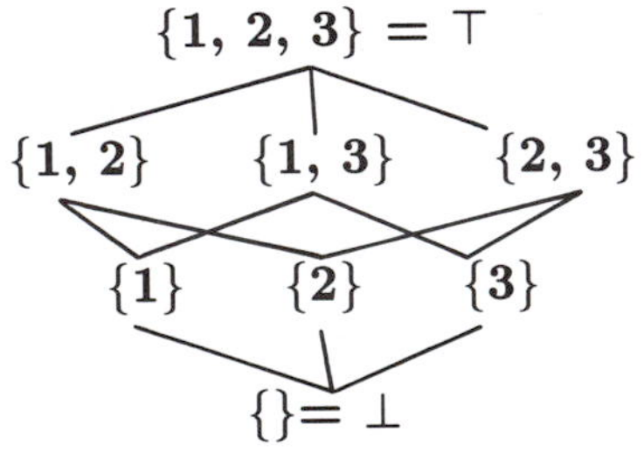

In this example, the join (least upper bound) of a set of elements is simply their union, and the meet (greatest lower bound) of a set of elements is their intersection.

We will also want to consider domains of functions. (After all, our aim is to provide a semantics for the lambda calculus.) As a simple example, consider a domain of unary partial functions on the nonnegative integers, with the approximates relation defined by

$$\mathbf{f} \sqsubseteq \mathbf{g} \qquad \text{if, for all } \mathbf{n} \in \mathbf{Z}, \text{ if } \mathbf{f(n)} \text{ is defined then } \mathbf{f(n)} = \mathbf{g(n)}$$

Then $\bot$ is the totally undefined function. Note that if we think of the functions as sets of ordered pairs (restricted, of course, to containing no more than one pair with a given first component — i.e., the functions must be well-defined), then the approximates relation may again be defined as the subset relation. However, such a domain has no well-defined element that could serve as the $\top$ element. We simply add $\top$ to this domain to represent functions providing inconsistent or conflicting information about their values on given arguments.

As a function, $\top$ is ill-defined. As a set of ordered pairs, it contains all ordered pairs of nonnegative integers; thus, it is a superset of every function (set of ordered pairs) in the domain. In this domain the join of two elements (and, by obvious extension, of sets of elements) is defined by

$$\mathbf{f} \sqcup \mathbf{g} = \begin{cases} \top & \text{if } \exists \mathbf{n} \text{ such that both } \mathbf{f}(\mathbf{n}) \text{ and } \mathbf{g}(\mathbf{n}) \\ & \text{are defined and } \mathbf{f}(\mathbf{n}) \neq \mathbf{g}(\mathbf{n}) \\ \mathbf{h} & \text{otherwise} \end{cases}$$

where

$$\mathbf{h}(\mathbf{n}) = \begin{cases} \mathbf{f}(\mathbf{n}) & \text{if } \mathbf{f}(\mathbf{n}) \text{ is defined} \\ \mathbf{g}(\mathbf{n}) & \text{if } \mathbf{g}(\mathbf{n}) \text{ is defined} \\ \text{undefined} & \text{otherwise} \end{cases}$$

Again, if we look at these functions as sets of ordered pairs, then

$$\mathbf{f} \sqcup \mathbf{g} = \begin{cases} \top & \text{if } \exists \mathbf{n}, \text{ such that } (\mathbf{n}, \mathbf{m}) \in \mathbf{f} \\ & (\mathbf{n}, \mathbf{k}) \in \mathbf{g} \text{ and } \mathbf{m} \neq \mathbf{k} \\ \mathbf{f} \cup \mathbf{g} & \text{otherwise} \end{cases}$$

(Aside: If we wish to consider the semantics of nondeterministic or parallel programs, then the notion of inconsistent information takes on new meaning. A program is no longer seen as necessarily computing a function; it may compute a relation. That is, it may be reasonable to drop the restriction that only one value is possible for a given argument. With this interpretation in mind, we may understand the top element attached to the domain of functions above as the meaning assigned to programs that were intended to be deterministic, but are in fact nondeterministic.)

We have seen several example domains; now we wish to investigate certain properties of functions on such domains.

DEFINITION: A function $\mathbf{f} : \mathbf{D} \to \mathbf{D}$ is ***monotonic*** if for all $\mathbf{x}, \mathbf{y} \in \mathbf{D}$, if $\mathbf{x} \sqsubseteq \mathbf{y}$ then $\mathbf{f}(\mathbf{x}) \sqsubseteq \mathbf{f}(\mathbf{y})$. ■

DEFINITION: A subset $\mathbf{X}$ of a domain is a ***directed set*** if and only if every finite subset of $\mathbf{X}$ has an upper bound in $\mathbf{X}$. ■

DEFINITION: A function $\mathbf{f{:}D \rightarrow D}$ is said to be ***continuous*** if for all directed subsets $\mathbf{X}$ of the domain $\mathbf{f}(\bigsqcup \mathbf{X}) = \bigsqcup \mathbf{f}(\mathbf{X})$ ■

(In the above we wrote $\mathbf{f(X)}$ as an abbreviation for $\{\mathbf{f(x)} \mid \mathbf{x} \in \mathbf{X}\}$.

LEMMA 5.5.1 If **f** is continuous, then **f** is monotonic.

Proof: By the definition of $\bigsqcup$, $\mathbf{x} \sqsubseteq \mathbf{y}$ implies that $\bigsqcup\{\mathbf{x}, \mathbf{y}\} = \mathbf{y}$. Thus, $\{\mathbf{x}, \mathbf{y}\}$ is a directed set, and $\mathbf{f}(\bigsqcup\{\mathbf{x}, \mathbf{y}\}) = \mathbf{f}(\mathbf{y})$. Since **f** is continuous, we know

$$\mathbf{f}(\bigsqcup\{\mathbf{x}, \mathbf{y}\}) = \bigsqcup\{\mathbf{f}(\mathbf{x}), \mathbf{f}(\mathbf{y})\}$$

Therefore, $\bigsqcup\{\mathbf{f}(\mathbf{x}), \mathbf{f}(\mathbf{y})\} = \mathbf{f}(\mathbf{y})$ and so, by the definition of $\bigsqcup$ we have $\mathbf{f}(\mathbf{x}) \sqsubseteq \mathbf{f}(\mathbf{y})$. ■

A recursive definition of a function **f** can be viewed as a function τ of the identifier **f**.

For example, on page 177 we gave a definition of a program to compute factorials. We could rewrite that program as a function of the identifier **F** as follows:

$$\tau(\mathbf{F}) = \mathbf{f} \text{ such that } \mathbf{f}(\mathbf{n}) = \begin{cases} \mathbf{1} & \text{if } \mathbf{n} = \mathbf{0} \\ \mathbf{n} \cdot \mathbf{F}(\mathbf{n} - \mathbf{1}) & \text{if } \mathbf{n} > \mathbf{0} \end{cases}$$

Then our sequence of partial functions $\mathbf{f_i}$ (page 177) could be defined as

$$\begin{aligned} \mathbf{f_0} &= \tau(\bot) \\ \mathbf{f_{n+1}} &= \tau(\mathbf{f_n}) \end{aligned}$$

DEFINITION: A ***fixed point*** of a function **f** is an element $\mathbf{x} \in \mathbf{D}$ such that $\mathbf{f}(\mathbf{x}) = \mathbf{x}$. ■

DEFINITION: A ***fixed point operator*** is a function **g** such that $\mathbf{g}(\mathbf{f}) = \mathbf{x}$ implies that **x** is a fixed point of **f** — that is, $\mathbf{f}(\mathbf{x}) = \mathbf{x}$. Thus, if **g** is a fixed point operator, then $\mathbf{f}(\mathbf{g}(\mathbf{f})) = \mathbf{g}(\mathbf{f})$. ■

DEFINITION: A ***least fixed point operator*** produces the least fixed points of continuous functions. That is, if $\mathbf{g}$ is a least fixed point operator and $\mathbf{f}$ is a continuous function, then $\mathbf{f(g(f)) = g(f)}$ (i.e., $\mathbf{g(f)}$ is a fixed point of $\mathbf{f}$, and for all fixed points $\mathbf{x}$ of $\mathbf{f}$, $\mathbf{g(f)} \sqsubseteq \mathbf{x}$). ■

We define the sequence $\mathbf{f_n}$ by

$$\mathbf{f_0} = \tau(\perp)$$

$$\mathbf{f_{n+1}} = \tau(\mathbf{f_n})$$

DEFINITION: The lattice theoretic least fixed point operator $\mathbf{Y}$ is defined by

$$\mathbf{Y(f)} = \bigsqcup\{\mathbf{f_n} \mid \mathbf{n} \geq \mathbf{0}\}$$

and produces the least fixed points of continuous functions. ■

DEFINITION: The join (l.u.b.) $\bigsqcup\mathbf{X}$ of a set $\mathbf{X}$ may properly be called the ***limit*** of the set only when $\mathbf{X}$ is directed. A directed set is ***interesting*** if it does not contain its own least upper bound. ■

A particular case of an interesting directed set is an infinite sequence of elements that forms a chain.

DEFINITION: A sequence $\mathbf{x_0}$, $\mathbf{x_1}$, $\mathbf{x_2}$, ... forms a ***chain*** if and only if $\mathbf{x_0} \sqsubseteq \mathbf{x_1} \sqsubseteq \mathbf{x_2} \sqsubseteq \cdots$. For chains, we generally write $\bigsqcup \mathbf{x_n}$ for $\bigsqcup\{\mathbf{x_n} \mid \mathbf{n} \geq \mathbf{0}\}$. ■

For example, the sequence of functions $\mathbf{f_n}$ defined above forms a chain. The proof of Lemma 5.5.2 is left as an exercise.

LEMMA 5.5.2 The following properties are derived from these definitions:

1. A set $\mathbf{X}$ is directed iff it is nonempty and every pair of elements in $\mathbf{X}$ has an upper bound in $\mathbf{X}$.

2. All interesting directed sets are infinite.

3. Every countably infinite directed set contains a chain with the same limit.

DEFINITION: An element $\mathbf{x}$ of a domain $\mathbf{D}$ is a ***limit point*** if and only if $\mathbf{x} = \bigsqcup \mathbf{X}$ for some interesting directed $\mathbf{X} \subset \mathbf{D}$. ■

For example, the factorial function is a limit point since it is $\bigsqcup \mathbf{f_n}$ and $\mathbf{f_n}$ is an interesting directed subset of the domain of unary functions on nonnegative integers. In flat domains there are no limit points since there are no interesting directed sets.

As mentioned at the beginning of this section, in order to provide a semantics for computable objects (as defined by the enumeration model) we need to be assured that all infinite objects can be determined by their finite approximations. Thus, we want to restrict our domains to those in which each element can be described as the join of a set of finitely representable elements.

Let $\mathbf{E} \subseteq \mathbf{D}$ be the set of finitely representable elements of $\mathbf{D}$. Then for each $\mathbf{x} \in \mathbf{D}$, there must exist a set $\mathbf{E_x} \subseteq \mathbf{E}$, such that $\mathbf{x} = \bigsqcup \mathbf{E_x}$. Note that if $\mathbf{x} = \bigsqcup \mathbf{E_x}$ then $\mathbf{x} = \bigsqcup(\mathbf{E_x} \cup \{\mathbf{e} \mid \mathbf{e} \in \mathbf{E} \text{ and } \mathbf{e} \sqsubseteq \mathbf{x}\})$, since if $\mathbf{e} \sqsubseteq \mathbf{x}$ then $\mathbf{e} \sqsubseteq \bigsqcup \mathbf{E_x}$. Thus we are led to the following definition.

DEFINITION: A ***sub-basis*** of a domain $\mathbf{D}$ is a subset $\mathbf{E}$ of $\mathbf{D}$ such that, for all $\mathbf{x} \in \mathbf{D}$,

$$\mathbf{x} = \bigsqcup \{\mathbf{e} \mid \mathbf{e} \in \mathbf{E} \text{ and } \mathbf{e} \sqsubseteq \mathbf{x}\}$$ ■

We insist, in order to provide a semantics consistent with our notion of computation as the enumeration of finite approximations, that $\mathbf{E}$ consist only of finitely representable elements, and that an algorithm can be described to generate its elements. Thus $\mathbf{E}$ must be countable. In fact, since the join of a finite number of finite approximations can contain only a finite amount of information, we can define a basis as follows:

DEFINITION: A sub-basis $\mathbf{E}$ of $\mathbf{D}$ is a ***basis*** of $\mathbf{D}$ if and only if for all finite $\mathbf{E}' \subset \mathbf{E}$, $\bigsqcup \mathbf{E}' \in \mathbf{E}$. ■

Since the set $\{\bigsqcup \mathbf{E}' \mid \mathbf{E}' \subset \mathbf{E},\ \mathbf{E}' \text{ finite}\}$ of finite joins of sub-basis elements is countable whenever the sub-basis itself is countable, we insist that every domain have a countable basis.

This requirement limits the size of allowable domains. Since there are at most a continuum number of subsets of a countable set, and every element of the domain is the least upper bound of a subset of a basis, this implies that all domains we consider have cardinality no larger than that of the real numbers.

Lemma 5.5.3 The following properties are consequences of the definitions just given: Let $\mathbf{E}$ be a basis for $\mathbf{D}$, then

1. For all $\mathbf{x} \in \mathbf{D}$, $\mathbf{x} \neq \top$, the set $\{\mathbf{e} \mid \mathbf{e} \in \mathbf{E}$ and $\mathbf{e} \sqsubseteq \mathbf{x}\}$ is directed.
2. If $\mathbf{x} \in \mathbf{D}$ is not a basis element, then $\mathbf{x}$ is a limit point.
3. When $\mathbf{E}$ is countable, every limit point $\mathbf{x} \in \mathbf{D}$ can be expressed as the limit of a chain of basis elements.

Exercises 5.5.1

1. Consider the domain of real numbers represented as closed intervals with rational endpoints. That is, an interval $[\mathbf{l}, \mathbf{u}]$ is an approximation to the real number $\mathbf{x}$ if $\mathbf{l} \leq \mathbf{x} \leq \mathbf{u}$. Thus we define $[\mathbf{l_1}, \mathbf{u_1}] \sqsubseteq [\mathbf{l_2}, \mathbf{u_2}]$ if and only if $\mathbf{l_1} \leq \mathbf{l_2}$ and $\mathbf{u_2} \leq \mathbf{u_1}$.
   a. Describe how to find the join of two elements of this domain.
   b. Describe how to find the meet of two elements of this domain.
2. Prove Lemma 5.5.2.
3. Prove Lemma 5.5.3.
4. Prove that lattice equality is an equivalence relation.

5.5.2 The Models

> The lambda-calculus is a curious language; one of my aims in life is to make it somewhat less curious.
>
> *D. Scott*

In order to provide a model for the lambda calculus we need as domain a complete lattice, with more than one element, that is isomorphic to its own continuous function space. This isomorphism is required because every term of the λ-calculus can stand on its own, representing an element of the domain, or can appear as rator of a combination, representing a function on the domain.

For our purposes we assume the existence of such a domain $\mathcal{D}_\infty$ that is isomorphic with its continuous function space $[\mathcal{D}_\infty \rightarrow \mathcal{D}_\infty]$. (For construction of the models represented by $\mathcal{D}_\infty$ see Scott [33] or Stoy [37].) The isomorphism is expressed by two continuous functions

$$\Phi : \mathcal{D}_\infty \rightarrow [\mathcal{D}_\infty \rightarrow \mathcal{D}_\infty]$$

and

$$\Psi : [\mathcal{D}_\infty \rightarrow \mathcal{D}_\infty] \rightarrow \mathcal{D}_\infty$$

with the properties:

1. $\boldsymbol{\Psi}(\boldsymbol{\Phi}(\mathbf{x})) = \mathbf{x}$, for all $\mathbf{x} \in \mathcal{D}_\infty$.

2. $\boldsymbol{\Phi}(\boldsymbol{\Psi}(\mathbf{f})) = \mathbf{f}$, for all $\mathbf{f} \in [\mathcal{D}_\infty \rightarrow \mathcal{D}_\infty]$.

To interpret the λ-calculus in $\mathcal{D}_\infty$, we must first introduce some terminology and notation.

Definition: Let Id represent the set of all identifiers of the λ-calculus. An ***environment*** ρ is a mapping of all identifiers to values (denotations) in $\mathcal{D}_\infty$:

$$\rho : Id \rightarrow \mathcal{D}_\infty$$ ■

Intuitively, we see that an environment is just a symbol table, an assignment of values to variable symbols (identifiers). We will use the following abbreviations:

Id	for the set of all identifiers (variables)
Exp	for the set of all terms
Env	for the set of all environments (i.e., the set of all functions from Id to $\mathcal{D}_\infty$)

The meaning of a term can be specified in terms of the meanings of its immediate subterms by a mapping $\mathcal{V}$ that takes a term as argument and produces a function from Env to $\mathcal{D}_\infty$ as result:

$$\mathcal{V} : Exp \rightarrow [Env \rightarrow \mathcal{D}_\infty]$$

One might prefer to think of $\mathcal{V}$ as a binary function, taking a term and an environment in which to find values for the free variables of the term as arguments and producing a value in $\mathcal{D}_\infty$ as result. However, we are simply currying again, considering $\mathcal{V}$ a unary function whose value is a unary function.

Before providing the definition of $\mathcal{V}$, we define what is meant by an extended environment $\rho[\mathbf{d}/x]$.

DEFINITION: Given an environment ρ, an element of the domain $\mathbf{d}$, and an identifier x, we define the ***extended environment*** $\rho[\mathbf{d}/x]$ as follows:

$$\rho[\mathbf{d}/x][\![y]\!] = \begin{cases} \mathbf{d} & \text{if } y \equiv x \\ \rho[\![y]\!] & \text{if } y \not\equiv x \end{cases}$$ ∎

Now we are ready to define the semantic function $\mathcal{V}$.

DEFINITION: We define $\mathcal{V}$ by structural induction based on the syntax of terms of the lambda calculus:

1. Identifiers: The value of an identifier x is the value assigned to it by the environment. Thus, the value of x, given an environment ρ, is the result of applying ρ to x:

$$\mathcal{V}[\![x]\!](\rho) = \rho[\![x]\!]^{9}$$

2. Combinations, MN: A combination is interpreted as a function application. Given an environment ρ, we can interpret the value of the rator M as a function by applying Φ to it. This function can then be applied to the value of the rand.

$$\mathcal{V}[\![MN]\!](\rho) = \Phi(\mathcal{V}[\![M]\!](\rho))(\mathcal{V}[\![N]\!](\rho))$$

3. Abstractions: An abstraction $\lambda x.M$ is interpreted as a function from $\mathcal{D}_\infty$ to $\mathcal{D}_\infty$. Given an environment ρ, the result of applying this function to any argument $\mathbf{d}$ from $\mathcal{D}_\infty$ is the value of the body M in the extended environment $\rho[\mathbf{d}/x]$ (where the value of the argument $\mathbf{d}$ is assigned to the formal parameter x). Thus, as $\mathbf{d}$ varies over $\mathcal{D}_\infty$, $\mathcal{V}[\![M]\!](\rho[\mathbf{d}/x])$ determines a continuous function, which, by application of Ψ, is mapped to an element of $\mathcal{D}_\infty$.

$$\mathcal{V}[\![\lambda x.M]\!](\rho) = \Psi(\lambda \mathbf{d} \in \mathcal{D}_\infty.\mathcal{V}[\![M]\!](\rho[\mathbf{d}/x]))$$ ∎

[9] We use emphatic brackets, $[\![$ and $]\!]$ to enclose the terms of the λ-calculus being mapped by the semantic function $\mathcal{V}$.

In the last equation we used the notation $\lambda\mathbf{d} \in \mathcal{D}_\infty$. The term thus built is *not* a term of the formal λ-calculus. We are using the notation informally to describe a function on the domain $\mathcal{D}_\infty$, and thus the argument $\mathbf{d}$ is restricted to being an element of that domain.

To establish that this interpretation of terms provides a model for the λ-calculus, we must show that every theorem of the λ-calculus is true in $\mathcal{D}_\infty$. In order to accomplish this we must know how to interpret equations between terms in $\mathcal{D}_\infty$; then we can show that all the rules of inference of the λ-calculus preserve truth in $\mathcal{D}_\infty$. (Recall that the axioms were given as rules of inference with no hypotheses.)

DEFINITION: We define two terms M and N to be ***semantically equivalent***, or ***equal in*** $\mathcal{D}_\infty$, if they have the same value in $\mathcal{D}_\infty$ for all values of their free variables:

$$M =_{\mathcal{D}_\infty} N \quad \text{iff } \mathcal{V}[\![M]\!](\rho) = \mathcal{V}[\![N]\!](\rho) \text{ for all } \rho$$ ■

Since $\mathcal{D}_\infty$ is a complete lattice, we know that $=_{\mathcal{D}_\infty}$ is a substitutive equivalence relation. Therefore rules (ρ), (σ), (τ), (μ), (ν), and (ξ) are valid. To prove the validity of the conversion rules, since they are defined in terms of substitution, we need a lemma relating substitution and extended environments similar to the substitution lemma (3.2.1 on page 53) of predicate calculus. First, however, we list some properties of environments that follow from the definitions.

LEMMA 5.5.4 For all $\rho \in Env; \mathbf{d}, \mathbf{d}' \in \mathcal{D}_\infty; x, x' \in Id$, and $M \in Exp$,

1. $x' \equiv x$ implies $\rho[\mathbf{d}/x][\mathbf{d}'/x'] = \rho[\mathbf{d}'/x']$ — that is, if you change the binding of the same variable twice, the effect on the environment is the same as if you had made only the latest change.

2. $x' \not\equiv x$ implies $\rho[\mathbf{d}/x][\mathbf{d}'/x'] = \rho[\mathbf{d}'/x'][\mathbf{d}/x]$ — that is, it makes no difference in what order you modify the bindings of two distinct variables (note that we are binding a variable with a value in the domain, not an expression that may involve other variables).

3. If $x \notin \mathcal{FV}(M)$, then

   a. $\mathcal{V}[\![M]\!](\rho[\mathbf{d}/x]) = \mathcal{V}[\![M]\!](\rho)$

   b. $\mathcal{V}[\![M]\!](\rho[\mathbf{d}/x][\mathbf{d}'/x']) = \mathcal{V}[\![M]\!](\rho[\mathbf{d}'/x'])$

Intuitively, we understand that the binding of x has no effect on the value of a term with no free occurrences of x.

The next lemma, the analogue of Lemma 3.2.1, says that extending environments correctly reflects substitution.

Lemma 5.5.5 (The substitution lemma) For all $M, N \in Exp$, $x \in Id$, and $\rho \in Env$,[10]

$$\mathcal{V}[\![[N/x]M]\!](\rho) = \mathcal{V}[\![M]\!](\rho[\mathcal{V}[\![N]\!](\rho)/x])$$

The proof of this lemma is not difficult, but it is very long and tedious, and is omitted here. One may find it in Wadsworth [41]. Now we are ready to prove that the conversion rules are valid in $\mathcal{D}_\infty$.

Theorem 5.5.6 If $M = N$ by one of the conversion rules, (α), (β), or (η), then $M =_{\mathcal{D}_\infty} N$ — i.e.,

(α) $\lambda x.M =_{\mathcal{D}_\infty} \lambda y.[y/x]M$, provided $y \notin \mathcal{FV}(M)$

(β) $(\lambda x.M)N =_{\mathcal{D}_\infty} [N/x]M$

(η) $\lambda x.Mx =_{\mathcal{D}_\infty} M$, provided $x \notin \mathcal{FV}(M)$

Proof: In the following we use $=$ rather than $=_{\mathcal{D}_\infty}$ for the lattice equality relation.

(α) 1. $\mathcal{V}[\![\lambda y.[y/x]M]\!](\rho) = \Psi(\lambda \mathbf{d} \in \mathcal{D}_\infty.\mathcal{V}[\![[y/x]M]\!](\rho[\mathbf{d}/y]))$
by 3 of the definition of $\mathcal{V}$, page 189

2. $= \Psi(\lambda \mathbf{d} \in \mathcal{D}_\infty.\mathcal{V}[\![M]\!](\rho[\mathbf{d}/y][\mathcal{V}[\![y]\!](\rho[\mathbf{d}/y])/x]))$
by Lemma 5.5.5

3. $= \Psi(\lambda \mathbf{d} \in \mathcal{D}_\infty.\mathcal{V}[\![M]\!](\rho[\mathbf{d}/y][\mathbf{d}/x]))$
by the definition of $\mathcal{V}$, $\mathcal{V}[\![y]\!](\rho[\mathbf{d}/y]) = \mathbf{d}$

4. $= \Psi(\lambda \mathbf{d} \in \mathcal{D}_\infty.\mathcal{V}[\![M]\!](\rho[\mathbf{d}/x]))$
by Lemma 5.5.4, 3b, since $y \notin \mathcal{FV}(M)$

5. $= \mathcal{V}[\![\lambda x.M]\!](\rho)$ by 3 of the definition of $\mathcal{V}$

[10] Note the difference between the notations $\rho[\mathbf{d}/x]$, and $[d/x]M$. In the first, we get the extended environment where $\mathbf{d}$ is substituted for the value of x. In $[d/x]M$, we get the expression M with all free occurrences of x replaced by the identifier d.

(β) 1. $\mathcal{V}[\![(\lambda x.M)N]\!](\rho) = \Phi(\Psi(\lambda \mathbf{d} \in \mathcal{D}_\infty.\mathcal{V}[\![M]\!](\rho[\mathbf{d}/x])))(\mathcal{V}[\![N]\!](\rho))$ by 2 and 3 of the definition of $\mathcal{V}$

2. $= (\lambda \mathbf{d} \in \mathcal{D}_\infty.\mathcal{V}[\![M]\!](\rho[\mathbf{d}/x]))(\mathcal{V}[\![N]\!](\rho))$ since $\Phi(\Psi(\mathbf{f})) = \mathbf{f}$

3. $= \mathcal{V}[\![M]\!](\rho[\mathcal{V}[\![N]\!](\rho)/x])$ by function application in the domain

4. $= \mathcal{V}[\![[N/x]M]\!](\rho)$ by the substitution lemma

(η) By the (informal) definition of the typed lambda notation (page 190), we know that for all $\mathbf{f} \in [\mathcal{D}_\infty \rightarrow \mathcal{D}_\infty]$ and $\mathbf{d} \in \mathcal{D}_\infty$, $(\lambda \mathbf{d} \in \mathcal{D}_\infty.\mathbf{f}(\mathbf{d}))(\mathbf{d}) = \mathbf{f}(\mathbf{d})$. So, by the definition of equality in the function space $[\mathcal{D}_\infty \rightarrow \mathcal{D}_\infty]$ (that is, that two functions are equal if and only if they have the same value on all arguments in the domain), we know that

$$(\lambda \mathbf{d} \in \mathcal{D}_\infty.\mathbf{f}(\mathbf{d})) = \mathbf{f}, \quad \text{for all } \mathbf{f} \in [\mathcal{D}_\infty \rightarrow \mathcal{D}_\infty] \qquad (5.5)$$

Then, considering the rule (η),

1. $\mathcal{V}[\![\lambda x.Mx]\!](\rho) = \Psi(\lambda \mathbf{d} \in \mathcal{D}_\infty.\mathcal{V}[\![Mx]\!](\rho[\mathbf{d}/x]))$ by 3 of the definition of $\mathcal{V}$

2. $= \Psi(\lambda \mathbf{d} \in \mathcal{D}_\infty.\Phi(\mathcal{V}[\![M]\!](\rho[\mathbf{d}/x]))(\mathcal{V}[\![x]\!](\rho[\mathbf{d}/x])))$ by 2 of the definition of $\mathcal{V}$

3. $= \Psi(\mathcal{V}\mathbf{d} \in \mathcal{D}_\infty.\Phi(\mathcal{V}[\![M]\!](\rho))(\mathbf{d}))$ since $x \notin \mathcal{FV}(M)$, and by 1 of the definition of $\mathcal{V}$

4. $= \Psi(\Phi(\mathcal{V}[\![M]\!](\rho)))$ by (5.5) with $\mathbf{f} \equiv \Phi(\mathcal{V}[\![M]\!](\rho))$

5. $= \mathcal{V}[\![M]\!](\rho)$ since $\Psi(\Phi(\mathbf{x})) = \mathbf{x}$

■

THEOREM 5.5.7 The interpretation defined by the function $\mathcal{V}$ and the relation $=_{\mathcal{D}_\infty}$, constitutes a model for the λ-calculus system based on $\alpha\beta\eta$-conversion — that is,

$$M \ \alpha\beta\eta\text{-}cnv \ N \text{ implies } M =_{\mathcal{D}_\infty} N$$

The proof is just a combination of the results from Lemmas 5.5.4 and 5.5.5, and Theorem 5.5.6.

5.6 Completeness

We have shown that the interpretation given by $\mathcal{V}$ and $=_{\mathcal{D}_\infty}$ provides a model for the λ-calculus. It is convenient at this point to simplify notation by:

1. allowing the terms themselves to stand for their values in $\mathcal{D}_\infty$ — i.e., writing M rather than insisting on $\mathcal{V}[\![M]\!](\rho)$.

2. identifying elements of $\mathcal{D}_\infty$ with their images in $[\mathcal{D}_\infty \rightarrow \mathcal{D}_\infty]$ under Φ (and correspondingly identifying functions in $[\mathcal{D}_\infty \rightarrow \mathcal{D}_\infty]$ with their images in $\mathcal{D}_\infty$ under Ψ), rather than writing in all the explicit uses of Φ and Ψ.

To be precise, we have lost no information in this simplification of notation, allowing terms to denote their values in $\mathcal{D}_\infty$, if we understand that:

1. Free variables range over $\mathcal{D}_\infty$.

2. By the abstraction $\lambda x.M$, we mean the image under Ψ of the function described by the value of M where x is restricted to ranging over $\mathcal{D}_\infty$.

3. When a term occurs as the rator of a combination, we really mean its image under Φ.

By virtue of Theorem 5.5.7, we may use the conversion rules to manipulate these (terms denoting) elements of $\mathcal{D}_\infty$ and their images in $[\mathcal{D}_\infty \rightarrow \mathcal{D}_\infty]$. When necessary for clarity or emphasis, we can fall back on the formal notation and write in the appropriate $\mathcal{V}$, ρ, Φ, or Ψ, but most of the time we are willing to accept the ambiguity in order to simplify the notation.

A model is not very interesting if all terms are equal; thus, we might ask whether there are terms that are not equal in $\mathcal{D}_\infty$. We know that $\mathcal{D}_\infty$ is a complete lattice, and thus, just as lattice equality determined the relation $=_{\mathcal{D}_\infty}$ between terms, so the partial order of the lattice $\sqsubseteq$ induces a partial order relation between terms:

$$M \sqsubseteq N \qquad \text{iff } \mathcal{V}[\![M]\!](\rho) \sqsubseteq \mathcal{V}[\![N]\!](\rho) \text{ for all } \rho \in Env^{11}$$

[11] We use the uncluttered symbol, $\sqsubseteq$ instead of $\sqsubseteq_{\mathcal{D}_\infty}$, for the relation induced by the partial order of the lattice.

This partial order is substitutive — that is, $M \sqsubseteq N$ implies that $C[M] \sqsubseteq C[N]$ for all contexts $C[\,]$.

We now show that not only are there terms that are unequal in the model, but there are terms that are unrelated by the partial order as well. (Remember: We are stating these results about the *elements* of $\mathcal{D}_\infty$ that are *denoted by* the terms used in the statement.)

LEMMA 5.6.1

1. The terms K and KI are incomparable.[12]

2. The terms I and K are incomparable.

Proof:

1. Suppose $K \sqsubseteq KI$. Then, since $\sqsubseteq$ is substitutive,

   $$x = Kxy \sqsubseteq KIxy = y \text{ holds for all } x, y \in \mathcal{D}_\infty.$$

   But then $x \sqsubseteq y$ and $y \sqsubseteq x$ (i.e., $x = y$, for all $x, y \in \mathcal{D}_\infty$), contradicting our assumption that $\mathcal{D}_\infty$ contains more than one element. Hence $K \not\sqsubseteq KI$. Similarly, $KI \not\sqsubseteq K$.

2. Note that $II(Kx)y = x$, while $KI(Kx)y = y$. Then the proof follows as in 1, showing that $I \not\sqsubseteq K$ and $K \not\sqsubseteq I$. ■

Theorem 5.5.7 guarantees that if $M = N$ is provable (by the conversion rules) then $M =_{\mathcal{D}_\infty} N$. Are there any circumstances under which we can claim that $M =_{\mathcal{D}_\infty} N$ implies $\vdash M = N$? In fact, we can show that *if* M and N have normal forms, then they are equal in the model if and only if M *cnv* N. This shown as a consequence of Böhm's Theorem (5.6.2), which deals with the separability of terms with distinct normal forms.

DEFINITION: Two terms M and N are said to be ***separable*** if there is a context $C[\,]$ such that $C[M]$ *cnv* I and $C[N]$ *cnv* K. ■

THEOREM 5.6.2 (Böhm's Theorem) If M and N have distinct — not α-convertible — normal forms, then M and N are separable.

[12] K and I are defined on page 164.

We will not prove it here.[13] Böhm's proof provides an effective procedure for finding the separating context, which, in the case of closed terms is just

$$[\,]X_1 \ldots X_k, \quad k > 0, \text{ where } X_i \text{ is closed for each } i, \ 0 < i \leq k$$

We knew by the Church–Rosser Theorem that if M and N have distinct normal forms, then we cannot prove $M = N$ using the conversion rules. Böhm's Theorem leads to a stronger statement — if we ever added as an extra axiom for the λ-calculus an equality between two distinct normal forms, the theory would be inconsistent.

Corollary 5.6.2.1 If M and N have distinct normal forms, and $M = N$ is provable, then $X = Y$ is provable for all terms X and Y (and thus the theory is inconsistent by def2 on page 162).

Proof: Assume M and N have distinct normal forms. Then there is a context $C[\,]$ such that $C[M]$ *cnv* I and $C[N]$ *cnv* K, but then, since $=$ is substitutive,

$$\begin{aligned} C[M]I(KX)Y &= C[N]I(KX)Y \\ II(KX)Y &= KI(KX)Y \\ I(KX)Y &= IY \\ KXY &= Y \\ X &= Y \end{aligned}$$

and thus $X = Y$ for all terms X and Y. ■

Corollary 5.6.2.2 If M and N have distinct normal forms, then M and N are incomparable in $\mathcal{D}_\infty$.

Proof: Let $C[\,]$ be the context determined by Theorem 5.6.2. If $M \sqsubseteq N$, then $I =_{\mathcal{D}_\infty} C[M] \sqsubseteq C[N] =_{\mathcal{D}_\infty} K$, contradicting Lemma 5.6.1. ■

So the conversion rules are complete for terms having normal forms. That is, for all terms M, N having normal forms, $M = N$ is provable

[13] The original reference in Italian is Böhm, C., "Alcune proprieta delle forme β-η-normali nel λ-κ-calcols," Consiglio Nazionali delle Richerche, No. 696, Roma, 1968. It has since been reprinted in [10], pages 156–162.

if and only if $M =_{\mathcal{D}_\infty} N$ if and only if M and N both *red* to the same (up to α-*cnv*) normal form by normal order reduction.

However, we have no such results for terms without normal forms. In particular, Corollary 5.6.2.2 tells us nothing if either M or N fails to have a normal form. All the claims made so far apply to all lattice models of the λ-calculus; the properties of terms without normal forms depend on the deeper structure of particular models, and we have yet to discuss an ordering of these terms from a computational point of view.

For an explicit construction of the models discovered by Scott in 1969, see [33], [37], or [40]. It is worth noting that we do not expect completeness of the conversion rules for all equations between terms; in particular, there are examples, such as unsolvable terms, that are not interconvertible but do behave alike from a computational point of view. We want such terms to be considered equal even though we know we cannot prove them equal. For Scott's original models there is a kind of "completeness in the limit" of the rules of conversion that does hold. This leads to a characterization of the relation $\sqsubseteq$ (and also of the relation $=_{\mathcal{D}_\infty}$) between terms that has a natural interpretation as the notion of computational approximation discussed at the beginning of Section 5.5.1.

The following theorems are proved in Wadsworth, [41] using laws obtained from the properties of the construction of Scott's models.

THEOREM 5.6.3

1. For $\Delta \equiv \lambda x.xx$, $\Delta\Delta \;=\; \bot$.
2. For $Y_\lambda \;\equiv\; \lambda f.(\lambda x.f(xx))(\lambda x.f(xx))$, $Y_\lambda \;=\; \mathbf{Y}$, where $\mathbf{Y}$ is the lattice-theoretic least fixed point operator (see page 185).
3. For $J \;\equiv\; Y_\lambda F$ with $F \equiv \lambda f.\lambda x.\lambda y.x(fy)$, $J \;=\; I$.

We have made use of the notational convenience of representing values in $\mathcal{D}_\infty$ by the terms denoting them in the λ-calculus. For example, to state part 1 of the theorem precisely, we would say:

$$\mathcal{V}[\![\Delta\Delta]\!](\rho) \;=\; \bot \qquad \text{for all } \rho$$

And in part 2 we should explain that we know from lattice theory that the function

$$\mathbf{Y} : [\mathcal{D}_\infty \to \mathcal{D}_\infty] \to \mathcal{D}_\infty$$

defined by

$$\mathbf{Y}(\mathbf{f}) = \bigsqcup\{\mathbf{f_n}\}$$

maps continuous functions to their least fixed points. Moreover, $\mathbf{Y}$ itself is continuous, so $\mathbf{Y} \in [\mathcal{D}_\infty \rightarrow \mathcal{D}_\infty]$ and we can use Ψ to map $\mathbf{Y}$ onto an element of $\mathcal{D}_\infty$; that is, $\mathbf{Y}$ is the element $\mathbf{Y}_\infty \in \mathcal{D}_\infty$ given by

$$\mathbf{Y}_\infty \equiv \Psi(\lambda f \in \mathcal{D}_\infty.\mathbf{Y}(\Phi(f))) = \Psi(\mathbf{Y} \circ \Phi)$$

Then, properly stated, 2 reads: For all ρ, $\mathcal{V}[\![Y_\lambda]\!](\rho) = \mathbf{Y}_\infty$.

Theorem 5.6.4 *I is the only fixed point of $F \equiv \lambda f.\lambda x.\lambda y.x(fy)$ in $\mathcal{D}_\infty$.*

Lemma 5.6.5 For $G \equiv \lambda y.\lambda f.f(yf)$ we have $\mathbf{Y}(G) = \mathbf{Y} = G(\mathbf{Y})$.

Again, the proofs of the above depend upon specific properties that follow from the construction of Scott's original models and thus are not presented here.

Theorem 5.6.6 Let

$$\begin{aligned} Y^0 &\equiv Y_\lambda \\ Y^{i+1} &\equiv Y^i(G) \quad i \geq 0 \end{aligned}$$

then, for all $i \geq 0$, $Y^i = \mathbf{Y}$

Proof:

Basis case: $i = 0$. This is just Theorem 5.6.3, part 2.

Induction step: Assume $Y^k = \mathbf{Y}$ for all $k \leq i$; show $Y^{i+1} \equiv \mathbf{Y}$.

1. $Y^{i+1} \equiv Y^i(G)$ — by definition
2. $Y^i = \mathbf{Y}(G)$ — by the induction hypothesis
3. $\mathbf{Y}(G) = \mathbf{Y}$ — by Lemma 5.6.5.

■

David Park showed (see [30]) that although $Y^0 = Y^1$ in Scott's models, we cannot prove this equation using the conversion rules, and therefore the λ-calculus, as defined on page 155, is incomplete (with respect to Scott's models). The notions of approximations and approximate normal forms provide motivation for expecting that the Y^i's are all equal. Perhaps more surprising is the equality between I and J, since one of these terms has a normal form while the other does not. In fact, as the following corollary states, *every* term with a normal form is equal to some term having no normal form.

Corollary 5.6.6.1 For any normal form N, there is a λ-term X, with no normal form, such that $N =_{\mathcal{D}_\infty} X$.

Proof: We need to replace a part of N with another term that is equal to the part being replaced, in such a way that we can guarantee that the new term does not have a normal form. We choose to replace the rightmost occurrence of an identifier y in N by the term $Y_\lambda(F)(y)$ to get the desired term X. We know that $Y_\lambda(F)(y) = y$ since $Y_\lambda(F) = I$. Thus, $N = X$ and since N was in normal form, we know that the only redex of the new term is $Y_\lambda(F)$, which has no normal form, thus causing X to have no normal form. ■

This result may seem surprising at first, but in fact we shall see several computational analogues of this relationship.

Exercises 5.6

1. What is a fixpoint?

2. What is a fixpoint operator?

3. Let $A \equiv \lambda z.\lambda x.x(zzx)$ and $F \equiv AA$ Prove that F is (or is not) a fixpoint operator.

5.6.1 The λ-Ω-calculus

We have seen several examples of terms that are equal in Scott's models but cannot be proved so by the theory of conversion. We have indicated that this is as we should expect. Given the rule of functional extensionality (page 156), together with the fact that any term can be rator of a combination, an equation between terms tells us an infinite number of facts — specifically, that applying the left hand function to any argument gives the same result as applying the right hand function. In general, it is impossible (because of Gödel's incompleteness results) to effectively axiomatize all true equations of such a functional kind. (We might also note that all of recursive function theory is representable in the λ-calculus. We hinted at this possibility in the exercises at the end of Section 5.3.)

In spite of the fact that the theory is too weak to prove all true equations between terms in $\mathcal{D}_\infty$, all implementations of the λ-calculus are based on the reduction rules. In programming, as in Section 5.3, we are not as concerned with proving terms equal as we are with computing the values (normal forms) of terms by successive reduction. Of course, a programming language allows a richer variety of structures than the identifiers, combinations, and abstractions of the pure λ-calculus. However, the computations performed on these structures (stacks, arrays, symbol tables, trees, queues, etc.) are conceptually equivalent to the process of reduction. We evaluate an expression by reducing it to a normal form. So, if our model is to be relevant to computation, there should be some connection between our semantics for the λ-calculus, given via $\mathcal{D}_\infty$ and the function $\mathcal{V}$, and the means of computation, given by the reduction rules.

To establish this connection, we formalize the notion of approximation. We extend the ordinary (syntactic) theory of the λ-calculus to allow partial terms and partial, or approximate, reductions, in much the same way that Scott's more general (semantic) theory of computation extends the conventional notion of discrete data types to allow partial (and infinite) objects and approximations to them. Then we can discuss limits of better and better approximations and tie these in with the notion of limit we already have in the lattice models.

To simplify matters, we will be concerned only with β-reductions (ignoring η-reductions). Suppose we wish to evaluate a term M. We begin by reducing M according to the conversion rules. If the reduction terminates with a normal form, we take it as the value of M. However, even if the reduction does not terminate, we may be able to learn something about the value of M from the intermediate terms in the reduction. For example, suppose we have reduced M to the term

$$M_1 \equiv \lambda x.\lambda y.y(x((\lambda z.P)Q))(xy)((\lambda w.R)S)$$

where P, Q, R, and S are terms. We don't know whether or not M has a normal form, because there are still at least two β-redexes in M_1, $((\lambda z.P)Q)$ and $((\lambda w.R)S)$. However, we can say that if M_1 is going to have a normal form, it must be of the form

$$\lambda x.\lambda y.y(x(\ ?\ ))(xy)(\ ?\ )$$

because any further β-reduction of M_1 can affect only the parts where ? is written.

DEFINITION: We adjoin to the λ-calculus the special constant symbol Ω to stand for the undetermined parts of normal forms. Replacing each ? by Ω, we get

$$A_1 \equiv \lambda x.\lambda y.y(x(\Omega))(xy)(\Omega)$$

A_1 is called a ***partial normal form*** of M because it gives us partial information about the normal form of M (if it exists). ■

Since we have extended the language, we also need to extend the definition of the semantic function $\mathcal{V}$(page 189). We add the clause:

$$4.\ \ \mathcal{V}[\![\Omega]\!](\rho) = \perp$$

Thus, under the induced partial ordering between terms, Ω must approximate every term (i.e., $\Omega \sqsubseteq M$ for all terms M; by substitutivity we have $A_1 \sqsubseteq M_1$; and since reductions preserve values in $\mathcal{D}_\infty$, we have $A_1 \sqsubseteq M$).

DEFINITION: A partial normal form A_1 is called an ***approximate normal form*** of every term that it approximates. ■

Thus A_1 is an approximate normal form of M (as well as of M_1). So, to obtain an approximate normal form of a term M, we reduce it to an intermediate term M_1, then replace any remaining β-redexes by Ω. Since this process can be performed on all terms to which M reduces, we can obtain a set of approximate normal forms of M. The limit of this set in $\mathcal{D}_\infty$ is equal to the value of the term M.

This is the "completeness in the limit" referred to earlier. Although the reductions of a term may not terminate, producing a normal form in a finite amount of time, we can say these reductions produce approximate normal forms that converge to the value of the term in the limit. We formalize these ideas in the following.

DEFINITION: The theory that allows the term Ω is called the ***λΩ-calculus***. Terms of this calculus will be called ***approximate terms***, or ***λΩ-terms***, those of the usual λ-calculus will continue to be called terms. ■

We have added to our language; we also need to add new rules of inference dealing with the new term Ω.

DEFINITION: The $\lambda\Omega$-calculus has all the rules of inference of the λ-calculus, with the additional rules:

$$\begin{array}{lrcl} (\Omega_1) & \Omega M & = & \Omega \\ (\Omega_2) & \lambda x.\Omega & = & \Omega \end{array}$$ ■

From the interpretation of Ω as $\bot$, it is immediate that the two ***Ω-conversion*** rules defined above are valid in $\mathcal{D}_\infty$. As expected, the left hand sides of these rules are called ***Ω-redexes***, and ***Ω-reductions***, etc., are defined analogously to the β- and η- terminology.

DEFINITION: A $\lambda\Omega$-term is said to be in ***approximate normal form*** if it does not contain a β-redex, and in ***Ω-normal form*** if it is not Ω-reducible. An approximate normal form is called a ***proper normal form*** if it does not contain any occurrences of Ω. ■

DEFINITION: An ***Ω-match of*** M is a $\lambda\Omega$-term A that is identical to M except at subterms that are occurrences of Ω in A. A is a ***direct approximant*** of M if A is an Ω-match of M and is in approximate normal form, and is the ***best direct approximant*** of M if Ω occurs in A only at the subterms corresponding to the β-redexes in M. A is an ***approximate normal form*** of M if A is a direct approximant of a term to which M is reducible; if A is in Ω-normal form, A is said to be a ***reduced approximant*** of M. ■

For example, M reduces to

$$M_1 \equiv \lambda x.\lambda y.y(x((\lambda x.P)Q)(xy)((\lambda w.R)S)$$

$$\begin{array}{rcl} A_1 & \equiv & \lambda x.\lambda y.y\Omega(xy)\Omega \\ A_2 & \equiv & \lambda x.\lambda y.\Omega \end{array}$$

$$A_3 \equiv \lambda x.\lambda y.\Omega(x\Omega)\Omega\Omega$$
$$A_4 \equiv \lambda x.\lambda y.y(x\Omega)(xy)\Omega$$
$$A_5 \equiv \lambda x.\lambda y.y\Omega\Omega((\lambda w.R)S)$$

Each of A_1–A_4 is in approximate normal form (no β-redexes).

A_1, A_4, and A_5 are in Ω-normal form (no Ω-redexes).
Each A_i is an Ω-match of M_1.
Each of A_1–A_4 is a direct approximant of M_1.
A_4 is the best direct approximant of M_1.
Each of A_1–A_4 is an approximate normal form of M.
A_1 and A_4 are reduced approximants of M.

It follows from the definitions above that every direct approximant $\sqsubseteq$ the best direct approximant. As another example, consider the paradoxical combinator:

$$\begin{array}{rcl} Y_\lambda & \equiv & \lambda f.(\lambda x.f(xx))(\lambda x.f(xx)) \\ & \textit{red} & \lambda f.f((\lambda x.f(xx))(\lambda x.f(xx))) \\ & \textit{red} & \lambda f.f(f((\lambda x.f(xx))(\lambda x.f(xx)))) \\ & \vdots & \\ & \textit{red} & \lambda f.f(f(\ldots f((\lambda x.f(xx))(\lambda x.f(xx)))\ldots)) \end{array}$$

The set of approximate normal forms of Y_λ is[14]

$$\{\lambda f.f^n(\Omega) \mid n \geq 0\}$$

Thus there is a close relationship between the computational approximation to Y_λ and the definition of the fixpoint operator $\mathbf{Y}$ as the function of $\mathbf{f}$ that produces fixed points by taking the limit as $\mathbf{n} \to \infty$ of $\mathbf{f^n}(\bot)$ — that is,

$$\mathbf{Y} = \lambda \mathbf{f}. \bigsqcup_{\mathbf{n=0}}^{\infty} \mathbf{f^n}(\bot)$$

DEFINITION: We write $\mathcal{A}(M)$ for the set of all approximate normal forms of a term M. ■

[14] f^n is defined as on page 165.

In the limit theorem we need to consider *all* approximate normal forms of a term. We can no longer rely on normal order reduction (or any other order) to produce enough approximations to guarantee convergence to the term in the limit. For example, consider the term:

$$M \equiv \lambda x.x(\Delta\Delta)((\lambda y.P)Q)$$

Since $(\Delta\Delta)$ is the leftmost redex, using normal order reduction reduces M only to itself. Thus, the only approximate normal form derivable in this way is

$$A \equiv \lambda x.x\Omega\Omega$$

Certainly M is not equal to the "limit" of this one-element set, as $M \not\sqsubseteq A$ (unless $((\lambda y.P)Q)$ has value $\bot$ in the model). To get all the information available about M, we must consider what happens when $((\lambda y.P)Q)$ is reduced. In particular, if it reduces to a normal form N, then $\lambda x.x\Omega N$ is an approximate normal form of M that must be considered.

Lemma 5.6.7 If M_0 *β-red* M_1, and if A_0 and A_1 are the best direct approximants of M_0 and M_1 respectively, then $A_0 \sqsubseteq A_1$. (The process of taking best direct approximants is monotonic with respect to β-reduction.)

The proof of this lemma is not difficult but it is very long and tedious. It is given in Appendix 1 to Chapter 6 of Wadsworth ([41]).

Corollary 5.6.7.1 For any term M, the set $\mathcal{A}(M)$ is directed.

Proof: From Lemma 5.5.2, page 185, we know that $\mathcal{A}(M)$ is directed if and only if it is nonempty and every pair of elements in $\mathcal{A}(M)$ has an upper bound in $\mathcal{A}(M)$.

1. $\mathcal{A}(M)$ is nonempty since $\Omega \in \mathcal{A}(M)$ for any term M.

2. Suppose A_1 and A_2 are two elements of $\mathcal{A}(M)$. Let M_1 and M_2 be the terms to which M is reducible for which A_1 and A_2 are direct approximants. Let A_1' and A_2' be the best direct approximants of M_1 and M_2. (Clearly $A_1 \sqsubseteq A_1'$ and $A_2 \sqsubseteq A_2'$.)

   Now, M_1 *cnv* M_2, so by the Church–Rosser Theorem, there exists a term M_3, such that M_1 *red* M_3 and M_2 *red* M_3. Let A_3 be the best direct approximant of M_3; thus, $A_3 \in \mathcal{A}(M)$. A_3 is an upper bound of A_1 and A_2, since $A_1 \sqsubseteq A_1'$, $A_2 \sqsubseteq A_2'$, and by Lemma 5.6.7 $A_1' \sqsubseteq A_3$ and $A_2' \sqsubseteq A_3$. ■

We state the limit theorem precisely, using $\mathcal{V}$ and ρ to emphasize the distinction between syntactic terms of the λ-calculus and values in $\mathcal{D}_\infty$.

Theorem 5.6.8 For all terms M and environments ρ,

$$\mathcal{V}[\![M]\!](\rho) = \bigsqcup\{\mathcal{V}[\![A]\!](\rho) \mid A \in \mathcal{A}(M)\}$$

(All terms are the limit of their approximate normal forms.)

This theorem (for proof see Wadsworth [41]) expresses precisely how we can consider the reduction rules to be complete in the limit. We can use the reduction rules to enumerate the set of terms to which some term M reduces. From these terms we can generate the approximate normal forms of M. Thus, there is an effective procedure for generating the elements of $\mathcal{A}(M)$. The theorem thus establishes that we can approximate the value of a term M by computing the values of its approximate normal forms.

We can also interpret the theorem as an assertion that *every* term has a normal form, but the normal form may be an infinite expression. If we were to allow such infinite expressions in the language we would have to guarantee that two terms have the same value in $\mathcal{D}_\infty$ if and only if they have the same infinite normal form. We will not pursue this possibility here.

Earlier we related truth, deduction, and computation (defined as normal order reduction) for terms with normal forms. Now, thanks to Theorem 5.6.8, we can relate truth, deduction, and computation (defined as head reduction) for those terms without normal forms that denote $\bot$ in the models.

Theorem 5.6.9 The following three conditions are equivalent:

1. $M =_{\mathcal{D}_\infty} \Omega$
2. M is unsolvable
3. M does not have a head normal form.

Proof:

1. $\Rightarrow$ 2. Suppose $M =_{\mathcal{D}_\infty} \Omega$ but M is solvable. Then there exists a head context $C_1[]$, such that $C_1[M]$ has a normal form

$$\begin{array}{rll} C_1[] & <\equiv & (\lambda x_1 \ldots x_n.[])X_1 \ldots X_m, \quad n \geq 0, \ m \geq 0 \\ C_1[M] & \mathit{red} & M_{C_1} \equiv (\lambda y_1 \ldots y_k.zM_1 \ldots M_n) \ \ k \geq 0, n \geq 0, \end{array}$$

Define $C_1'[]$ as follows:

$$C_1'[] \equiv \begin{cases} \lambda z.C_1[] & \text{if } z \text{ is free in } M_{C_1} \\ C_1[] & \text{if } z \text{ is bound in } M_{C_1} \end{cases}$$

Note that $\lambda z.C_1[M]$ *red* $\lambda z.M_{C_1}$, which is in normal form. Thus,

$$C_1'[M] \ \mathit{red} \ \lambda w_1 \ldots w_n.zM_1 \ldots M_m$$

where $n \geq 1$, $m \geq 0$, and $z \equiv w_i$ for some i, $1 \leq i \leq n$.
Define

$$X_j \equiv \begin{cases} I & \text{if } j \neq i \\ K^m X & \text{if } j = i \end{cases}$$

Then

$$\begin{array}{ll} C_1'[M]X_1 \ldots X_n & \\ \quad \mathit{red} & (\lambda w_1 \ldots w_n.zM_1 \ldots M_m)X_1 \ldots X_n \\ \quad \mathit{red} & K^m X[I \ldots K^m I \ldots I/w_1 \ldots w_i \ldots w_n]M_1 \ldots M_m \\ \quad \mathit{red} & X \end{array}$$

while

$$C_1[\Omega] \equiv (\lambda x_1 \ldots x_n.\Omega)X_1 \ldots X_m \ \mathit{red} \ \Omega$$

and so $C_1'[\Omega]$, which is either $\lambda z.C_1[\Omega]$ or simply $C_1[\Omega]$, also reduces to Ω. That is,

$$X =_{\mathcal{D}_\infty} C_1'[M]X_1 \ldots X_n =_{\mathcal{D}_\infty} \omega X_1 \ldots X_n =_{\mathcal{D}_\infty} \Omega$$

for all terms X, which is a contradiction.

2. $\Rightarrow$ 3. M is unsolvable. Suppose M has a head normal form

$$H \ \equiv \ \lambda x_1 \ldots x_n.zX_1 \ldots X_m \quad n, m \geq 0$$

where $z \ \equiv \ x_i$ for some i (since M is closed). Define $C[]$ to be $\lambda z.[]$ if z is free in H, and $[]$ otherwise. Then

$$C[H] = \lambda x_1 \ldots x_k.zX_1 \ldots X_m$$

where $k \geq 1$, $m \geq 0$, and $z \equiv x_i$ for some i, $1 \leq i \leq n$.

Let

$$N_j \equiv \begin{cases} I & \text{if } j \neq i \\ K^m I & \text{if } j = i \end{cases}$$

Then $C[M]N_1 \ldots N_k$ *red* I, so M is solvable, contradicting our initial assumption.

3. $\Rightarrow$ 1. Suppose M has no head normal form. Then no term M' to which M reduces is in head normal form. Thus every direct approximant of any term to which M reduces is of the form

$$A' \equiv \lambda x_1 \ldots x_n.\Omega X_1 \ldots X_m$$

But $A' =_{\mathcal{D}_\infty} \Omega$ by the rules (Ω_1) and (Ω_2). Since all the approximate normal forms of M are $=_{\mathcal{D}_\infty} \Omega$, their limit must also be $=_{\mathcal{D}_\infty} \Omega$, so $M =_{\mathcal{D}_\infty} \Omega$ by Theorem 5.6.8. ■

The idea of using approximate normal forms to compute approximations to the value of a term is further supported by the following theorem relating the results produced when terms and their approximants are used in the context of larger expressions.

Theorem 5.6.10 For all terms M and contexts $C[\,]$,

1. $C[M]$ has a normal form iff there exists $A \in \mathcal{A}(M)$, such that $C[A]$ has the same normal form.

2. $C[M]$ has a head normal form iff there exists $A \in \mathcal{A}(M)$, such that $C[A]$ has a similar head normal form.

Proof: Part 1 is proved in [41] by syntactic arguments based on the relative lengths of the normal order reductions of terms and their Ω-matches. We will prove part 2, which can be accomplished more easily by using Theorems 5.6.8 and 5.6.9.

$\Rightarrow$: $C[M]$ has a h.n.f. $\Rightarrow$ $C[M] \neq_{\mathcal{D}_\infty} \Omega$ by Theorem 5.6.9
$\lambda x.C[x]$ denotes a continuous function mapping the value of its argument x to the value of the term $C[x]$. Thus,

$$(\lambda x.C[x])(\bigsqcup\{A \mid A \in \mathcal{A}(M)\}) =_{\mathcal{D}_\infty} \bigsqcup\{C[A] \mid A \in \mathcal{A}(M)\}$$

So, by Theorem 5.6.8 and β-reduction,

$$C[M] =_{\mathcal{D}_\infty} \bigsqcup\{C[A] \mid A \in \mathcal{A}(M)\}$$

Then, since $\bigsqcup\{C[A] \mid A \in \mathcal{A}(M)\} \neq_{\mathcal{D}_\infty} \Omega$, there must exist an $A \in \mathcal{A}(M)$, such that $C[A] \neq_{\mathcal{D}_\infty} \Omega$, and thus, by Theorem 5.6.9, $C[A]$ has a head normal form.

$\Leftarrow$: $A \in \mathcal{A}(M)$ and $C[A]$ has a h.n.f. implies that $C[A] \neq_{\mathcal{D}_\infty} \Omega$ by Theorem 5.6.9.

Since $A \sqsubseteq M$, we know that $C[A] \sqsubseteq C[M]$, and thus $C[M] \neq_{\mathcal{D}_\infty} \Omega$, which, by Theorem 5.6.9, implies that $C[M]$ has a head normal form.

The head normal forms (h.n.f.'s) involved must be similar, for it can be shown that dissimilar head normal forms are incomparable under $\sqsubseteq$, while we know that

$$hnf\_of(C[A]) =_{\mathcal{D}_\infty} C[A] \sqsubseteq C[M] =_{\mathcal{D}_\infty} hnf\_of(C[M])$$

where $hnf\_of(X)$ stands for the head normal form of X. ∎

Corollary 5.6.10.1 Suppose U is unsolvable and $C[\,]$ is any context. Then

1. $C[U]$ has a normal form
   iff $C[\Omega]$ has the same normal form
   iff for all terms M, $C[M]$ has the same normal form
2. $C[U]$ has a head normal form
   iff $C[\Omega]$ has a similar head normal form
   iff for all terms M, $C[M]$ has a similar head normal form

So it makes sense to consider the unsolvable terms as representations of $\perp$, the least defined value in the models. We get no useful information from any term with an unsolvable subterm that we could not have gotten by completely ignoring that subterm. Theorem 5.6.10 guarantees that working with the approximations to a term, we can derive the same results we get with the complete term.

Not only can we guarantee, via Theorem 5.6.8, that every term M is the limit of its approximate normal forms, we can extend this result to approximate normal forms of $C[M]$ for any context $C[\,]$.

That is, the value of $C[M]$ is determined by the values of the approximations $C[A]$ where A is an approximate normal form of M.

Corollary 5.6.10.2 For all terms M and contexts $C[\,]$,

$$C[M] = \bigsqcup\{C[A] \mid A \in \mathcal{A}(M)\}$$

Proof: Consider the term $\lambda x.C[x]$, where $x \notin \mathcal{FV}(C[\,])$. This term denotes a continuous function in $[\mathcal{D}_\infty \to \mathcal{D}_\infty]$ that maps the value of its argument x to the value of the term $C[x]$. Thus,

$$\begin{array}{lll}
\multicolumn{3}{l}{\mathcal{V}[\![C[M]]\!]\rho} \\
= & \mathcal{V}[\![(\lambda x.C[x])M]\!]\rho & \text{by } (\beta) \text{ and def of substitution} \\
= & \Phi(\mathcal{V}[\![\lambda x.C[x]]\!]\rho)(\mathcal{V}[\![M]\!]\rho) & \text{def of } \mathcal{V} \\
= & \Phi(\mathcal{V}[\![\lambda x.C[x]]\!]\rho)(\bigsqcup\{\mathcal{V}[\![A]\!]\rho \mid A \in \mathcal{A}(M)\}) & \text{Theorem 5.6.8} \\
= & \bigsqcup\{\Phi(\mathcal{V}[\![\lambda x.C[x]]\!]\rho)(\mathcal{V}[\![A]\!]\rho) \mid A \in \mathcal{A}(M)\} & \text{by continuity} \\
= & \bigsqcup\{\mathcal{V}[\![C[A]]\!]\rho \mid A \in \mathcal{A}(M)\} & \text{def of } \mathcal{V}
\end{array}$$

■

In the case of functional application, taking $C[\,] \equiv F[\,]$, this specializes to

$$\mathcal{V}[\![FM]\!]\rho = \bigsqcup\{\mathcal{V}[\![FA]\!]\rho \mid A \in \mathcal{A}(M)\}$$

In other words, we can gain information about a function application if we can discover information about its argument. In particular, to get an approximate normal form of the application all we need is an approximate normal form of the argument.

We have investigated relationships between terms (and their approximate normal forms) and values in the models, but we have not yet shown a connection with a computation method. Theorems 5.6.8 and 5.6.9 capture the intuitive ideas that: (a) the behavior of terms is determined by their approximate normal forms, and (b) unsolvable terms behave as totally undefined functions.

We now wish to investigate the relationship between our means of computation and truth in the models. We will show that the equality $=_{\mathcal{D}_\infty}$ (and the partial order $\sqsubseteq$) can be characterized syntactically as a relation definable from the conversion rules.[15] Of course, we already

[15]Since the conversion rules are incomplete for these models, we know that *cnv* and $=_{\mathcal{D}_\infty}$ are not the same relation, but still a reasonable equivalence relation between terms should be characterizable via the conversion rules.

know that the formal λ-calculus is incomplete and therefore *cnv* and $=_{\mathcal{D}_\infty}$ cannot be equivalent. However, we can characterize some form of equivalence, using the conversion rules, that is not quite so limited as being able to prove equations between terms.

The following are several equivalence relations between terms definable from our discussion so far:

1. Syntactic identity: $M \equiv N$
   $M \equiv N$ iff M and N are identical terms

2. Interconvertibility: $M\,cnv\,N$
   $M\,cnv\,N$ iff $\lambda\beta\eta \vdash M = N$

3. Equality in $\mathcal{D}_\infty$: $M =_{\mathcal{D}_\infty} N$
   $M =_{\mathcal{D}_\infty} N$ iff $\mathcal{V}[\![M]\!](\rho) = \mathcal{V}[\![N]\!](\rho)$ for all $\rho \in Env$

4. Approximate normal form equivalence: $M \sim_a N$
   $M \sim_a N$ iff M and N have the same set of (Ω-reduced) approximate normal forms.

5. Normal form equivalence: $M \sim_n N$
   $M \sim_n N$ iff $(\forall C[\,],\ C[M]$ has a normal form iff $C[N]$ has the same normal form)

6. Head normal form equivalence: $M \sim_h N$
   $M \sim_h N$ iff $(\forall C[\,],\ C[M]$ has a h.n.f. iff $C[N]$ has a similar h.n.f.)

7. Solvably equivalent: $M \sim_s N$

DEFINITION: M and N are ***solvably equivalent*** if each is solvably extended by the other. ■

DEFINITION: M is ***solvably extended by*** N, written $M \leq_s N$, if and only if $\forall C[\,]$, $C[M]$ is solvable implies $C[N]$ is solvable. ■

The known implications among these equivalence relations are summarized by:

$$
\begin{array}{cl}
M \equiv N & \\
\Downarrow \quad \not\Uparrow & \\
M\, cnv\, N & \\
\Downarrow \quad \not\Uparrow & \text{take } M \equiv Y^0,\ N \equiv Y^1 \\
M \sim_a N & \\
\Downarrow \quad \Uparrow ? & \text{probably holds} \\
M \sim_n N & \\
\Downarrow \quad \not\Uparrow & \text{take } M \equiv I,\ N \equiv J \\
M =_{\mathcal{D}_\infty} N & \\
\Downarrow \quad \Uparrow & \text{to be shown} \\
M \sim_h N & \\
\Downarrow \quad \Uparrow & \\
M \sim_s N &
\end{array}
$$

We know that when terms have the same set of approximate normal forms, they will not only yield (the same) normal forms in the same contexts — i.e.,

$$M \sim_a N \text{ implies } M \sim_n N \qquad \text{from Theorem 5.6.10}$$

they will also have the same values in Scott's models — i.e.,

$$M \sim_a N \text{ implies } M =_{\mathcal{D}_\infty} N \qquad \text{from Theorem 5.6.8}$$

For arbitrary terms M and N it can be shown that

$$M \sim_n N \qquad \text{implies } M =_{\mathcal{D}_\infty} N \tag{5.6}$$

But the reverse implication does not hold. For example; let $M \equiv I$ and $N \equiv J \equiv Y_\lambda(\lambda f.\lambda x.\lambda y.x(fy))$, and consider the null context $[\,]$. In the null context, I has a normal form while J does not, so it is not the case that $I \sim_n J$; but we know $I =_{\mathcal{D}_\infty} J$ by Theorem 5.6.3.

The property of having a normal form is too restrictive for the converse of (5.6) to hold. However, if we consider the weaker property of having a head normal form then the implications can be established in both directions. Equivalently, since the property of having a h.n.f. is equivalent to that of being solvable (the proof of Lemma 5.4.1, page 169, required only h.n.f.), we shall show that:

$$M =_{\mathcal{D}_\infty} N \qquad \text{iff } M \sim_s N$$

From left to right, this is a consequence of terms being unsolvable only if they have value $\perp$ in $\mathcal{D}_\infty$. In the other direction the full proof is rather intricate but the result can be derived quite straightforwardly with the aid of a lemma we shall state here without proof (Lemma 5.6.13, below).

We introduce a weak version of the concept of separability introduced on page 194.

DEFINITION: The partial order relation $M \models\!\leq N$ of M being ***semi-separable*** from N is defined as follows:

$$M \models\!\leq N \qquad \text{iff } \exists C[\,],\ C[M]\ \mathit{red}\ \ I,\ C[N] \text{ is unsolvable}$$

and we say that two terms are semi-separable if either is semi-separable from the other. ■

LEMMA 5.6.11 If S is solvable, then there exists a context $C[\,]$ such that $C[S]$ *red* I, while uniformly for all unsolvable terms U, $C[U]$ is unsolvable. Thus, in particular:

$$S \text{ solvable and } U \text{ unsolvable implies } S \models\!\leq U$$

Proof: S is solvable implies that S has a head normal form (by Theorem 5.6.9), say,

$$S = \lambda x_1 \ldots x_n.xX_1 \ldots X_k$$

If $x = x_i$ for some i:

Let $C[\,] \equiv M_1 \ldots M_n$ where $M_i \equiv \lambda y_1 \ldots y_k I$ and $M_j \equiv I$ for $j \neq i$. Then $C[S]$ *red* I.

Since U has no head normal form and the head redex of $C[U]$ is the head redex of U, we know $C[U]$ has no head normal form, and thus, $C[U]$ is unsolvable.

If $x \neq x_i$ for all i:

Let $C[\,] \equiv (\lambda x.[\,])M_1 \ldots M_{n+1}$, where $M_1 \equiv \lambda y_1 \ldots y_k.I$ and $M_j \equiv I$ for $j > 1$. Then $C[S]$ *red* I. By Corollary 5.6.10.1, $C[U]$ has a head normal form if and only if $C[M]$ has a similar head normal form for all M. But, $C[S]$ *red* I and $C[\lambda x_1 \ldots x_n.xX_1 \ldots X_k(KI)]$ *red* KI and I

and KI are dissimilar. Thus, $C[U]$ has no head normal form and thus, by Theorem 5.6.9, $C[U]$ is unsolvable. ■

Corollary 5.6.11.1 Terms are semi-separable iff they are not solvably equivalent; further

$$M \mid\!\leq N \qquad \text{iff } M \not\leq_s N$$

Proof:

$M \mid\!\leq N$:

Then $\exists C[\,]$ such that $C[M]$ *red* I, while $C[N]$ is unsolvable. But then $C[\,]$ is a context showing M is *not* solvably extended by N, and so $M \not\leq_s N$ and thus $M \not\sim_s N$.

$M \not\sim_s N$:

Then either $M \not\leq_s N$ or $N \not\leq_s M$. (Without loss of generality, we'll assume the first.)

$M \not\leq_s N$ implies $\exists C[\,]$ such that $C[M]$ is solvable, while $C[N]$ is not. Therefore, $C[M]$ is I-solvable, so $\exists C'[\,]$ such that $C'[C[M]]$ *red* I, while $C'[C[N]]$ is unsolvable (by Lemma 5.6.11).

Let $C^*[\,] \equiv C'[C[\,]]$. Then

1. $C^*[M]$ *red* I

2. $C^*[N]$ is unsolvable So, by definition, $M \mid\!\leq_s N$. ■

Lemma 5.6.12 If U is unsolvable, then $I = U$ is inconsistent with the equality of all unsolvable terms.

Proof: If $I = U$ then $X = IX = UX$ for all terms X, which says that every term X is equal to an unsolvable term UX. Since we assume all unsolvable terms are equal we must conclude that *all* terms are equal — i.e., the theory is inconsistent. ■

Corollary 5.6.12.1 The equality of a solvable term and an unsolvable term is inconsistent with the equality of all unsolvable terms.

Proof: We will use λ^* to denote the extended theory of the λ-calculus with the additional inference rule:

$$\text{Uns:} \quad M,\ N \text{ both unsolvable} \vdash M = N$$

Let S be a solvable term and U be unsolvable. Suppose we postulate that $S = U$.

Let $C[\,]$ be the context given by Lemma 5.6.11. Then:
$\lambda^* + (S = U) \vdash$

1. $I = C[S]$ since $C[S]$ *red* I
2. $I = C[U]$ from $S = U$ by substitutivity
3. $I = U'$ where U' is unsolvable by choice of $C[\,]$

which implies inconsistency by Lemma 5.6.12. ■

Thus: S solvable, U unsolvable implies $\lambda^* + S = U$ is inconsistent. Since λ^* is consistent, this implies that it is not the case that $\lambda^* \vdash S = U$.

Lemma 5.6.13 Suppose A is in approximate normal form, N is an arbitrary term such that $A \not\sqsubseteq N$. Then A is not solvably extended by N, whence also A is semi-separable from N. (Proof omitted.)

Now we provide as close to a syntactic characterization of $=_{\mathcal{D}_\infty}$ as we have been able to establish. We state and prove this for the inequality $\neq_{\mathcal{D}_\infty}$ along with the stronger characterization of $(\not\sqsubseteq)$.[16]

Theorem 5.6.14 The following four conditions are equivalent:

1. $M \neq_{\mathcal{D}_\infty} N$ $(M \not\sqsubseteq N)$
2. M and N are semi-separable $(M \,|\!\leq N)$
3. M and N are not solvably equivalent $(M \not\leq_s N)$
4. $\lambda^* + (M = N)$ is inconsistent

Proof: Since 2 and 3 are equivalent by Corollary 5.6.11.1, it suffices to show that $1 \Rightarrow 2 \Rightarrow 4 \Rightarrow 1$.

$1 \Rightarrow 2$: Since every term is the limit of its approximate normal forms, $M \not\sqsubseteq N$ holds iff $A \not\sqsubseteq N$ for some $A \in \mathcal{A}(M)$. Hence:

[16] The latter written in parentheses for the first three conditions of Theorem 5.6.14.

1. $A \not\leq N$ by Lemma 5.6.13
2. $\exists C[\,]$, $C[A]\,red\ \ I$, $C[N]$ unsolvable by def of $\not\leq$
3. $\exists\ C[\,]$, $C[M]\,red\ \ I$, $C[N]$ unsolvable by Theorem 5.6.10, since $A \in \mathcal{A}(M)$
4. $M \not\leq N$ by definition of $\not\leq$

$2 \Rightarrow 4$: Suppose $M \not\leq N$ and let $C[\,]$ be a context that semi-separates them; i.e.,

$$C[M]\,red\ \ I,\ \ C[N] = U' \text{ is unsolvable.}$$

Then, as for the proof of Corollary 5.6.12.1:

$$\lambda^* + (M = N)\ \vdash\ I = C[M] = C[N] = U'$$

and, by Lemma 5.6.12, $\lambda^* + (M = N)$ is inconsistent.

$4 \Rightarrow 1$: Assume $\lambda^* + (M = N)$ is inconsistent. Since $\mathcal{D}_\infty$ models λ^*, if $M =_{\mathcal{D}_\infty} N$, then $\mathcal{D}_\infty$ also provides a model of $\lambda^* + (M = N)$, which is therefore consistent, since the $\mathcal{D}_\infty$ model is consistent. Thus $M \neq_{\mathcal{D}_\infty} N$. ∎

For closed terms, the characterization of $\not\sqsubseteq$ and similarly $\neq_{\mathcal{D}_\infty}$ specializes to the following theorem.

Theorem 5.6.15 For all closed terms M and N, the following three conditions are equivalent:

1. $M \not\sqsubseteq N$
2. There exist closed terms $X_1, \ldots, X_k$ $(k \geq 0)$ such that:
   $M X_1 \ldots X_k\ red\ \ I$
   $N X_1 \ldots X_k$ is unsolvable
3. There is a closed term F such that
   $FM\ red\ \ I$
   FN is unsolvable

Proof:

$3 \Rightarrow 1$: M and N are semi-separable, taking $C[\,] \equiv F[\,]$ and thus $M \not\sqsubseteq N$ by Theorem 5.6.14.

1 $\Rightarrow$ 2: This is a consequence of the construction of a semi-separating context for closed terms in a proof of Lemma 5.6.13 (which we omitted).

2 $\Rightarrow$ 3: Simply set $F \equiv \lambda z.zX_1 \ldots X_k$. ∎

We can gain some insight into the content of our characterization by looking back at the intuitive interpretation of $\not\sqsubseteq$ in Scott's theory in terms of information content. For domain elements **a** and **b**, $\mathbf{a} \sqsubseteq \mathbf{b}$ if **b** contains all the information of **a** (and possibly more). Thus $\mathbf{a} \not\sqsubseteq \mathbf{b}$ implies that **a** contains some information not provided by **b**. Then Theorem 5.6.14 shows that when there is a difference in the information content of (the values of) terms, this can be detected in their computational behavior — that is, when $M \not\sqsubseteq N$, there are two terms $A \equiv C[M]$ and $B \equiv C[N]$, differing only in one occurrence of M or N, such that the computation (normal order reduction) for A halts and yields the identity as output, while the computation for B fails to produce even a head normal form (which could at least provide partial information about the value of the term).

This computational aspect of our characterization of $\neq_{\mathcal{D}_\infty}$ has an obvious counterpart for programming languages. Suppose ϵ_1 and ϵ_2 are two phrases (well-formed program fragments) of a language $\mathcal{L}$.

Definition: Two phrases ϵ_1 and ϵ_2 are ***computationally semi-discrete*** if there are two programs $\mathcal{P}_1$ and $\mathcal{P}_2$ of language $\mathcal{L}$, differing only in that $\mathcal{P}_1$ contains an occurrence of ϵ_1 where $\mathcal{P}_2$ contains an occurrence of ϵ_2, such that the computation for $\mathcal{P}_1$ halts (say with output 0) while that for $\mathcal{P}_2$ is nonterminating and provides no output while running. ∎

Given a semantics for a programming language $\mathcal{L}$, we hope to establish that if ϵ_1 and ϵ_2 are semantically distinct (i.e., have different meanings), then they are computationally semi-discrete. If this and the converse holds, we can reasonably claim that the given semantics for $\mathcal{L}$ has the appropriate properties for reasoning about the computational behavior of programs of $\mathcal{L}$ — that is, it provides a reasonable model for $\mathcal{L}$. This is as close as we can hope to get (in light of Gödel's results) to establishing completeness for our computation method.

The characterization of $\neq_{\mathcal{D}_\infty}$ in terms of the inconsistency of extensions to λ^* (part 4, Theorem 5.6.14) also has some interesting consequences.

COROLLARY 5.6.15.1 There is no consistent extension of the relation $=_{\mathcal{D}_\infty}$ as an equivalence relation between terms; indeed, $=_{\mathcal{D}_\infty}$ provides the unique, maximal, consistent model of the theory λ^*.

Proof: Let $\approx$ be any equivalence relation between terms that provides a consistent model of λ^*. Then:

$$\begin{array}{lll} M \approx N & \Rightarrow \lambda^* + (M = N) \text{ is consistent} & \text{since} \approx \text{models } \lambda^* \\ & \Rightarrow M =_{\mathcal{D}_\infty} N & \text{by Theorem 5.6.14.} \end{array}$$

■

This corollary states that two terms are equal in $\mathcal{D}_\infty$ if and only if we have no compelling reason to say they are unequal — of course, being computationally semi-discrete is a necessary and sufficient reason to consider them unequal. Thus, extending the relation $=_{\mathcal{D}_\infty}$ to terms M and N that were not $=_{\mathcal{D}_\infty}$ causes an inconsistency.

Exercises 5.6.1

1. Reduce each of the following expressions to Ω-normal form, if possible. If not, state why not.

   a. $\lambda x.\lambda y.y((\lambda z.\Omega zz)y)(\lambda x.x\Omega x)$

   b. $\lambda x.\lambda y.y(\lambda x.((\lambda z.\Omega)yx)(xy)(\Omega yzy))$

5.6.2 Another look at I and J

We consider again the terms I and J where

$$\begin{array}{lll} I & \equiv & \lambda x.x \\ J & \equiv & Y_\lambda F \equiv (\lambda f.(\lambda x.f(xx))(\lambda x.f(xx)))(\lambda f.\lambda x.\lambda y.x(fy)) \end{array}$$

These are equal in Scott's models, although I has a normal form while J does not. These terms certainly do not look alike as presented here, and the fact that one has a normal form and the other does not makes one (initially) expect that they should represent different values. However, we've seen that we can get some information (through head normal forms) from terms with no normal form, so we do not wish to equate all terms without normal forms. Thus we've concluded that J is not equal to the (least defined) unsolvable terms, but why should it be equal to I? We've seen formal justification (see Theorem 5.6.3, page 196), but there are also intuitive reasons.

1. $I = J$ is a λ-calculus analogue of $3 = 2.999\ldots$. Attempting to reduce J to normal form leads to an infinite sequence of β-reductions producing terms of the form:

$$J = \lambda x_0.\lambda x_1.x_0(\lambda x_2.(x_1(\lambda x_3.x_2(\lambda x_4.x_3(\ldots))))) \qquad (5.7)$$

   The remaining redexes are always in the innermost parentheses, and with each reduction the part of the term not in normal form gets deeper and deeper. We might be tempted to consider (5.7) as an infinite normal form, while I is a finite normal form of the same value, just as 3 is a finite and $2.999\ldots$ an infinite representation of the same number.

2. J represents an infinite number of applications of the η-expansion operation. The operation η of η-expansion (replacing the right hand side of the (η) rule by the left hand side) can be expressed by

$$\eta(x) = \lambda y.xy, \quad \text{where } y \not\equiv x.$$

   By the (η) rule we know that η is an identity operation. We define an infinite η-expansion operator η_∞, obtained by recursively applying η-expansion to the newly introduced variable — i.e., the recursive operation

$$\eta_\infty(x) = \lambda y.x(\eta_\infty(y)), \quad \text{where } y \not\equiv x.$$

   J is a solution to this equation, thus J represents an infinite number of applications of an identity operation.

3. I and J are "interconvertible in the limit". We can illustrate this by the conversions of I and J in Figure 5.1.

In Figure 5.1 we perform several β-reductions in going from one row of the table to the next. The steps are derived as follows: We first show that $Y_\lambda M = M(Y_\lambda M)$, for any M

$$\begin{array}{rcl} Y_\lambda M & \equiv & (\lambda f.(\lambda x.f(xx))(\lambda x.f(xx)))M \\ & \beta\text{-}red & (\lambda x.M(xx))(\lambda x.M(xx)) \\ & \beta\text{-}red & M((\lambda x.M(xx))(\lambda x.M(xx))) \\ & = & M(Y_\lambda M) \end{array}$$

This is not surprising as we already knew that Y_λ is a fixed point operator (see Theorem 5.6.3, part 2, page 196). Therefore, we have:

$$\begin{array}{rcll} J\ (\equiv Y_\lambda F) & = & FJ & \\ & \equiv & (\lambda f.\lambda x.\lambda y.x(fy))J & \\ & \beta\text{-}red & \lambda x.\lambda y.x(Jy) & \text{(second line in table)} \end{array}$$

and Jy is thus

$$(\lambda x.\lambda y.x(Jy))y\ \ \beta\text{-}red\ \ (\lambda x.\lambda y.x(\lambda z.y(Jz))$$

Thus, in Figure 5.1, we have applied η-expansions to I and $\alpha\beta$-reductions to J, making the resulting terms look more and more alike and pushing the subterms at which they differ deeper and deeper inside the terms. That is, although we cannot establish that I *cnv* J through a finite sequence of conversions, we can show that I *cnv* M and J *cnv* N where M and N can be made syntactically identical to an arbitrarily large finite depth.

Since we have already decided (Section 5.5.1) that any reasonable computation model must deal with infinite objects and that we can consider such objects computable if they can be obtained as effective limits of their finite approximations, we are led to conclude that we should consider I and J as equal. More generally, the characterization of $=_{\mathcal{D}_\infty}$ in terms of limits of approximate normal forms (Theorem 5.6.8) is a natural consequence of the validity of the (η) rule.

5.6.3 Completeness Results

We have shown that the λ-calculus is incomplete in that, even though the theory is sound (everything provable is true in the models — Theorem 5.5.7), the models contain true statements (equations between

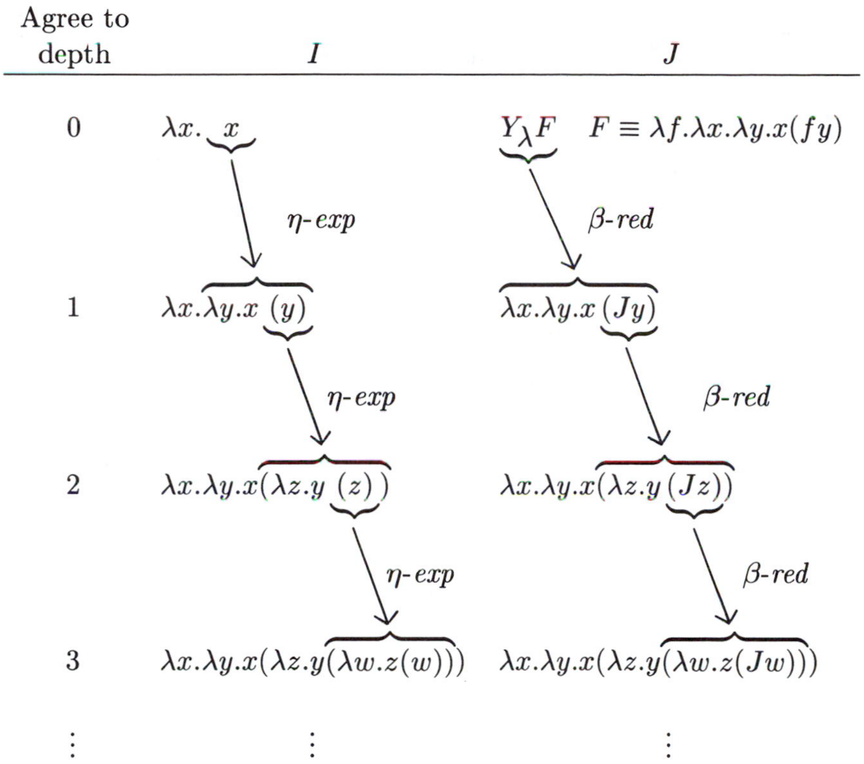

Figure 5.1 Interconvertibility of I and J

terms) that are not provable (Corollary 5.6.6.1). If we restrict our attention to terms with normal forms, then the λ-calculus is complete — but this is much too restrictive for a theory of computation. We want to be able to deal with infinite objects that have no finite representation (normal form). Looking at head normal forms or (equivalently) solvability, we seem to fare better. At first glance it seems that λ^* (λ-calculus + Uns, the axiom stating the equality of unsolvable terms — see page 212) is a complete theory. However, we have a problem. The axiom (Uns) that allowed us to assert the equality of any two unsolvable terms is not effective. That is, we have no decision procedure for determining when an equation is an instance of that axiom, because unsolvability of terms is undecidable.

We have completeness with respect to truth in the models and computation, for *solvable* terms — that is, two solvable terms are equal in the models if and only if they have similar head normal forms in every context. This does not give us a decision procedure for truth. We know that if we have two solvable terms that are in fact equal, then we can compute similar h.n.f.'s for them; if it were possible to compute similar h.n.f.'s for two terms in every context, then they would in fact be equal in the models. However, we have no algorithm for computing all contexts even though we do have an algorithm for computing h.n.f.'s in a particular context.

It is possible to describe an algorithm to enumerate all possible contexts, since there are only a countable number of them. Of course, the algorithm would not terminate, so we could never decide that two terms were in fact equal. However, we would eventually generate a context in which two unequal terms produced dissimilar h.n.f.'s. Thus we might say we have a partial decision procedure in that, given two solvable terms that are unequal in the models, we could, in an arbitrarily long but finite time, compute the fact that they were unequal. One problem with this procedure, as in our algorithm for $\mathcal{PC}$, is that we can put no bound on our computation. Thus we have, at best, only a partial decision procedure for solvable terms.

Exercises 5.6.3

1. a. How (and under what conditions) can you show two terms of the λ-calculus are equal to each other:
      i. when they both have normal forms?
      ii. when they do not both have normal forms?
      iii. when they both have head normal forms?
   b. How (and under what conditions) can you show two terms of the λ-calculus are not equal to each other:
      i. when they both have normal forms?
      ii. when they do not both have normal forms?
      iii. when they both have head normal forms?
   c. Will your method(s) in a work for every possible pair of terms that are equal in the model?
   d. Will your method(s) in b work for every possible pair of terms that are unequal in the model?

e. Will you ever get any wrong answers from the methods described in a and b?

2. Determine, wherever possible, whether or not each of the following wffs is a theorem of the λ-calculus. State whether the wff is a theorem, the wff is not a theorem, or it is not possible to show whether or not it is a theorem.

   a. $(\lambda x.\lambda y.\lambda z.xz(yz))(\lambda x.x)(\lambda x.\lambda y.x)$
   $= ((\lambda x.xy)(\lambda z.z))((\lambda x.\lambda w.y)((\lambda x.xx)(\lambda x.xx))$

   b. $(\lambda x.xx)(\lambda x.f((\lambda x.xx)x)) = f((\lambda x.xx)(\lambda x.f((\lambda x.xx)x)))$

   c. $(\lambda x.\lambda y.x)(\lambda x.x) = (\lambda x.\lambda y.x)(\lambda x.x)(\lambda x.x)$

   d. $(\lambda x.xx)(\lambda y.xy)((\lambda x.xxx)(\lambda x.xx))$
   $= x(\lambda w.xw)((\lambda x.xx)(\lambda y.yy)(\lambda z.zz))$

3. We have not shown that there exists a decision procedure for determining whether or not two terms have similar h.n.f.'s in any given context. In general, a term has many head normal forms. Head normal reduction always generates a h.n.f. when one exists. Does that guarantee that it will generate all h.n.f.'s of a term? Does it need to?

Appendix A

SELECTED ANSWERS AND WORKED EXAMPLES

A.1 Preliminary Definitions

Exercises 1.0

1. Review the definitions of sound, complete, consistent, and decidable. Is it conceivable that a theory might be:

   a. sound, but not complete?
   Yes, a theory in which you can prove only true things, but not all true things.

   b. sound, but not consistent?
   No. If the theory is not consistent, then there is a wff A, such that both A and $\neg A$ are provable. These cannot both be tautologies, so the theory is not sound.

   c. consistent, but not sound?
   Yes. It may be possible to prove something false and still not be able to prove the negation of anything provable. For example you may be able to prove only false things.

   d. complete, but not decidable?
   Yes. The existence of a proof for every true wff does not give

us an algorithm for deciding whether or not a wff is provable.

e. consistent and complete, but not sound?
No, IF we insist that all axioms are schema. From the assumption that we can prove a wff A that is not a tautology (i.e., that the theory is not sound), we can construct a wff A' that is provable and is always false. Since $\neg A'$ is thus always true, and the theory is complete, we can also prove $\neg A'$. Thus the theory cannot be consistent.

A.2 Propositional Logic

Exercises 2.2

2. Determine whether each of the following is unsatisfiable, a tautology, both, or neither:

   Of course, if one has read the definitions carefully, it is clear that nothing could be both unsatisfiable and a tautology. A truth table can be constructed to establish each of the following results.

   a. $(\neg A \rightarrow B) \rightarrow (\neg B \rightarrow A)$: tautology
   b. $(A \rightarrow B) \rightarrow (B \rightarrow A)$: neither
   c. $\neg(A \rightarrow (B \rightarrow A))$: unsatisfiable
   d. $\neg(A \rightarrow B) \rightarrow A$: tautology
   e. $\neg(A \rightarrow B) \rightarrow \neg(B \rightarrow A)$: neither

4. Is "$\rightarrow$" associative? No. Consider the truth tables for $(A \rightarrow B) \rightarrow C$ and $A \rightarrow (B \rightarrow C)$. For example, when A is false, B is true, and C is false, $(A \rightarrow B) \rightarrow C$ is false and $A \rightarrow (B \rightarrow C)$ is true.

7. A NOR B, written $A \uparrow B$, is defined to be $\neg(A \vee B)$. Is {NOR} a sufficient set of connectives? Yes. In Theorem 2.2.1 we showed that $\{\neg, \wedge, \vee\}$ is a sufficient set, and anything expressed in terms of $\neg$, $\wedge$, and $\vee$ can be reexpressed in terms of NOR using the following equivalences:

$$\begin{aligned} \neg A &\equiv A \uparrow A \\ A \wedge B &\equiv (A \uparrow A) \uparrow (B \uparrow B) \\ A \vee B &\equiv (A \uparrow B) \uparrow (A \uparrow B) \end{aligned}$$

Exercises 2.3

There are advantages and disadvantages to working with a minimal theory such as $\mathcal{L}$. Since there is little machinery available for use, intuition does not serve us well; however, at the same time, fewer choices provide fewer chances for choosing incorrectly. Two heuristics are very useful in attempting proofs in $\mathcal{L}$:

1. Whenever attempting to prove an implication, consider using the Deduction Theorem. Assume the left hand side of the implication as a hypothesis, then derive the right hand side, and finally, apply the Deduction Theorem to conclude the original implication. This can be used several times in the same proof. For example, to prove $A \rightarrow (B \rightarrow (C \rightarrow D))$, assume A and attempt to prove $B \rightarrow (C \rightarrow D)$. This is again an implication, so assume B and attempt to prove $C \rightarrow D$. Again, assume C and attempt to prove D. If you are successful, you can then apply the deduction theorem three times to work your way back out to the proof of the initial wff.

2. Whenever attempting to prove a wff that involves a change in negations (that is, a subformula appears both negated and unnegated in the same wff), consider using **L3**. This is the only axiom that explicitly deals with negations. It is closely related to proof by contradiction. Intuitively, it states that if something implies a wff and also implies its negation, then that something must be wrong. In finding the needed instance of this rather complicated-looking axiom, one can fill it in piecemeal, starting with the wff needed as result. This becomes the final conclusion of the axiom and determines the antecedants of the two subimplications.

   $$(\neg \mathit{wanted\_wff} \rightarrow \neg \_\_\_) \rightarrow ((\neg\ \mathit{wanted\_wff} \rightarrow \_\_\_) \rightarrow\ \mathit{wanted\_wff})$$

   In order to fill in the remaining blanks, one needs to find some wff such that both it and its negation will be derivable from the assumption $\neg \mathit{wanted\_wff}$. Usually, one of these implications will be true, and provable independently of any extra assumptions, while the other will only be provable because of hypotheses specific to this problem.

These two heuristics are applicable in a surprisingly large number of cases. Of course, after you have proved several theorems, your bag of tools expands and you gain many new shortcuts to proving new theorems. As with anything, it all becomes easier with practice.

1. Prove: $\neg\neg A \rightarrow A$

1. $\neg\neg A$	hypothesis
2. $(\neg A \rightarrow \neg\neg A) \rightarrow ((\neg A \rightarrow \neg A) \rightarrow A)$	**L3**
3. $\neg\neg A \rightarrow (\neg A \rightarrow \neg\neg A)$	**L1**
4. $\neg A \rightarrow \neg\neg A$	MP 1,3
5. $(\neg A \rightarrow \neg A) \rightarrow A$	MP 2,4
6. $\neg A \rightarrow \neg A$	Lemma 2.3.2
7. A	MP 2,5
8. $\neg\neg A \rightarrow A$	Deduction Theorem 1,7

2. Prove: $A,\ B \vdash \neg(A \rightarrow \neg B)$

1. A	hypothesis
2. B	hypothesis
3. $(\neg\neg(A \rightarrow \neg B) \rightarrow \neg B) \rightarrow ((\neg\neg(A \rightarrow \neg B) \rightarrow B) \rightarrow \neg(A \rightarrow \neg B))$	**L3**
4. $\neg\neg(A \rightarrow \neg B) \rightarrow (A \rightarrow \neg B)$	Exercise 1
5. $A \rightarrow \neg B$	hypothesis
6. $\neg B$	MP 1,5
7. $(A \rightarrow \neg B) \rightarrow \neg B$	Deduction Theorem 5,6
8. $\neg\neg(A \rightarrow \neg B) \rightarrow \neg B$	Lemma 2.3.4 (4,7)
9. $(\neg\neg(A \rightarrow \neg B) \rightarrow B) \rightarrow \neg(A \rightarrow \neg B)$	MP 8,3
10. $B \rightarrow (\neg\neg(A \rightarrow \neg B) \rightarrow B)$	**L1**
11. $\neg\neg(A \rightarrow \neg B) \rightarrow B$	MP 2,10
12. $\neg(A \rightarrow \neg B)$	MP 11,9

5. Show: $\neg(A \rightarrow \neg B) \vdash B$

1. $\neg(A \rightarrow \neg B)$	hypothesis
2. $(\neg B \rightarrow \neg(A \rightarrow \neg B)) \rightarrow ((\neg B \rightarrow (A \rightarrow \neg B)) \rightarrow B)$	**L3**

3. $\neg(A\to\neg B)\to(\neg B\to\neg(A\to\neg B))$ **L1**
4. $\neg B\to\neg(A\to\neg B)$ MP 1,3
5. $(\neg B\to(A\to\neg B))\to B$ MP 2,4
6. $\neg B\to(A\to\neg B)$ **L1**
7. B MP 5,6

6. Show: If $A,\ B\vdash C$, then $\neg(A\to\neg B)\vdash C$.
   From Exercise 5, we know that $\neg(A\to\neg B)\vdash B$, if we can show that $\neg(A\to\neg B)\vdash A$ then we'll have the result we want by the third property of deducibility.

   1. $\neg(A\to\neg B)$ hypothesis
   2. $(\neg A\to\neg(A\to\neg B))\to((\neg A\to(A\to\neg B))\to A)$ **L3**
   3. $\neg(A\to\neg B)\to(\neg A\to\neg(A\to\neg B))$ **L1**
   4. $\neg A\to\neg(A\to\neg B)$ MP 1,3
   5. $((\neg A\to(A\to\neg B))\to A)$ MP 2,4
   6. $\neg A\to(\neg\neg B\to\neg A)$ **L1**
   7. $(\neg\neg B\to\neg A)\to(A\to\neg B)$ Lemma 2.3.5
   8. $\neg A\to(A\to\neg B)$ Lemma 2.3.4 (6,7)
   9. A MP 5,8

9. Prove: $\neg A\to(A\to B)$

   1. $\neg A$ hypothesis
   2. A hypothesis
   3. $(\neg B\to\neg A)\to((\neg B\to A)\to B)$ **L3**
   4. $\neg A\to(\neg B\to\neg A)$ **L1**
   5. $A\to(\neg B\to A)$ **L1**
   6. $\neg B\to\neg A$ MP 1,4
   7. $(\neg B\to A)\to B$ MP 3,6
   8. $\neg B\to A$ MP 2,5
   9. B MP 7,8
   10. $A\to B$ Deduction Theorem 2,9
   11. $\neg A\to(A\to B)$ Deduction Theorem 1,10

Exercises 2.4

It is very important to keep in mind that CLE is a refutation procedure, and therefore, if successful, shows that something is a contradiction. We then conclude that the negation of the wff that was refuted must be true. Be careful to start with the correct wff, and be careful in transforming it to reduced conjunctive normal form. The actual refutation is the easy part.

1. Exhibit a refutation of the NEGATION of each of the following wffs.

   c. $((\neg B \rightarrow \neg A) \rightarrow ((\neg B \rightarrow A) \rightarrow B))$

   First, take the negation of the wff and transform it to reduced conjunctive normal form:

$$\neg[((\neg B \rightarrow \neg A) \rightarrow ((\neg B \rightarrow A) \rightarrow B))]$$
$$\neg[\neg(\neg B \rightarrow \neg A) \vee ((\neg B \rightarrow A) \rightarrow B)]$$
$$\neg[\neg(\neg\neg B \vee \neg A) \vee \neg(\neg\neg B \vee A) \vee B]$$
$$\neg[\neg(B \vee \neg A) \vee \neg(B \vee A) \vee B]$$
$$\neg\neg(B \vee \neg A) \wedge \neg\neg(B \vee A) \wedge \neg B$$
$$(B \vee \neg A) \wedge (B \vee A) \wedge \neg B$$

   Then perform Complementary Literal Elimination:

   B_1: $B \vee \neg A$ $\quad$ B_2: $B \vee A$

   B_3: B $\quad$ B_4: $\neg B$

   B_5: $\Box$

2. (a new one) Reduce the following wff to reduced conjunctive normal form and exhibit a refutation of it by CLE:

$$\neg[(A \rightarrow (B \rightarrow \neg C)) \rightarrow (B \wedge C \rightarrow \neg A)]$$
$$\neg[\neg(A \rightarrow (B \rightarrow \neg C)) \vee (\neg(B \wedge C) \vee \neg A)]$$
$$\neg[\neg(\neg A \vee (\neg B \vee \neg C)) \vee (\neg B \vee \neg C \vee \neg A)]$$
$$(\neg A \vee \neg B \vee \neg C) \wedge B \wedge C \wedge A$$

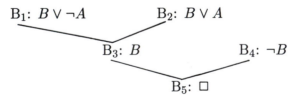

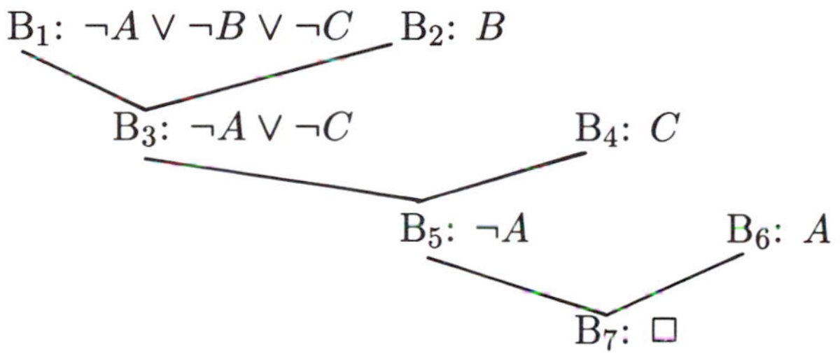

3. (and another) Show that

$$(\neg A \rightarrow (\neg B \vee \neg C)) \wedge \neg(\neg(A \vee B) \vee (\neg A \rightarrow \neg C))$$

is unsatisfiable by transforming it into reduced conjunctive normal form and exhibiting a refutation.

$$(\neg A \rightarrow (\neg B \vee \neg C)) \wedge \neg(\neg(A \vee B) \vee (\neg A \rightarrow \neg C))$$
$$(A \vee \neg B \vee \neg C) \wedge (A \vee B) \wedge \neg(A \vee \neg C)$$
$$(A \vee \neg B \vee \neg C) \wedge (A \vee B) \wedge \neg A \wedge C$$

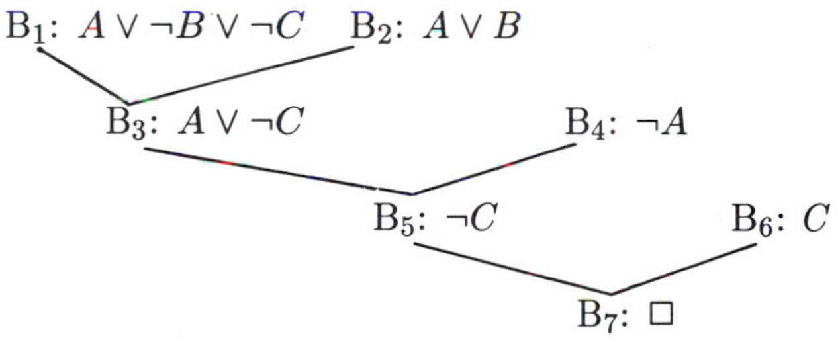

Exercises 2.5

Of the four metatheoretic properties (soundness, completeness, consistency, and decidability) only one can be checked in an algorithmic way. To determine whether or not a theory is sound one can, using truth tables, see whether each axiom is a tautology and whether each rule of inference leads from tautologies to tautologies. The other properties are not so easily disposed of. Rather than trying to determine whether each property holds individually, one's time is better spent stepping back from the individual questions for a moment and trying to characterize the set of provable wffs in the theory. For example, all instances of the axioms are provable, next, you should consider what can be derived from them using the rules of inference. If one can get a feeling for what is provable, even if it is only a partial characterization, one is in a better position to ask whether all tautologies are provable or whether it is possible that a wff and its negation might be provable. In the process of trying to characterize what is provable, one often develops an algorithm establishing the decidability of a theory.

1. In each of the following cases, determine, if possible, whether the theory described is sound, consistent, complete, and/or decidable. If there is insufficient information to determine any of these, state why. (Assume that all axioms and rules are given as schema, standing for many axioms or rules as instances.)

   b. The language of $\mathcal{L}$, with one axiom: $A \rightarrow \neg B$
   and one rule of inference: $A \rightarrow B,\ B \rightarrow C \vdash B$

   The theory is not sound. Its axiom is not a tautology.

   What can be proved in this theory? In order to use the rule of inference, we have to be able to derive two implications, and the consequent of one must be the antecedant of the other. We have only one axiom with which to generate the hypotheses for the first application of the rule of inference. We can use it in the following way:

   1. $A \rightarrow \neg B$ — by the axiom
   2. $\neg B \rightarrow \neg C$ — again, by the axiom
   3. $\neg B$ — by the rule of inference

   Thus, in this theory we can derive all instances of the axiom, as well as all negations (instances of $\neg B$). Since the rule of inference did not generate something that could again be used as hypothesis for another application of the rule of inference (being a negation, not an implication), all provable wffs must be an instance of one or the other. Thus the issue of decidability is simply a parsing problem. The theory is decidable: Given any wff, if it is an instance of $A \rightarrow \neg B$ or of $\neg B$ then it is provable, otherwise it is not provable.

   The theory is not complete, since $A \rightarrow A$ is a tautology that is not of either of the two forms, and thus, is not provable. (Note that $\neg\neg(A \rightarrow A)$ is provable, but that is a different wff.)

   The theory is not consistent, since $\neg B$ and $\neg\neg B$ are both provable.

f. The language of $\mathcal{L}$ with one axiom and no rules of inference.

The theory will be sound *if* the axiom is a tautology. However, since we do not know what the axiom is, we have insufficient information to determine soundness.

If the axiom is an implication, then the theory will be consistent. However, if the axiom is something such as $\neg B$, in which the negation of the axiom is an instance of the axiom, the theory is inconsistent. Thus, we have insufficient information to determine whether or not the theory is consistent.

If the axiom is simply A, then everything is provable, and thus all tautologies are provable, so the theory is complete. However, if the axiom is $\neg(A \rightarrow B)$, then $A \rightarrow A$ is not provable, so the theory is not complete. Thus, we have insufficient information to determine completeness.

The theory *is* decidable! No matter what the axiom is, we can certainly devlop an algorithm to determine whether or not a given wff is an instance of that axiom.

2. What relationships, if any, exist among the metatheoretic notions of completeness, soundness, consistency, and decidability? (Are they totally independent, or does knowing one property imply that another must hold?)

Soundness implies consistency. If every provable wff is a tautology, then you cannot prove something and its negation, since both cannot be tautologies.

A theory can be consistent and yet not be sound. However, if all axioms and rules are given as schemata (and thus each theorem is a schema standing for all its instantiations), then a theory that is complete as well as consistent must also be sound.

> Assume that a theory is consistent and complete but not sound. Then there exists a wff A that is provable and is not a tautology. One can generate an instance of A (which is therefore provable) that is always false. Simply consider an interpretation (line in the truth table for A) in which A is false: for each proposition letter that takes the value **f** under the interpretation, substitute the wff $\neg(A \rightarrow A)$; for each proposition letter that takes

the value **t** under the interpretation, substitute the wff $(A \to A)$. The wff thus constructed is provable, since it is an instance of A, and by its construction it is always false. Its negation is thus always true, and is also provable since the theory is complete. But this contradicts the fact that the theory was consistent.

Every other combination of the metatheoretic properties is possible.

Some more examples:

3. Determine, if possible, whether each of the following theories is sound, complete, and/or consistent.

a. The language of theory $\mathcal{L}$

axioms: $(A \to (B \to C)) \to ((A \to B) \to (A \to C))$
$(A \to (B \to C)) \to (D \to (E \to D))$
$(\neg B \to \neg A) \to ((\neg B \to A) \to B)$

rule of inference: Modus Ponens

Sound: The axioms are all tautologies, and we already know that Modus Ponens is a valid rule of inference.

Complete and consistent: The first and second axioms can be used with Modus Ponens to derive the first axiom, **L1**, of the theory $\mathcal{L}$. Then we have all the axioms and the rule of inference of $\mathcal{L}$, together with the second axiom above, which is a tautology and thus provable in $\mathcal{L}$ by completeness, and so this theory is equivalent to $\mathcal{L}$. Thus, it is complete and consistent.

b. The language of $\mathcal{L}$

axioms: $(A \to (B \to A))$
$(A \to (B \to C)) \to ((A \to B) \to (A \to C))$
$(\neg B \to \neg A) \to ((\neg B \to A) \to B)$
$(A \wedge (A \to B)) \to B$

rule of inference: $A \to B,\ B \to C \vdash A \to C$

Sound: Each axiom is a tautology, and the rule of inference leads from tautologies to tautologies.

Not complete, and consistent: Everything that is provable is a tautology, but you can't prove all tautologies. For example, $A \rightarrow A$ is not provable. Thus, the theory is not complete, though it is consistent.

c. The language of theory $\mathcal{L}$

axioms: $(A \rightarrow (A \rightarrow B))$
$(\neg B \rightarrow \neg A) \rightarrow ((\neg B \rightarrow A) \rightarrow B)$

rule of inference: Modus Ponens

Not sound: The first axiom is not a tautology, and so the theory is not sound.

Complete, and not consistent: Using the first axiom together with Modus Ponens it is possible to prove everything in this theory.

1. $A \rightarrow (A \rightarrow B)$ — first axiom
2. $(A \rightarrow (A \rightarrow B)) \rightarrow ((A \rightarrow (A \rightarrow B)) \rightarrow B$ — first axiom
3. $((A \rightarrow (A \rightarrow B)) \rightarrow B$ — MP 1,2
4. B — MP 1,3

Therefore, the theory is complete and not consistent.

d. The language of theory $\mathcal{L}$

axioms: $(A \rightarrow (B \rightarrow C)) \rightarrow ((B \rightarrow A) \rightarrow (B \rightarrow C))$
$(\neg B \rightarrow \neg A) \rightarrow (B \rightarrow A)$

rule of inference: $A \vdash B \rightarrow A$

Not sound: The theory is not sound because the second axiom is not a tautology.

Not complete, and consistent: All theorems are implications. Each of the axioms is an implication, and the rule of inference allows one to derive implications. (This is not to say that all implications are provable, but only implications are provable.) Thus, the theory is not complete: $\neg\neg(A \rightarrow A)$ is a tautology that is not provable. The theory is consistent, since no negations are provable.

e. The language of theory $\mathcal{L}$

axioms: $(A \rightarrow (B \rightarrow C)) \rightarrow ((A \rightarrow B) \rightarrow (A \rightarrow C))$
$(A \rightarrow (B \rightarrow C)) \rightarrow (A \rightarrow (B \rightarrow A))$
$(\neg B \rightarrow \neg A) \rightarrow ((\neg B \rightarrow A) \rightarrow B)$

rule of inference: Modus Ponens

Sound: The theory is sound because the axioms are tautologies and the rule of inference preserves logical validity.

Not complete, and consistent: The theory is not complete because we cannot prove $(A \rightarrow (B \rightarrow A))$, although we can prove some instances of it. (Note the difference between this problem and part a.)
It is consistent because it is sound.

f. The language of theory $\mathcal{L}$

axioms: $A \rightarrow A$
$(A \rightarrow (B \rightarrow A))$
$(A \rightarrow (B \rightarrow C)) \rightarrow ((A \rightarrow B) \rightarrow (A \rightarrow C))$
rules of inference: Modus Ponens
$A,\ B \vdash \neg(A \rightarrow \neg B)$

Sound: The axioms are tautologies and the rules of inference preserve logical validity (note that the second rule of inference is equivalent to stating that $A,\ B \vdash A \vee B$)

Not complete, and consistent. For example, we cannot prove $(\neg B \rightarrow \neg A) \rightarrow ((\neg B \rightarrow A) \rightarrow B)$.
It is consistent because it is sound.

g. The language of theory $\mathcal{L}$

axioms: $(A \rightarrow (B \rightarrow A))$
$(A \rightarrow (B \rightarrow C)) \rightarrow ((A \rightarrow B) \rightarrow (A \rightarrow C))$
$(\neg B \rightarrow \neg A) \rightarrow ((\neg B \rightarrow A) \rightarrow B)$
rules of inference: Modus Ponens
$\neg A \rightarrow B,\ A \rightarrow C \vdash \neg B \rightarrow C$

Sound: The theory is sound because all the axioms are tautologies and the rules of inference preserve logical validity.

Complete and consistent: The theory is complete since it contains all the axioms and rules of inference of $\mathcal{L}$ and we know $\mathcal{L}$ is complete.
It is consistent because it is sound. (Actually, the "new" rule of inference could be proven in $\mathcal{L}$, so this theory is equivalent to $\mathcal{L}$.)

4. I have an algorithm that can produce a proof of any theorem of the theory M in a finite amount of time. I claim that the theory

M is undecidable. Is this possible? Why or why not?

Yes, it is possible. I have said nothing about what the algorithm might do when given a nontheorem. A decision procedure must be able to answer yes to a theorem AND no to a nontheorem in a finite amount of time.

5. Theory T is a formal theory with the language of Propositional Logic. You do not know what the axioms and rules of inference of T are, but you do know that T is sound.

   a. Is $A \rightarrow (B \rightarrow A)$ provable in T?
   The fact that T is sound is not enough information to determine whether or not a specific tautology is provable.
   b. Is $(A \rightarrow (B \rightarrow C)) \rightarrow (A \rightarrow C)$ provable in T?
   No, since T is sound we know that every theorem must be a tautology, i.e., no nontautologies are provable, and this wff is not a tautology.

6. Decide whether or not the wff:

$$(A \rightarrow (B \rightarrow C)) \rightarrow ((B \rightarrow A) \rightarrow (B \rightarrow C))$$

is a theorem of $\mathcal{L}$. JUSTIFY your answer.

Yes. You can prove it in $\mathcal{L}$; or exhibit a truth table, showing it is a tautology (then since $\mathcal{L}$ is complete it must be a theorem); or you could refute the negation of it by CLE and since we know that $\neg A \xrightarrow{*} \Box$ implies $\vdash A$, then it is provable.

7. Is the following wff a theorem of $\mathcal{L}$? JUSTIFY YOUR ANSWER!!

$$((A \rightarrow B) \rightarrow (A \rightarrow C)) \rightarrow (A \rightarrow (B \rightarrow C))$$

Yes — and it can be justified by:

   a. Proving it in the formal theory $\mathcal{L}$;
   b. Showing via a truth table that it is a tautology AND stating that since we know $\mathcal{L}$ is complete this also shows it is a theorem; or
   c. Exhibiting a resolution refutation of the negation of it AND stating that since we know $\neg A \xrightarrow{*} \Box$ implies $\vdash A$ this also shows it is a theorem of $\mathcal{L}$.

A.3 Predicate Calculus

Exercises 3.1

1. Determine whether each of the variables x, y, and z is *free, bound,* or *both* in each of the wffs a–d.

   a. $(\forall x)P(f(x), y, z) \rightarrow \neg P(z, x, y)$
      x is both, y and z are free.

   b. $(\forall z)P(g(z), a, y) \wedge (\forall y)\neg Q(x, y)$
      x is free, y is both, and z is bound.

   c. $(\forall x)(P(x, y, z) \wedge (\forall y)S(f(x), z, y) \vee R(z))$
      x is bound, y is both, and z is free.

   d. $(\forall y)P(y, a, z) \rightarrow (\forall z)(Q(x, z) \wedge P(x, a, z))$
      x is free, y is bound, and z is both.

2. Determine whether or not each of the terms:

$$h(x, y) \text{ and } g(a, f(y, z))$$

   is free for each of the variables x, y, and z in each of the following wffs (that is 18 questions):

   a. $(\forall z)(P(z, y, a) \wedge (\forall x)Q(g(z)))$
      $h(x, y)$ is free for x, y, and z, vacuously in the first and third cases, since there are no free occurrences of x or z in the wff.
      $g(a, f(y, z))$ is free for x and z but not free for y.

   b. $(\forall x)P(f(x), y) \rightarrow \neg P(f(x), z)$
      $h(x, y)$ is free for x and z, but not free for y.
      $g(a, f(y, z))$ is free for x, y, and z.

   c. $P(f(x), x) \rightarrow (\forall z)\neg P(f(y), z)$
      $h(x, y)$ is free for x, y, and z.
      $g(a, f(y, z))$ is free for x and z, but not free for y.

3. (one more) In each of the following wffs:

   a. $(\forall z)P(X, y, z) \wedge (\forall y)Q(f(x), z, y)$

   b. $(\forall x)((\exists z)P(z, y) \rightarrow (\forall y)R(f(z, y, x)))$

indicate whether each variable is free, bound, or both:

a. x is free, y is both, z is bound.

b. x is bound, y is both, z is both.

indicate whether each of the terms, $h(y, z)$ and $g(x, a)$, is free for each variable:

a. $h(y, z)$ is free for z only.
   $g(x, a)$ is free for x, y, and z.

b. $h(y, z)$ is free for x only.
   $g(x, a)$ is free for x only.

Exercises 3.2

1. Determine whether each of the following wffs is true, false, or neither in the interpretation:

$$\text{Domain} = \text{Integers}$$
$$P(x, y) \text{ means } x \le y$$

a. $(\forall x)(\exists y)P(x, y) \rightarrow (\exists y)(\forall x)P(x, y)$
   This wff means that if for all integers **x** one can find an integer **y** such that $\mathbf{x} \le \mathbf{y}$, then there is an integer **y** such that for all integers **x**, $\mathbf{x} \le \mathbf{y}$. That is, the wff claims that there is a greatest integer, which is false.

b. $(\forall x)(\forall y)P(x, y) \rightarrow (\forall y)(\forall x)P(x, y)$
   This wff is true in the interpretation. It states that *if* for all integers **x** it is the case that for all integers **y**, $\mathbf{x} \le \mathbf{y}$, *then* it is the case that for all integers **y** it is true that for all integers **x**, $\mathbf{x} \le \mathbf{y}$. An implication is always true if its antecedant is false (i.e., **false** $\rightarrow$ *anything* is true).

c. $(\exists x)(\forall y)P(x, y)$
   This states that there is a least integer, which is false.

d. $(\forall y)(\exists x)P(x, y)$
   This states that for any integer **y** one can find an integer **x** such that $\mathbf{x} \le \mathbf{y}$, which is true. (Note that sometimes it makes more sense to read $\forall$ as "for any" or "for each." It

is important to take note of the scope of quantifiers so that you are careful when combining statements, "for each x one can find (there exists) a y" is very different in meaning from "there is a y such that for each x."

2. Indicate *as many* of the following as apply to each of the wffs listed below:

   a. logically valid

   b. true in an interpretation, but not logically valid

   c. satisfiable but not true, in some interpretation

   d. false in an interpretation

   e. unsatisfiable (contradictory)

   i. $\forall x A(z,x) \vee B(x,y) \rightarrow (\forall x A(z,x) \vee \forall x B(x,y))$
   b, c, d —
   b: Consider any interpretation in which $B(x,y)$ is always true.
   c: Consider the domain of integers, with $A(x,y)$ meaning $\mathbf{x}+\mathbf{y}$ is even, and $B(x,y)$ meaning $\mathbf{x}$ is even. Then the wff will be true for even values of $\mathbf{z}$ (since the antecedant will be false), and it will be false for odd values of $\mathbf{z}$.
   d: With the domain of integers, let $A(x,y)$ mean $\mathbf{y}$ is even, and $B(x,y)$ mean $\mathbf{x}$ is odd.

   iii. $P(x,y) \rightarrow P(y,x)$
   b, c — Let the domain be integers in each of the following.
   b: $P(x,y)$ means $\mathbf{x}=\mathbf{y}$
   c: $P(x,y)$ means $\mathbf{x} \leq \mathbf{y}$
   (Note that it is impossible for this wff to be false in an interpretation.)

   v. $\forall x P(x) \rightarrow P(f(x))$
   a — If $P(x)$ is true for all $\mathbf{x}$, then it must certainly be true for $\mathbf{f}(\mathbf{x})$.

And some more:

vi. $\forall x P(f(x)) \rightarrow \exists x \neg P(x)$
<u>b, d</u> —
b: Choose an interpretation in which $P(x)$ is mapped to a relationship that is false for some value.
d: Choose an interpretation in which $P(x)$ is always true.

vii. $\neg(P(f(x)) \rightarrow P(x))$
<u>c, d</u> — Consider the domain of integers.
c: $P(x)$ means $\mathbf{x} > \mathbf{0}$, and $f(x)$ means $\mathbf{x^2}$.
d: $P(x)$ means $\mathbf{x} + \mathbf{x}$ is even.

viii. $(\forall x)(\exists y)P(x, y, z) \rightarrow (\exists y)(\exists x)P(x, y, z)$
<u>a</u> — In fact $(\forall x)(\exists y)A \rightarrow (\exists y)(\exists x)A$ is logically valid for any wff A.

ix. $P(x) \wedge \neg P(f(x))$
<u>c, d</u> — Consider the domain of integers.
c: $P(x)$ means x is even, $f(x)$ is $x + 1$.
d: f is the identity function.

x. $P(x) \wedge ((\exists x)P(x) \rightarrow \neg((\forall z)Q(z, x) \rightarrow (\exists z)Q(z, x)))$
<u>e</u> — For this to be satisfied both sides of the conjunction must be satisfied. If $P(x)$ holds then $(\exists x)P(x)$ also holds. Thus, for the implication to be satisfied, the consequent $\neg((\forall z)Q(z, x) \rightarrow (\exists z)Q(z, x)))$ must hold. However, $(\forall z)Q(z, x) \rightarrow (\exists z)Q(z, x)$ is logically valid, and so its negation is unsatisfiable.

xi. $(\forall x)P(x) \vee \neg P(f(x))$
<u>b, d</u> — Consider the domain of integers.
b: Let f be the identity function.
d: Let $f(x)$ be $x + 1$, and $P(x)$ be x is even.

And a few more for you to work out:

xii. $P(x) \rightarrow \forall x P(f(x))$

xiii. $(\exists x A(x) \rightarrow \exists x B(x)) \rightarrow \exists x (A(x) \rightarrow B(x))$

xiv. $P(x) \rightarrow P(f(x))$

3. Make up a wff of $\mathcal{PC}$ for each set of conditions given below. Justify your answer (providing interpretations wherever appropriate).

HINT: Remember that a necessary (though not sufficient) condition for a wff to be satisfiable but not true in an interpretation, is that it contain at least one free variable.

Exercises 3.3

1. Prove each of the following in the formal theory $\mathcal{PC}$:

   a. $\forall x \forall y(P(x,y) \rightarrow Q(x)) \rightarrow \forall y \forall x(P(x,y) \rightarrow Q(x))$
   Actually, one can prove the more general result that

   $$\forall x \forall y A \rightarrow \exists y \exists x A$$

   of which the current problem is an instance.

1.	$\forall x \forall y A$	hypothesis
2.	$\forall x \forall y A \rightarrow \forall y A$	**PC4**
3.	$\forall y A$	MP 1,2
4.	$\forall y A \rightarrow A$	**PC4**
5.	A	MP 3,4
6.	$\forall x A$	Gen 5
7.	$\forall y \forall x A$	Gen 6
8.	$\forall x \forall y A \rightarrow \forall y \forall x A$	Theorem 3.3.5

   b. $\neg \forall x \neg \forall y A \rightarrow \forall y \neg \forall x \neg A$
   By the definition of $\exists$, this is just $\exists x \forall y A \rightarrow \forall y \exists x A$. (So it does make sense, and, by the way, it is not an equivalence.)

   c. $\forall x \forall y P(x,y) \rightarrow \forall x \forall y P(y,x)$
   HINT: This is just another variation on the Lemma proved in a.

   d. $\forall x_1 \ldots \forall x_n(P \wedge Q) \rightarrow (\forall x_1 \ldots \forall x_n P) \wedge (\forall x_1 \ldots \forall x_n Q)$
   First show that $\forall x(P \wedge Q) \rightarrow (\forall x P \wedge \forall x Q)$, then establish the more general result by induction on n.
   To show that $\forall x(P \wedge Q) \rightarrow (\forall x P \wedge \forall x Q)$, use the results of the exercises from Section 2.3, together with **PC4** and Gen, in showing that:

   1. $\forall x(P \wedge Q) \vdash \forall x P$;
   2. $\forall x(P \wedge Q) \vdash \forall x Q$; and thus
   3. $\forall x(P \wedge Q) \vdash \forall x P \wedge \forall x Q$.

Then the deduction theorem for $\mathcal{PC}$ gives the desired result.

e. $\forall x_1 \ldots \forall x_n P \rightarrow \forall x_n \forall x_1 \ldots \forall x_{n-1} P$

Again, make use of the result proved in a, then generalize with a proof by induction on n.

f. (new) $\exists x \exists y A \rightarrow \exists y \exists x A$, i.e., $\neg \forall x \neg \neg \forall y \forall A \rightarrow \neg \forall y \neg \neg \forall x \neg A$, or $\neg \forall x \forall y \neg A \rightarrow \neg \forall y \forall x \neg A$

1.	$\forall y \forall x \neg A \rightarrow \forall x \forall y \neg A$	proof in part a, above.
2.	$(\forall y \forall x \neg A \rightarrow \forall x \forall y \neg A) \rightarrow (\neg \forall x \forall y \neg A \rightarrow \neg \forall y \forall x \neg A)$	Exercise 4, Section 2.3
3.	$(\neg \forall x \forall y \neg A \rightarrow \neg \forall y \forall x \neg A)$	MP 1,2

g. (new) $\forall x A \rightarrow \exists x A$, i.e., $\forall x A \rightarrow \neg \forall x \neg A$

1.	$\forall x A$	hypothesis
2.	$(\neg\neg \forall x \neg A \rightarrow \neg A) \rightarrow ((\neg\neg \forall x \neg A \rightarrow A) \rightarrow \neg \forall x \neg A)$	**PC3**
3.	$\neg\neg \forall x \neg A \rightarrow \forall x \neg A$	Exercise 1, Section 2.3
4.	$\forall x \neg A \rightarrow \neg A$	**PC4**
5.	$\neg\neg \forall x \neg A \rightarrow \neg A$	Lemma 2.3.4
6.	$((\neg\neg \forall x \neg A \rightarrow A) \rightarrow \neg \forall x \neg A)$	MP 5,2
7.	$\forall x A \rightarrow A$	**PC4**
8.	A	MP 1,7
9.	$A \rightarrow (\neg\neg \forall x \neg A \rightarrow A)$	**PC1**
10.	$\neg\neg \forall x \neg A \rightarrow A$	MP 8,9
11.	$\neg \forall x \neg A$	MP 10,6
12.	$\forall x A \rightarrow \neg \forall x \neg A$	Theorem 3.3.5

Exercises 3.4.1

2. Supply a most general unifier for each of the following pairs of terms. If no unifier exists for a pair, state why not. (w, x, y, and z are variables; a, b, c, and d are constant symbols.)

a.	h(x, f(a, x))	h(b, y)
b.	h(x, f(g(a, x), z))	h(b, f(g(a, f(w, c)), h(y, x)))
c.	f(a, f(b, f(c, x)))	f(a, y)
d.	h(x, f(g(a, y), z))	h(b, f(g(a, f(w, c)), h(y, x)))
e.	f(x, f(a, f(y, c)))	f(z, f(z, f(f(a, c), w)))

b. Not possible, since x is first matched with b, and then b must unify with f(w, c), which is impossible.

d. [(b, x), (f(w, c), y), (h(f(w, c), b), z)]

3. Exhibit a resolution refutation of each of the following sets of clauses. (Recall that f, g, and h are function symbols; a, b, c, and d are constant symbols; and w, x, y, and z are variables.) Remember to:

- Standardize apart a pair of clauses *before* attempting unification.
- Indicate each unifying substitution *clearly.*
- Make the unifying substitution throughout *both* clauses.

Also, remember that there is no limit (upper or lower) to the number of times that you may use a particular clause.

b. Q(x, a, a)
Q(x, f(x, y), z) ∨ ¬Q(x, y, z)
Q(x, f(y, z), f(y, w)) ∨ ¬Q(x, z, w)
¬Q(b, f(b, f(c, f(b, a))), x)

As in the example on page 79, we show the pair of clauses we intend to resolve upon (standardized apart), then the most general unifier, then the unified version of the clauses, before exhibiting the resolvent.

$\neg Q(b, f(b, f(c, f(b, a))), x) \qquad Q(x_1, f(x_1, y_1), z_1) \lor \neg Q(x_1, y_1, z_1)$

$[(b, x_1),\ (f(c, f(b, a)), y_1),\ (x, z_1)]$

$\neg Q(b, f(b, f(c, f(b, a))), x)$

$Q(b, f(b, f(c, f(b, a))), x) \lor \neg Q(b, f(c, f(b, a)), x)$

$\neg Q(b, f(c, f(b, a)), x) \qquad Q(x_2, f(y_2, z_2), f(y_2, w_2)) \lor \neg Q(x_2, z_2, w_2)$

$[(b, x_2),\ (c, y_2),\ (f(b, a), z_2),\ (f(c, w_2), x)]$

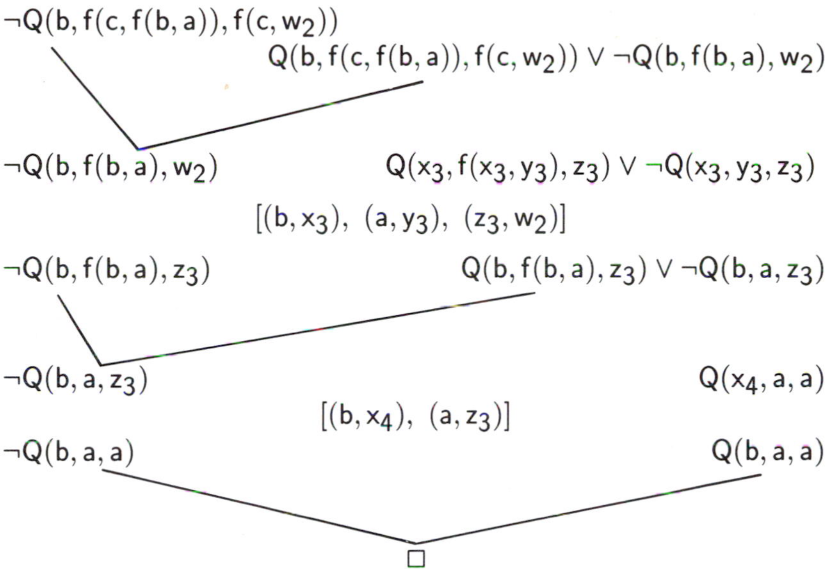

d. (One more to work on)
$L(a, b)$
$L(f(x, y), g(z)) \vee \neg L(y, z)$
$\neg L(x, g(g(w)))$

5. (a new one) Supply a most general unifier for each of the following pairs of terms, if possible. If no unifier exists, state why not. Letters from the beginning of the alphabet are constant symbols, from the end are variables, and f, g, and h are function symbols. (Note: Unification is one small part of the process of resolution; you are asked here to unify two terms only. It is assumed that they have occurred in an appropriate context within atomic formulas that are being unified.)

a. f(a, f(g(x), x))   f(y, z)
[(a, y), (f(g(x), x), z)]

b. f(a, f(g(x), x))   f(y, f(g(h(y, a)), z))
[[(a, y), (h(a, a), x), (h(a, a), z)]

c. $\mathsf{f(a, f(g(x), x))}$ $\quad\quad$ $\mathsf{f(a, f(b, c))}$
   not possible, $\mathsf{g(x)} \rightarrow\leftarrow \mathsf{b}$

d. $\mathsf{f(a, f(g(x), x))}$ $\quad\quad$ $\mathsf{f(x, f(y, z))}$
   $\mathsf{[(a, x), (g(a), y), (a, z)]}$

e. $\mathsf{f(a, f(g(x), x))}$ $\quad\quad$ $\mathsf{f(y, f(z, g(z)))}$
   not possible, $\mathsf{g(g(x))} \rightarrow\leftarrow \mathsf{x}$

6. (another) Exhibit a resolution refutation of the following set of clauses:

$\mathsf{P(x, a, x)}$
$\mathsf{P(x, f(y), f(z))} \vee \neg\mathsf{P(x, y, z)}$
$\neg\mathsf{P(z, f(f(a)), f(w))}$

$\neg\mathsf{P(z_1, f(f(a)), f(w_1))}$ $\quad\quad$ $\mathsf{P(x, f(y), f(z))} \vee \neg\mathsf{P(x, y, z)}$

$\mathsf{[(x, z_1), (f(a), y), (w_1, z)]}$

$\neg\mathsf{P(x, f(f(a)), f(w_1))}$ $\quad\quad$ $\mathsf{P(x, f(f(a)), f(w_1))} \vee \neg\mathsf{P(x, f(a), w_1)}$

$\neg\mathsf{P(x, f(a), w_1)}$ $\quad\quad$ $\mathsf{P(x_2, f(y_2), f(z_2))} \vee \neg\mathsf{P(x_2, y_2, z_2)}$

$\mathsf{[(x, x_2), (a, y_2), (f(z_2), w_1)]}$

$\neg\mathsf{P(x, f(a), f(z_2))}$ $\quad\quad$ $\mathsf{P(x, f(a), f(z_2))} \vee \neg\mathsf{P(x, a, z_2)}$

$\neg\mathsf{P(x, a, z_2)}$ $\quad\quad$ $\mathsf{P(x_3, a, x_3)}$

$\mathsf{[(x_3, x), (x_3, z_2)]}$

$\neg\mathsf{P(x_3, a, x_3)}$ $\quad\quad$ $\mathsf{P(x_3, a, x_3)}$

$\square$

Exercises 3.4.2

2. We have seen definitions of family relationships, some given by facts asserting that the relationship holds between specific individuals (for example, mother(theresa, aaron) and father(rob, bev)),

and others given by rules describing the conditions under which the relationship holds (such as parent(Par, Child) and grandparent(Gpar, Gchild)).

Assume that you are provided with definitions of the following relationships:

- mother(X, Y) — X is the mother of Y
- father(X, Y) — X is the father of Y
- female(X) — X is female
- male(X) — X is male
- parent(X, Y) — X is a parent of Y
- grandparent(X, Y) — X is a grandparent of Y
- diff(X,Y) — X and Y are different

a. Define some new relationships:

- sibling(X, Y) — X is a sibling of Y

```
sibling(X, Y) :- parent(P, X),
                 parent(P, Y),
                 diff(X, Y).
```

Note that we must include the condition that X and Y are different in order to avoid concluding that one is a sibling of oneself. (Two variables, X and Y in this case, can be bound to the same individual.)

- sister(X, Y) — X is a sister of Y

```
sister(X, Y) :- sibling(X, Y), female(X).
```

- ancestor(X, Y) — X is an ancestor of Y

```
ancestor(X, Y) :- parent(X, Y).
ancestor(X, Y) :- parent(X, Z), ancestor(Z, Y).
```

We have defined ancestor recursively, by moving down from the ancestor to descendant. We might also have defined the second clause above by moving from the descendant up to the ancestor as follows:

```
ancestor(X, Y) :- parent(Z, Y), ancestor(X, Z).
```

Consider the difference this would make in the computation of ancestors vs. descendants in each case.

- kin(X, Y) — X and Y are related.

    kin(X, Y) :- ancestor(Z, X), ancestor(Z, Y).

b. Do your definitions include half-relations? step-relations? What about "in-laws"? How might you change the definitions to include/exclude them?

    For example, in the definition of sibling given above, we require only that the two individuals share a single parent. Thus, we have included half-siblings in the relationship. If we wish to exclude half-siblings, we should insist that the individuals have the same mother and the same father.

    In order to include step-relations and in-laws, we need a relationship that states whether two individuals are married. In providing this information we must be careful about unstated assumptions, such as whether the order in which the individuals are given makes any difference (i.e., if married(X, Y) then is it also the case that married(Y, X)?).

    We also find that we need a way of stating that a relationship does not hold. For the purposes of this exercise, assume that you have a predicate not-, which can be a prefix to any relationship. [1] For example, we can define step-mother as follows:

```
step-mother(X, Y) :- married(X, Z),
                     father(Z, Y),
                     not-mother(X, Y).
```

3. Write logic programs to define the following utilities for dealing with list structures:

[1] Actually, the issue of negation in logic programming is a very complex one. In general, we prove that relationships hold, or we fail to prove that they hold. We don't really have the ability to prove that a relationship does not hold. In Prolog, negation is equated with failure to prove. Under certain circumstances it is safe to assume that a relationship does not hold if we are unable to prove that it does hold. See [6] for a discussion of this issue.

a. insert(X, NewL, OldL) — NewL is the result of inserting X (anywhere) into OldL.

```
insert(X, [X|L], L).
insert(X, [Y|L], [Y|Z]) :- insert(X, L, Z).
```

Note that the definition of insert is identical (except for the name of the relationship) to the definition of delete given on page 93. This is not surprising when you consider that the relationship being described is simply that one list differs from the other only in an occurrence of the item X. Whether you consider the relationship as expressing deletion or insertion of the item in question simply depends upon which values you are given and which you are expected to produce.

c. append(FrontL, BackL, L) — L is the list containing all the elements of the list FrontL followed by all the elements of the list BackL.

```
append([], L, L).
append([X|L], Back, [X|Rest]) :- append(L, Back, Rest).
```

d. sublist(X, Y) — The list X is a sublist of the list Y (i.e., the entire list X appears contiguously in the list Y). It is *not* simply that each element of X is also an element of Y. (Try defining it with and without using append.)

e.g., sublist([1, 2], [2, 1, 2, 3]) is true
sublist([1, 2], [1, 1, 2]) is true
sublist([1, 2], [2, 1, 3]) is false
sublist([1, 2], [1, 3, 2]) is false

With append:

```
sublist(X, Y) :-  append(Before, X, Front),
                  append(Front, After, Y).
```

That is, you can break the list Y up into three parts: (1) the list of elements that come before X in Y; (2) the list X; and (3) the list of elements that come after X in Y.

In order to define sublist without using append, split the problem into simpler pieces. Define a relationship that holds when X is an initial_sublist of Y. The X is a sublist of Y if it is an initial sublist, or if it is a sublist of the rest of Y.

f. max(L, X) — The maximum value in the list of numbers L is X. (Assume that you are given the relationship > (X, Y), which holds if X is greater than Y.)

A.4 Elementary Number Theory

Exercises 4.2.1

3. Show that parts $d - m$ and o of Lemma 4.2.2 are primitive recursive.

e.
$$\begin{aligned} \mathbf{x} \dot{-} \mathbf{0} &= \mathbf{x} \\ \mathbf{x} \dot{-} \mathbf{N}(\mathbf{y}) &= \delta(\mathbf{x}) \dot{-} \mathbf{y} \end{aligned}$$

f. $|\,\mathbf{x} - \mathbf{y}\,| = (\mathbf{x} \dot{-} \mathbf{y}) + (\mathbf{y} \dot{-} \mathbf{x})$

h. $\mathbf{min}(\mathbf{x}, \mathbf{y}) = \mathbf{x} \dot{-} (\mathbf{x} \dot{-} \mathbf{y})$

j. Actually, what is intended is to assert the existence of an **n**-ary function, $\mathbf{min_n}$, that produces the minimum of **n** arguments, for each natural number **n**. Assuming that **min(x, y)** is the binary minimum function defined in part h, we can define succeeding functions as follows:

$$\begin{aligned} \mathbf{min_3}(\mathbf{x_1}, \mathbf{x_2}, \mathbf{x_3}) &= \mathbf{min}(\mathbf{x_1}, \mathbf{min}(\mathbf{x_2}, \mathbf{x_3})) \\ \mathbf{min_{n+1}}(\mathbf{x_1}, \mathbf{x_2}, \ldots, \mathbf{x_{n+1}}) &= \mathbf{min}(\mathbf{x_1}, \mathbf{min_n}(\mathbf{x_2}, \ldots, \mathbf{x_{n+1}})) \end{aligned}$$

4. Show that the relations **even**(**x**) and **odd**(**x**) are primitive recursive.

$$\mathbf{even}(\mathbf{x}) = \mathbf{rm}(\mathbf{2}, \mathbf{x})$$

A.5 Lambda Calculus

Exercises 5.3

1. Show that it is possible that A *red* B and B *red* A and $A \not\equiv B$ — (i.e., that *red* is not antisymmetric).

$$
\begin{array}{rcl}
A & \equiv & (\lambda x.xx)(\lambda x.\lambda y.xxy) \\
 & \beta\!-\!red & (\lambda x.\lambda y.xxy)(\lambda x.\lambda y.xxy)
\end{array}
$$

$$
\begin{array}{rcl}
B & \equiv & (\lambda x.\lambda y.xxy)(\lambda x.\lambda y.xxy) \\
 & \eta\!-\!red & (\lambda x.xx)(\lambda x.\lambda y.xxy)
\end{array}
$$

Thus, A *red* B and B *red* A, but A and B are not identical.

3. Show the necessity of the restriction that $x \notin \mathcal{FV}(M)$ in the (η) rule, by showing that without this restriction the λ-calculus would be inconsistent (all terms A and B could be proved equal).

   Suppose that we allow η-reduction without restriction. Then, for example, we can claim that $\lambda x.xx$ $\eta\!-\!red$ x. (One should find this disturbing, for this leads one to conclude that the function that takes one argument and applies that argument to itself is equal to a free variable!) To construct a term that can be proven equal to arbitrary terms A and B we proceed as follows: We know that

$$\lambda x.(\lambda x.xx)N \;\beta\!-\!red\; (\lambda x.NN)$$

   and that

$$\lambda x.(\lambda x.xx)N \;\eta\!-\!red\; (\lambda x.xN)$$

   We need to find arguments to apply these terms to (and a value of N) such that one reduces to A and the other reduces to B. Consider first the form of these terms applied to a term M:

$$(\lambda x.NN)M \;\beta\!-\!red\; NN$$

   and

$$(\lambda x.xN)M \;\beta\!-\!red\; MN$$

   If we can find values of M and N such that NN *red* K and MN *red* KI then we can apply these terms to A

and B. We let $N \equiv \lambda z.K$ and $M \equiv \lambda z.KI$. Thus, the term we want to start with is

$$(\lambda x.(\lambda x.xx)(\lambda z.K))(\lambda z.KI)AB$$

Then,

$$\begin{array}{ll} \multicolumn{2}{l}{(\lambda x.(\lambda x.xx)(\lambda z.K))(\lambda z.KI)AB} \\ \quad \beta\text{--}red & (\lambda x.(\lambda z.K)(\lambda z.K))(\lambda z.KI)AB \\ \quad \beta\text{--}red & (\lambda x.K)(\lambda z.KI)AB \\ \quad \beta\text{--}red & KAB \\ \quad \beta\text{--}red & A \end{array}$$

$$\begin{array}{ll} \multicolumn{2}{l}{(\lambda x.(\lambda x.xx)(\lambda z.K))(\lambda z.KI)AB} \\ \quad \eta\text{--}red & (\lambda x.x(\lambda z.K))(\lambda z.KI)AB \\ \quad \beta\text{--}red & ((\lambda z.KI)(\lambda z.K))AB \\ \quad \beta\text{--}red & KIAB \\ \quad \beta\text{--}red & B \end{array}$$

4. Reduce each of the following to normal form if one exists; if not, then state that no normal form exists.

   b. $(\lambda x.\lambda y.xy)((\lambda y.yy)(\lambda y.yy))$

$$\begin{array}{ll} \multicolumn{2}{l}{(\lambda x.\lambda y.xy)((\lambda y.yy)(\lambda y.yy))} \\ \quad \beta\text{--}red & \lambda y.((\lambda y.yy)(\lambda y.yy))y \\ \quad \eta\text{--}red & (\lambda y.yy)(\lambda y.yy) \end{array}$$

   This will reduce to itself, infinitely. Thus, there is no normal form of this term.

   d. $(\lambda y.y(\lambda x.xx))(\lambda x.\lambda y.yx)$

$$\begin{array}{lll} (\lambda y.y(\lambda x.xx))(\lambda x.\lambda y.yx) & \beta\text{--}red & (\lambda x.\lambda y.yx)(\lambda x.xx) \\ & \beta\text{--}red & \lambda y.y(\lambda x.xx) \end{array}$$

   which is in normal form.

f. (another) $(\lambda f.\lambda g.\lambda x.f(gx))(\lambda y.y)$

$$\begin{array}{lll} (\lambda f.\lambda g.\lambda x.f(gx))(\lambda y.y) & \beta\text{--}red & \lambda g.\lambda x.(\lambda y.y)(gx) \\ & \beta\text{--}red & \lambda g.\lambda x.gx \\ & \eta\text{--}red & \lambda g.g \end{array}$$

which is in normal form.

g. (one more) $(\lambda x.(\lambda y.x))(\lambda z.y(\lambda w.zw))$

$$\begin{array}{ll} \multicolumn{2}{l}{(\lambda x.(\lambda y.x))(\lambda z.y(\lambda w.zw))} \\ \beta\text{--}red & (\lambda y_2.\lambda z.y(\lambda w.zw)) \\ \eta\text{--}red & (\lambda y_2.\lambda z.yz) \\ \eta\text{--}red & (\lambda y_2.y) \end{array}$$

Note that this is *not* the same as the identity.

5. (New one) We know that $(\lambda x.x)$ behaves as an identity function, when applied to any argument the value is always that argument. Is there a lambda expression that behaves as an "identity argument"? That is, an expression M, such that FM=F for all functions F.

   No. You explain why not.

Exercises 5.4

1. As further examples of its expressiveness, consider how we might begin to represent number theory in the lambda calculus. The general scheme for representing the nonnegative integers is as follows:

$$\begin{array}{ll} \text{Represent } \mathbf{0} & \text{by } \overline{0} \equiv \lambda x.\lambda y.y \\ \mathbf{1} & \text{by } \overline{1} \equiv \lambda x.\lambda y.xy \\ \mathbf{2} & \text{by } \overline{2} \equiv \lambda x.\lambda y.x(xy) \\ \mathbf{3} & \text{by } \overline{3} \equiv \lambda x.\lambda y.x(x(xy)) \\ \vdots & \quad \vdots \\ \mathbf{n} & \text{by } \overline{n} \equiv \lambda x.\lambda y.\underbrace{x(x\ldots(x}_{n \text{ times}}\,y)\ldots) \end{array}$$

We can represent the successor function as the λ-expression

$$\lambda x.\lambda y.\lambda z.y(xyz)$$

b. Find a λ-expression representing the addition function. That is, find *Add*, such that *Add X Y cnv* the representation for the sum of **x** and **y**, where X is the representation for **x** and Y is the representation for **y**.

We can define the addition of two numbers **m** and **n** in terms of the successor function. To add **m** to **n**, one can add one to **n**, **m** times. Since our representation of the number **m** is as a function that applies its first argument to its second argument **m** times, we can express the result of applying the successor function to **n**, **m** times, as the λ-term

$$\overline{m}(\lambda x.\lambda y.\lambda z.y(xyz))\overline{n}$$

And thus, the addition function is expressed as the λ-term

$$ADD \equiv \lambda m.\lambda n.m(\lambda x.\lambda y.\lambda z.y(xyz))n$$

c. Find a λ-expression representing multiplication.

We can define multiplication in terms of successive additions. To multiply **m** by **n**, we add **m**, **n** times. Since addition is a binary operation we need to say what we are adding **m** *to*. Of course **0** is the appropriate starting point.
Similarly to the way we defined addition, we want to express the notion of successive additions that define the product we want. The difference here is that we want to repeat an operation that is generally considered binary, not unary. However, if we recall the notion of Currying, we can consider addition to be a unary function whose value is a unary function. And to produce the product of **m** and **n** we want to apply the unary function **add-m** to **0** **n** times . Thus, the λ-term for multiplication can be expressed as:

$$MULT \equiv \lambda m.\lambda n.n(Add\ m)\overline{0}$$

2. (New) We might also consider representing symbolic expressions with λ-terms. We can build complex objects out of simpler ones by pairing them. The representation of a pair is not particularly important, as long as it is possible to both construct and decompose pairs. Suppose that we choose to represent the pairing function as the term

$$cons \equiv \lambda x.\lambda y.\lambda z.zxy$$

We need to define selector functions that return the parts of a pair. We call them *head* and *tail*.

   a. Find a λ-expression *head* that when applied to a pair $cons\ x\ y$ will return x.

   b. Find a λ-expression *tail* that when applied to a pair $cons\ x\ y$ will return y.

Exercises 5.5.1

1. Consider the domain of real numbers represented as closed intervals with rational endpoints. That is, an interval $[\mathbf{l}, \mathbf{u}]$ is an approximation to the real number $\mathbf{x}$ if $\mathbf{l} \leq \mathbf{x} \leq \mathbf{u}$. Thus we define $\sqsubseteq$ as follows: $[\mathbf{l_1}, \mathbf{u_1}] \sqsubseteq [\mathbf{l_2}, \mathbf{u_2}]$ if and only if $\mathbf{l_1} \leq \mathbf{l_2}$ and $\mathbf{u_2} \leq \mathbf{u_1}$.

   a. Describe how to find the join of two elements of this domain.

      If the intervals intersect, then the join is their intersection, i.e., the interval

$$[\mathbf{max}(\mathbf{l_1}, \mathbf{l_2}), \mathbf{min}(\mathbf{u_1}, \mathbf{u_2})]$$

      If they do not intersect, then their join is $\top$, since they give inconsistent information.

2. Prove Lemma 5.5.2.
   Proof of part 1: A set $\mathbf{X}$ is directed iff it is nonempty and every pair of elements in $\mathbf{X}$ has an upper bound in $\mathbf{X}$.

   Assume that $\mathbf{X}$ is directed. $\mathbf{X}$ is nonempty because it must contain an upper bound for $\{\}$. Every pair of elements constitutes a finite subset of $\mathbf{X}$, and thus must have an upper bound in $\mathbf{X}$ by the definition of directed.

Assume that $\mathbf{X}$ is nonempty and every pair of elements in $\mathbf{X}$ has an upper bound in $\mathbf{X}$. We can prove by induction on n, that $\forall n \geq 0$, every subset of $\mathbf{X}$ with n elements has an upper bound in $\mathbf{X}$.

$n = 0$: $\mathbf{X}$ is nonempty, and any element will suffice as an upper bound to the empty set. Assume that every subset of $\mathbf{X}$ with n elements has an upper bound in $\mathbf{X}$. Consider a subset $\mathbf{A}$ with $n+1$ elements. Let $\mathbf{x} \in \mathbf{A}$. $\mathbf{A} - \{\mathbf{x}\}$ is a subset of $\mathbf{X}$ with n elements, which thus, has an upper bound, $\mathbf{y}$, in $\mathbf{X}$. We know that the pair of elements $\{\mathbf{x}, \mathbf{y}\}$ must have an upper bound $\mathbf{z} \in \mathbf{X}$; $\mathbf{z}$ is also an upper bound of $\mathbf{A}$.

3. Prove Lemma 5.5.3.
Proof of part 1: Let $\mathbf{E}$ be a basis for $\mathbf{D}$, then for all $\mathbf{x} \in \mathbf{D}$, $\mathbf{x} \neq \top$, the set $\{\mathbf{e} \mid \mathbf{e} \in \mathbf{E} \textit{ and } \mathbf{e} \sqsubseteq \mathbf{x}\}$ is directed.

   The set is nonempty since, by the definition of basis, it must contain $\bigsqcup\{\,\}$. Every singleton contains an upper bound in the set, consisting of the single element.

   Let $\mathbf{y}$ and $\mathbf{z}$ be two elements of the set. By definition, $\mathbf{y} \sqsubseteq \mathbf{x}$ and $\mathbf{z} \sqsubseteq \mathbf{x}$, and thus $\mathbf{u} = \bigsqcup\{\mathbf{y}, \mathbf{z}\} \sqsubseteq \mathbf{x}$. By the definition of basis we know that $\mathbf{u} \in \mathbf{E}$, and therefore, it is in $\{\mathbf{e} \mid \mathbf{e} \in \mathbf{E} \textit{ and } \mathbf{e} \sqsubseteq \mathbf{x}\}$, and so, by Lemma 5.5.2, $\{\mathbf{e} \mid \mathbf{e} \in \mathbf{E} \textit{ and } \mathbf{e} \sqsubseteq \mathbf{x}\}$ is a directed set.

4. Prove that lattice equality is an equivalence relation. (Show that lattice equality is reflexive, symmetric, and transitive, as consequences of its definition in terms of the partial order, $\sqsubseteq$.)

Exercises 5.6

3. Let $A \equiv \lambda z.\lambda x.x(zzx)$ and $F \equiv AA$ Prove that F is (or is not) a fixpoint operator.

   (HINT: Try to show that $FX = X(FX)$ for all terms X.)

Exercises 5.6.1

1. Reduce each of the following expressions to Ω-normal form, if possible, if not, state why not.

   a. $\lambda x.\lambda y.y((\lambda z.\Omega zz)y)(\lambda x.x\Omega x)$ *red* $\lambda x.\lambda y.y\Omega$

Exercises 5.6.3

1. a. How (and under what conditions) can you show two terms of the λ-calculus are equal to each other in the model:

      i. when they both have normal forms?

         Reduce both terms to their normal forms. If these normal forms are α-convertible, then the terms are equal.

      ii. when they do not both have normal forms?

         If you can show that both terms are convertible to a common term (perhaps one or the other of the given terms, perhaps something they both convert to), then you know that the terms are equal.

      iii. when they both have head normal forms?

         Use the same methods described above.

   c. Will your method(s) in a work for every possible pair of terms that are equal in the model?

      No. If either of the terms has no normal form, then they may be equal even though we were unable to establish it by showing convertibility.

   e. Will you ever get any wrong answers from the methods described in a and b?

      For part a: No. We may not be able to get an answer in some cases, but when we do it is correct.

2. Determine, wherever possible, whether or not each of the following wffs is a theorem of the λ-calculus. State whether the wff is a theorem, the wff is not a theorem, or it is not possible to show whether or not it is a theorem.

b. $(\lambda x.xx)(\lambda x.f((\lambda x.xx)x)) = f((\lambda x.xx)(\lambda x.f((\lambda x.xx)x)))$
It is a theorem:

$$
\begin{array}{ll}
\multicolumn{2}{l}{(\lambda x.xx)(\lambda x.f((\lambda x.xx)x))} \\
\beta\text{-}red & (\lambda x.f((\lambda x.xx)x))(\lambda x.f((\lambda x.xx)x)) \\
\beta\text{-}red & f((\lambda x.xx)(\lambda x.f((\lambda x.xx)x)))
\end{array}
$$

d. $(\lambda x.xx)(\lambda y.xy)((\lambda x.xxx)(\lambda x.xx))$
$= x(\lambda w.xw)((\lambda x.xx)(\lambda y.yy)(\lambda z.zz))$
It is a theorem:

$$
\begin{array}{ll}
\multicolumn{2}{l}{(\lambda x.xx)(\lambda y.xy)((\lambda x.xxx)(\lambda x.xx))} \\
\beta\text{-}red & (\lambda y.xy)(\lambda y.xy)((\lambda x.xxx)(\lambda x.xx)) \\
\eta\text{-}red & x(\lambda y.xy)((\lambda x.xxx)(\lambda x.xx)) \\
\beta\text{-}red & x(\lambda y.xy)((\lambda x.xx)(\lambda x.xx)(\lambda x.xx)) \\
\alpha\text{-}cnv & x(\lambda w.xw)((\lambda x.xx)(\lambda y.yy)(\lambda z.zz))
\end{array}
$$

BIBLIOGRAPHY

[1] Artificial Intelligence, *13*, 1980. Special issue on non-monotonic logic.

[2] J. R. Allen. *Anatomy of LISP.* McGraw-Hill, New York, 1978.

[3] A. Bundy. *The Computer Modelling of Mathematical Reasoning.* Academic Press, London, 1983.

[4] A. Church. "An Unsolvable Problem of Elementary Number Theory". In M. Davis, editor, *The Undecidable*, pages 89–109, Raven Press, Hewlett, 1965.

[5] A. Church. *The Calculi of Lambda-Conversion.* Volume 6 of *Annals of Mathematical Studies*, Princeton University Press, Princeton, 1951.

[6] K. L. Clark. "Negation as Failure". In H. Gallaire and J. Minker, editors, *Logic and Data Bases*, pages 293–322, Plenum Press, New York, 1978.

[7] K. L. Clark and J. Darlington. "Algorithm Classification Through Synthesis". *Computer Journal*, 23(1), 1980.

[8] K. L. Clark, F. G. McCabe, and S. Gregory. "IC-PROLOG Language Features". In K. Clark and S.-A. Tarnlund, editors, *Logic Programming*, pages 253–266, Academic Press, New York, 1982.

[9] H. B. Curry and R. Feys. *Combinatory Logic.* Volume I, North Holland, Amsterdam, 1968.

[10] H. B. Curry, J. R. Hindley, and J. P. Seldin. *Combinatory Logic.* Volume II, North Holland, Amsterdam, 1972.

[11] M. Davis. "The Mathematics of Non-Monotonic Reasoning". *Artificial Intelligence*, 13:73–80, 1980.

[12] M. Davis, editor. *The Undecidable.* Raven Press, Hewlett, 1965.

[13] R. E. Davis. "Executable Specifications as Basis of Program Life Cycle". In *Proceedings of the 18th Hawaii International Conference on System Sciences*, pages 722–733, 1985.

[14] R. E. Davis. *"Keeping the Logic in Logic Programming"*. Technical Report, Santa Clara University, 1984.

[15] R. E. Davis. "Logic Programming and Prolog: A Tutorial". *IEEE Software*, 2(5):53–62, 1985.

[16] R. E. Davis. "Runnable Specifications as a Design Tool". In K. Clark and S.-A. Tarnlund, editors, *Logic Programming*, pages 141–150, Academic Press, 1982.

[17] M. J. C. Gordon. *Denotational Description of Programming Languages: An Introduction.* Springer-Verlag, New York, 1982.

[18] H. Hermes. *Introduction to Mathematical Logic.* Springer-Verlag, New York, 1970.

[19] K. Gödel. "On Formally Undecidable Propositions Of Principia Mathematica and Related Systems I". In M. Davis, editor, *The Undecidable*, pages 4–38, Raven Press, Hewlett, 1965.

[20] S. C. Kleene. *Introduction to Metamathematics.* Van Nostrand, New York, 1952.

[21] R. Kowalski. "Algorithm = Logic + Control". *Communications of the ACM*, 22(7):424–431, 1979.

[22] R. Kowalski. *Logic for Problem Solving.* North Holland, New York, 1982.

[23] R. A. Kowalski and M. H. van Emden. "The Semantics of Predicate Logic as a Programming Language". *Journal of the ACM*, 23(4):733–743, 1976.

[24] P. J. Landin. "The Mechanical Evaluation of Expressions". *Computer Journal*, 6:308–320, 1964.

[25] D. Luckham. "The Resolution Principle in Theorem Proving". In B. Meltzer and D. Michie, editors, *Machine Intelligence*, Elsevier, New York, 1966.

[26] R. C. Lyndon. *Notes on Logic.* Van Nostrand, Princeton, 1966.

[27] D. McDermott and J. Doyle. "Non-Monotonic Logic I". *Artificial Intelligence*, 13:41–72, 1980.

[28] E. Mendelson. *Introduction to Mathematical Logic.* Van Nostrand, Princeton, 1964.

[29] R. Milne and C. Strachey. *A Theory of Programming Language Semantics.* Chapman and Hall, London, 1976.

[30] D. M. R. Park. "The Y-combinator in Scott's Lambda-Calculus". (manuscript), Symposium on Programming Theory, Warwick, 1970.

[31] J. A. Robinson. *Logic: Form and Function.* North Holland, New York, 1979.

[32] R. M. Robinson. "Recursion and Double Recursion". *Bulletin of the American Mathematical Society*, 54:987–993, 1948.

[33] D. Scott. "Models for Various Type-Free Calculi". In P. Suppes et al., editors, *Logic, Methodology and Philosophy*, pages 157–187, North Holland, New York, 1973.

[34] D. Scott. "Outline of a Mathematical Theory of Computation". In *Proceedings of the Fourth Annual Princeton Conference on Information Sciences and Systems*, pages 169–176, Princeton, 1970.

[35] Y. Shoham and D. V. McDermott. "Directed Relations and Inversion of Prolog Programs". In *Fifth Generation Computer Systems 1984*, pages 307–316, Institute of New Generation Computer Technology (ICOT), North-Holland, Amsterdam, 1984.

[36] Sharon Sickel. "Invertibility of Logic Programs". In *Proceedings of the Fourth Workshop on Automated Deduction*, pages 103–109, Austin, 1979.

[37] J. Stoy. *Denotational Semantics: The Scott-Strachey Approach to Programming Language Theory.* MIT Press, Cambridge, 1977.

[38] C. Strachey. "The Varieties of Programming Language". In *Proceedings of the International Computing Symposium*, pages 222–233, Cini Foundation, 1972.

[39] A. Turing. "On Computable Numbers, with an Application to the Entscheidungsproblem". In M. Davis, editor, *The Undecidable*, pages 116–154, Raven Press, Hewlett, 1965.

[40] C. Wadsworth. "Approximate Reduction and Lambda-Calculus Models". *SIAM Journal on Computing*, 1976.

[41] C. Wadsworth. SIS830 Lecture Notes. A course at Syracuse University, 1974.

[42] C. Wadsworth. "The Relation Between Computational and Denotational Properties for Scott's $\mathcal{D}_\infty$ Models of the Lambda-Calculus". *SIAM Journal on Computing*, 5:488–521, 1976.

INDEX